# The Minds of the Chinese People

## Mental Health in New China

# The Minds of the Chinese People

## Mental Health in New China

Martha Livingston and
Paul Lowinger, M.D.

Prentice-Hall, Inc., Englewood Cliffs, New Jersey 07632

*Library of Congress Cataloging in Publication Data*

Livingston, Martha. date.
  The minds of the Chinese people.
  Bibliography: p.
  Includes index.
  1. Mental health services—China.  2. Mental illness—
China.  3. Psychiatry—China.  I. Lowinger, Paul: date.
II. Title.
RA790.7.C6L58    362.2'0951     82–3745
ISBN 0–13–583294–2          AACR2

This book is available at a special discount when ordered in bulk quantities.
Contact Prentice-Hall, Inc., General Publishing Division, Special Sales,
Englewood Cliffs, N. J. 07632.

10  9  8  7  6  5  4  3  2  1

Printed in the United States of America

Art Director: Hal Siegel

ISBN 0-13-583294-2

Prentice-Hall International, Inc., *London*
Prentice-Hall of Australia Pty. Limited, *Sydney*
Prentice-Hall Canada Inc., *Toronto*
Prentice-Hall of India Private Limited, *New Delhi*
Prentice-Hall of Japan, Inc., *Tokyo*
Prentice-Hall of Southeast Asia Pte. Ltd., *Singapore*
Whitehall Books Limited, *Wellington, New Zealand*
Editora Prentice-Hall do Brasil Ltda., *Rio de Janeiro*

To my husband David Bellin, from Martha; without your extraordinary love and support this book would never have been written.

To my family, from Paul; my wife, Margaret, and my children, whose love and ideas were always a presence.

# Contents

# Contents

# Acknowledgments

We are enormously grateful to our many friends and colleagues who have contributed much time, energy, love, and support to this project. A number of people read and criticized the present manuscript, and provided many valuable suggestions for changes. They are Dana Bramel, Ron Friend, Bill Livant, Carole Livingston, Margaret Lowinger, Diana Ralph, and Ruth S. Ralph. Our former editor at Prentice-Hall, Robert Stewart, worked closely with us, providing many helpful suggestions. Many thanks also to John Kirk, Senior Executive Editor, General Publishing Division, Prentice-Hall; Marlys Lehmann and Shirley Stein, Production Editors; and Nancy Velthaus, copy editor. Many other friends have helped in numerous ways; thank you, Anne Bellin, Eugene Bellin, Judy Bellin, Kathy Chamberlain, Don Cotton, Frank Kehl, Flo Kennedy, Ruth Misheloff, Helen Rosen, Linda Vogel, and Michael Zweig.

Martha's M.A. thesis, which provided much of the historical material contained in this work, owed a great deal to the support and criticisms of Doug Daniels, Hsieh Pei-chih, Bill Livant, Diana Ralph, Doris Rands, Stan Rands, Jo Roberts, and Joseph Roberts.

Special gratitude is due the *New York Guardian* for arranging the travel that took Paul to China in 1975, and the Acupuncture Association of America, which arranged the 1979 trip to China. Of course, among the many people in China who spoke helpfully of their life and experience, there are many; but in particular, Rewi Alley, C. C. Ching, Israel Epstein, Talitha Gerlach, David Ho, Hsia Chen-yi, Liu Xiehe, Ma Haide, Hans Müller, Sid Rittenberg, Julian Schuman, Sid Shapiro, Shen Yu-tsun, T'ao Kuo-t'ai, Ruth Weiss, Wu Chen-i, and our guides on both trips. Other old and new friends of China who personally helped with Paul's China travel, understanding, and research were C. S. Cheung, Joshua Horn, Victor Li, Fran and Phil Shapiro, H. C. Tien, Ann Tompkins, and Andrew Woods.

The staffs of numerous libraries provided invaluable and tireless assistance in tracking down often hard-to-get materials. Mrs. Carole Olive of the University of Regina, Saskatchewan Interlibrary Loan Department, deserves particular mention; thanks also to the staffs of the Columbia University East Asia and School of International Affairs Libraries, the New York Academy of Medicine Library, the State University of New York at Stony Brook libraries, the Queens College Library, the Medical Library of Wayne State University, the Cornell University Medical Center Library, the Library of the University of California, San Francisco, and the Library of Highland General Hospital in Oakland.

Many thanks to photographers Kathy Chamberlain, Howard Hyman, Norma Hyman, Marvin Miller, and Naomi Woronov for contributing their time and work.

Thanks to Stephen Katigbak for his excellent work in preparing the manuscript, and to Paul's secretary, Virginia McGarry.

Finally, thanks to our many friends and colleagues who have helped us over the years to gather information about mental health in China; in particular, we would like to thank our friends in the U.S.–China Peoples Friendship Association. Without their help, we would not have nearly as much information as we have. To all our friends, many thanks for all your help; we would like, however, to take sole responsibility for the many weaknesses of the work.

## A NOTE ON THE ROMANIZATION SYSTEM

In keeping with current practice, we have tried to use the *hanyu pinyin* system of romanization of Chinese names. Where the Wade-Giles system's spellings are more familiar to the reader, we have inserted them in parentheses after the first use of each *hanyu pinyin* name. In some cases, however, the Wade-Giles spelling is so well known that we have left it.

# Introduction

China, 1981: On the streets of Beijing (Peking) and Shanghai, the few cars and trucks are honking a path for themselves through thousands of cyclists. At early-morning exercises, thousands of people from six to ninety are gracefully performing the movements of t'ai-ch'i-ch'uan together in city parks before heading to work or school. The streets are washed and swept every morning. In the countryside China's peasants, 80 percent of her population, are at work, using animals—but few machines—to feed her one billion people.

A billion people, a quarter of the world's population, working together, taking care of each other, and building a new society within a four-thousand-year-old culture. Hardworking, dedicated, and self-sacrificing, the Chinese people are still very poor, yet without the signs of poverty so often seen in other countries of the Third World. They are fit and healthy; decently, if simply, clothed, fed, and housed; literate, educated, and studious. Each person actively participates in and contributes to the development of China, the advancement of something called socialist construction, and all are now purposefully engaged in the ambitious campaign to develop China into a strong, modern socialist country by the year 2000.

It wasn't always this way. Little more than thirty years ago, a population of 450 million was so devastated by famine, floods, disease, and a century of exploitation by warlords and foreign nations, that China was known as the "Sick Man of Asia." Far from pulling together, people fought over scraps of rice, ate the bark off trees, begged on the streets, and sold their children. Wagons went through Shanghai and other large cities every morning to collect the bodies of those who had died during the night; corpses were fished out of the Yangtze. In Shanghai, which was divided into concessions governed by several western nations, the park now called People's Park had a sign at the entrance which read, "No dogs or Chinese allowed." Drugs, prostitution, and misery were rampant.

What happened in China to cause such a transformation in so short a time? For over twenty years, mainly because of our government's lack of diplomatic relations with China, we in America were kept ignorant of developments there. We heard little about what was going on behind the "bamboo curtain" except for occasional fanciful pieces written by journalists from their vantage point in the bars of Hong Kong.

Then, ten years ago, the U.S. Ping-Pong Team went to China, and for the first time since the Revolution of 1949, we started to get a picture of a country in which some interesting and exciting social changes were taking place. For the authors of this book, some of the developments were so exciting that we started to learn everything we could about China, and haven't stopped yet.

Who are we? Paul is a psychiatrist with thirty years of practice in Iowa, New Orleans, Detroit, and San Francisco. He has worked in mental hospitals and community mental health programs, in private practice, in teaching and research. He has been actively involved in the human rights and antiwar movements, and is a past national chairperson of the Medical Committee for Human Rights, an organization formed during the 1960s to provide health care for Southern civil rights workers which later went on to organize for a national health plan.

On a hot muggy afternoon in 1970 it first occurred to him that the American mental health system might have something to learn from the People's Republic of China. He had just finished a dispiriting session interviewing heroin addicts in a Detroit inner-city clinic, and he and another doctor were sitting around grimly pondering the unrelenting American drug dilemma. As they searched their minds for some new direction to take in the struggle against this epidemic, they wondered whether what they had heard was true—that somehow China had ended the monstrous problem of opium addiction. Then and there Paul decided to investigate what had happened to drug addiction in China; maybe we in the United States might learn from what the Chinese had done. He wanted to go to China to see for himself what had happened, but at this time, 1970, before the rapprochement between the U.S. and China, a visit was very difficult to arrange, so he spent a lot of time talking to people who had special connections to China and reading old newspaper reports from the People's Republic to gather information about how China had solved its drug problem. As time went by his interest expanded to cover China's campaign against drugs, and also the effect of the Chinese style of socialism on the quality of life, and therefore on the mental well-being of the Chinese people.

Martha is a social psychologist who has been active in the civil rights, antiwar, and women's movements, and has worked as a union organizer for health-care workers. Her interest in the People's Republic was awakened when she saw Felix Greene's film *China!* in 1971. On the same day she also saw the film *La Dolce Vita,* and the contrast between the hard work, dignity, and sense of purpose of the Chinese people, and the bored, decadent, purposeless lives blazingly depicted by Fellini left a lasting impression. Later that year she learned more about China from William Hinton, the American farmer who spent many years living and working in China, and from a group of the first American scholars to travel to China, a 1972 delegation of the Committee of Concerned Asian Scholars. Her interest in the social causation of personal mental health problems—the way societies can produce either mental health or mental illness—led her to write an M.A. thesis on mental health in China in 1974.

Both of us are active members of the U.S.–China Peoples Friendship Association, an organization dedicated to spreading information, understanding, and friendship between the peoples of our two countries; and both of us have written and spoken about Chinese health care, mental health, and related social questions for years. It was at a national meeting of the U.S.–China Peoples Friendship Association in 1978 that we first met and discussed the possibility of combining our efforts to acquaint Americans with the valuable contributions the Chinese had made in the field of mental health. Although a number of articles by visitors to China had already appeared in the professional journals, the information contained in them had not been systematically or comprehensively collected.

We have tried, over the years, to gather and synthesize all the information there is in English about mental health in China. Our information comes from several kinds of sources. For the early years, up to about 1960, our chief sources are translations by the United States government of material written by the Chinese themselves. For the period after the start of the Cultural Revolution (1965), our major sources are western visitors to China who reported on their visits to Chinese mental hospitals and their interviews with Chinese psychiatrists. Since their exposure was limited, their information was limited, and therefore so is ours for this period. Our third source of information is articles written in English by the Chinese themselves, which are very valuable to us, considering the limitations of our understanding of their history. In addition, Paul has visited China twice and we have both met and talked with Chinese psychiatrists and psychologists. We have made every effort to gather what material there is, but as you will see, there is much that we do not know, and many questions are raised by the material which we cannot answer at this time. As the relations between our two countries develop and broaden, and the scholarly exchanges grow, all of us will learn a good deal more about China than we know now. But we cannot stress enough just how limited and often frustrating our present level of information is. We approach the writing of this book with deep humility.

In spite of the limitations of our knowledge, however, we feel that there is much we in the United States can learn from the Chinese experience. But there are two kinds of mistakes we can make in trying to learn from China. One is what we think of as the "East is East and West is West" fallacy—that is, that China's history and culture are so different from our own that there is little we can learn from the experience of the Chinese, except perhaps the odd mechanical technique, like acupuncture. Of course China's history and culture are very different from our own; every country's history and culture provide the unique conditions in which its people function. We need to sort out what aspects of their work are particular to one country and what aspects are universal and can be useful to people in other countries. (What's more, even the most culturally specific aspects of mental health care in China, like acupuncture and herbal medications, were beyond the means of most of the Chinese themselves until a change in the social system made them available.)

The second mistake is the flip side of the coin, to think that everything the Chinese do is applicable, because it works there, and all we have to do is follow their recipe. This "we're all human" fallacy fails to recognize first of all that China is a different country with a different history and, more importantly, that China is a socialist country. The social forms which are developed for the benefit of the masses of people cannot be transported into a capitalist setting without changing, sometimes into their opposite. For example, psychology is used to re-educate prisoners in Chinese jails; here it is used to stifle resistance to oppression. On the other hand, while we believe that we can learn much from the amount of involvement the Chinese people have in each other's everyday lives, some of this involvement would be seen by Americans as invasion of privacy.

Both of these approaches are less than helpful, because they both regard China as a collection of frozen achievements rather than as a society in the process of change and development. If we look at China simply in terms of triumphs and difficulties to date, then we wind up putting ourselves in the role of accountants, recording accomplishments as "credits" and the problems still remaining as "debits" in our China ledger. We're entitled to speculate, and to "like" certain aspects of what's happening in Chinese society and "dislike" others. But as observers of a living society in constant motion, we have to move beyond this kind of scorekeeping and try to develop an understanding of the history of socialism in China as a whole.

What we can learn from the Chinese is the *way* they are finding solutions to their problems, so that we can solve our own problems, which may be very different from theirs. In particular, we can learn the method of dialectical materialism, which the Chinese have tried to use to understand the world and to change it. One aspect of this method is what the Chinese call the mass line. The mass line, which embodies both the Marxist theory of knowledge and the Leninist theory of organization, may be defined as learning from the masses of ordinary people, taking their knowledge of the world and systematizing it, and giving it back to them in a more structured way so that their ideas about what needs changing in the real world can be used to make the changes. Mao Tsetung, in the classic statement of how the mass line works in practice, put it this way in 1943:

*In all the practical work of the Party, all correct leadership is necessarily "from the masses, to the masses." This means: take the ideas of the masses (scattered and unsystematic ideas) and concentrate them (through study turn them into concentrated and systematic ideas), then go to the masses and propagate and explain these ideas until the masses embrace them as their own, hold fast to them and translate them into action, and test the correctness of these ideas in such action. Then once again concentrate ideas from the masses and once again go to the masses so that the ideas are persevered in and carried through. And so on, over and over again in an endless spiral, with the ideas becoming more correct, more vital and richer each time. Such is the Marxist theory of knowledge.*[1]

According to Mao, the masses of people are the source of all knowledge, but in order for that knowledge to be usable, it must be summed up systematically by the most politically conscious representatives of the masses, the Communist Party. Decisions are made not by handing down orders, but by summing up the masses' ideas and putting them into practice, and then by summing up this practical work to determine the next step. Inherent in the mass line is respect for the thinking of ordinary people, who, when they understand what the problems are and what needs to be and can be done about them, are capable of achieving great things. But the mass line is different from populism in that it sees organization as a necessary prerequisite to accomplishing changes in the real world. In China's use of the mass line we see the relationship of theory and practice; the test of all ideas is in actual practice, through which mistakes can be corrected and people's understanding of their problems becomes more and more correct. It was in applying these massline principles that the Chinese people were able to overcome many major health problems with few resources.

The subject of this book is the People's Republic of China, which was proclaimed on October 1, 1949, when Mao Tse-tung, Chairman of the Communist Party of China, announced in Tian An Men Square in Beijing, "The Chinese people have stood up." The Chinese people refer to this time as their Liberation. Earlier, in 1911, the last dynasty—the Qing Dynasty—had ended, and the first republic was established, headed by Dr. Sun Yat-sen, the George Washington of China. At Dr. Sun's death in 1925, Chiang Kai-shek became China's ruler. The Communist Party was founded in 1924, and in the late 1920s a massacre of Communists was led by Chiang, resulting in the deaths of tens of thousands. (You may recall André Malraux's great novel *Man's Fate*,[2] which takes place during this period in China's history.) Following this massacre, Mao Tse-tung assumed leadership of the Communist Party, planning and leading the famous Long March, which took over a hundred thousand Communists and their followers to the hinterlands of China in 1934. Hardship and battle decimated their number, but those who survived became the core of the movement to liberate China. Establishing themselves in a base area in Yan'an Province, where they governed ninety-one million people, the Communists developed the principles of government, including the mass line, which they were later to use in governing all of China. After the start of the Sino-Japanese War in 1937, the Communists persuaded Chiang Kai-shek to unite with them to defeat the Japanese invaders; they did so, getting rid of the Japanese in 1945. Four years later, after a civil war, Chiang and his followers were defeated and departed for the island of Taiwan, and the Communists founded the People's Republic of China on October 1, 1949. Readers who want to learn more about the years before 1949 will enjoy Edgar Snow's classic, *Red Star Over China,* William Hinton's *Fanshen,* Jack Belden's *China Shakes the World,* or Israel Epstein's *From Opium War to Liberation.*[3]

There are historical landmarks in the history of post-Liberation China which we should identify. After the first decade of revolution had passed, the movement called the Great Leap Forward was launched in 1959. This was a period of rededication to socialist principles, when people learned to make steel in their backyards and cooperative farms were transformed into the People's Communes. Shortly thereafter, China and the Soviet Union began to part ways, and in 1960 the Soviet Union withdrew all technical assistance and advisers from China. This removal of aid, combined with several years of natural disasters such as floods and droughts, led to the "three hard years," 1959 to 1961, when many people went hungry.

In 1965 the Great Proletarian Cultural Revolution was launched.

This political movement attempted to transform the relations between people suddenly and all-encompassingly. Elitism and hierarchies were attacked; bureaucracy was attacked; the contradictions between mental and manual labor, between workers and peasants, and between city and countryside were attacked. The movement was hailed as a first in world history, a historical step no other socialist country had yet taken, a giant step toward communism. When it ended in 1976, after the death of Mao Tse-tung, it was condemned as a disaster, and the entire period has since been called "the ten lost years" by China's present leadership. It seems clear that in the later years of the Cultural Revolution, from about 1971–1976, during which time the individuals later known as the Gang of Four ruled China, terrible excesses were committed and there was much chaos. But whether the entire period should be written off remains to be seen; what we may be witnessing right now is a period of strong reaction to the excesses of the Cultural Revolution.

The present period in China is being called the modernization period. China has committed herself to becoming a strong, modern socialist nation by the year 2000, and in a country where 80 percent of the people must work simply to feed the population, that is no small task. (In the United States, only 7 percent of the population is engaged in food production.) After a decade of political upheaval, the ordinary people of China are settling down and getting to work to achieve a better standard of living. Some observers have expressed the fear that socialist principles will go by the board in the rush to produce more consumer goods and to advance technologically. We have confidence in the people of China, however, and we are sympathetic to their desire for a life that is not quite so hard as the one they lead now. Anyone who has seen first-hand the backbreaking labor that is involved in old-fashioned farming, or the factories where workers work very hard to produce very little because their machinery is antiquated, or simply the amount of work involved in daily living without refrigeration, hot water, or washing machines, can appreciate the desire of the Chinese people to modernize. What excites us about the Chinese people is that they have been able, since Liberation, to work together collectively, each person contributing, caring about one another, and cooperating to improve the whole of society. Far from threatening the achievements China has made thus far in human relations, modernization will free people from the least rewarding aspects of their work, providing them with more time and opportunity to develop still further their social and cultural life. As workers in the field of human relations, we will be delighted to help our Chinese colleagues "catch up" with international developments in our fields. In the process, we will count our country more fortunate if a little of the Chinese spirit of cooperation and working together for the good of all rubs off on our own individualist, competitive society.

# Notes

1. Mao Tse-tung, "Some Questions Concerning Methods of Leadership" (June 1, 1943), *Selected Readings from the Works of Mao Tse-tung* (Beijing: Foreign Languages Press, 1967), p. 236.
2. André Malraux, *Man's Fate* (New York: Random House/Vintage Books, 1961).
3. Edgar Snow, *Red Star Over China,* rev. ed. (New York: Grove Press, 1968); William Hinton, *Fanshen* (New York: Random House/Vintage Books, 1966); Jack Belden, *China Shakes the World* (New York and London: Monthly Review Press, 1970); Israel Epstein, *From Opium War to Liberation,* third ed. (Hong Kong: Joint Publishing Company, 1980).

# Chapter 1

# Mental Health and the Quality of Life

*If a couple is quarreling, the children, sometimes even children of eight or nine, will come to the residents' committee to ask for help. Whoever is available will go. We will talk separately with the husband and with the wife and then all talk together. If the children are at home, they will attend, and if older people live in the home, they may attend, too.*[1]

The Li family gets up at five-thirty in the morning. Mrs. Li goes out to the market first thing to get breakfast, which will consist of freshly cooked Chinese vegetables and tofu (bean curd). While she is marketing, Mr. Li is dressing their three-year-old daughter. Their son, seven years old, dresses himself. The family has breakfast together at six-thirty. Mrs. Li takes her daughter with her on her bicycle to the day care center connected to her factory. Mr. Li walks his son to school and then bicycles to work. Since the Lis both work quite close to home, they are at work at seven-thirty. While they are out, Mrs. Li's mother, Mrs. Lu, who lives with the Li family, first cleans up the two-room apartment, and then helps wash the sidewalk in front of the building. A retired worker, she puts in half a day at the neighborhood health center. There she checks up on the health of her neighbors, helping ill or homebound neighbors by doing errands and household chores for them.

On the way home from work, Mr. Li stops at a vegetable stand for freshly chopped vegetables, and at the butcher's for a little meat. The Lis have no refrigerator, so they need to market every day. Mrs. Lu will have made the rice in the afternoon; Mr. and Mrs. Li have but to stir-fry the meat and vegetables, and supper will be ready.

After supper their daughter goes to sleep, their son does his homework, and the dishes are washed with tap water from outside. The family listens to the radio, or reads, or Mrs. Li sews some clothing for one of the family. They have no telephone, and their social life is conducted in person; one of their friends will just knock on the door and pop in. Then the Lis will make tea and bring out some candy or dried fruit and have a visit. At nine o'clock, the Lis call it a night. Mom and Dad and their little girl sleep in the bedroom; the son and grandma sleep in the living room. Their apartment also has a tiny kitchen with a coal-burning stove. There is a shared lavatory which has a bathtub with running water, but no hot water. The Lis take their drinking water hot, and always have a huge thermos of hot water on hand for drinking or making tea. The Lis, and most people in China, have electricity; light is supplied by a single bulb in each of their rooms. Their apartment is decorated with photographs of the family, and embroidered doilies top the bureau, on which are the thermos, radio, a calendar, and several pretty prints. As two workers with two children and one mother who is a retired worker, their family unit is about average, though they are doing pretty well because there are two income-earning adults and one retired worker collecting a pension, 70 percent of her preretirement salary, in the family. If there were fewer working adults or more children, the family would be less well-off.

Outside the Lis' apartment, in a neighborhood in downtown Beijing (Peking), are crowds; the noise of hundreds of bicycle bells ringing as people make their way to work or school; trucks honking constantly to carve a path through the bicyclists; and voices shouting above the pervasive loudspeaker system which plays music or makes announcements. The architecture, except for some traditional buildings preserved since 1949 as museums, consists mainly of gray, western-style boxlike structures often much the worse for wear. Except in winter, hundreds of trees lining the streets transform the city. These trees were once almost obliterated; before Liberation, when times were very hard, they were cut down for firewood or the bark was eaten to stave off hunger. Now the trees are one of the glories of China.

The daily throngs on the streets of Chinese cities sometimes overwhelm Americans, but if one observes closely, the pace of Chinese life is slower, and although tremendous crowds fill the department stores, everyone moves sedately without pushing and shoving. A decorous space is left between bodies.

At night the streets are quieter; in the summer one sees people lounging in front of their houses, sitting in chairs pulled outside or on

Mental Health and the Quality of Life

the curb. A few people stroll on the street or walk to their night jobs with no fear of muggers. Bikes and trucks continue to travel the streets, but there is not the overwhelming bicycle traffic of daytime.

Homes in the cities are not isolated from the industrial districts but mingle among the shops, factories, and public buildings. They often lack fresh paint, but are very clean inside and outside. During the night, in some designated places in the city, vegetables grown on outlying farms are brought in and left on the sidewalk to be sold the next morning. No one steals them although they are unguarded, and in the early hours a line forms to buy this produce. A new phenomenon in the 1980s is the rise of small, private sellers' markets on certain streets set aside with the sanction of the government, where cooked foods, produce, and other things are sold for personal profit.

Although the cities are crowded to the bursting point, China is basically an agricultural country. Eight hundred million people live in the countryside, while two hundred million live in the cities. Traveling through the Chinese countryside on the double-laned, tree-lined roads, one always sees people. All China's arable land (13 percent) is cultivated, with much care given to arranging the earth to suit irrigation needs and the shape of the hills. (By comparison, the U.S. has 22 percent arable land.) Trucks and bicycles travel on roads, but more primitive ways of transporting goods are common as one goes deeper into the countryside, where hand- or animal-powered carts transport farm needs and produce.

The housing of the peasants in the rural communes is more primitive than in the city. Houses are often thatch-covered, and built of dried mud or maybe fired brick or concrete blocks if the commune is prosperous. Several generations of a family usually live in each house. There is one major water source in a village street and communal but separate latrines for men and women. The streets are narrow and unpaved.

An American teaching in Hunan Province, in central China, observed this bucolic scene:

*Today I went down to the Xiang Jiang River, walked along the bank, sat under the bridge. I sat for thirty minutes in one place watching the morning traffic on a little rock jutting out into the water. During the time one woman came to wash her clothes, a man came to pluck and clean the scrawniest chicken I have ever seen, and another came to wash his face and brush his teeth. The all-purpose rock. A little further down the way a fisherman in a tiny one-person sampan was arranging his hooks for the*

Mental Health and the Quality of Life

*day's fishing. He said he lived on the boat, fished every day, liked his work
and was happy on his boathouse. The size of the nets and the number of
hooks led me to believe that a full catch would sink that boat, but the
fisherman assured me of its seaworthiness with some knocking on wood,
gesticulations, and an explanation that I didn't understand.*[2]

In the city or in the countryside, life in China is a good deal harder
than it is for most Americans. A Canadian friend visiting China in the
early 1970s reported meeting an old woman in the countryside who
urged him to visit her home. She exclaimed proudly when he got there,
"Look at this house that Chairman Mao gave me! Isn't it wonderful?"
Jack looked at it. It was a one-room cottage with no running water. The
floor was of packed earth. It had a coal-burning stove in one corner, and
a *kang* (Chinese-style sleeping platform). It was dark, and not much to
look at. The old woman looked at Jack and said, "You don't think this
is much of a house, do you? Before Liberation, I never had a house
before. I slept out in the fields, and the cold and damp left me crippled
with arthritis. The new society gave me this house," she concluded proudly.[3]
This story reminds us that when studying China (or any other country,
for that matter), we need to compare it to its own past, not to what we
in America have. Ours is an extraordinarily rich country; we could do a
lot better for our people if the wealth was not concentrated in the hands
of a few, and if decisions were not made on the basis of the profit of a
few rather than the needs of most. In China—a poor, developing country—
people are doing a lot better than people in other countries with similar
resources and development. Social organization, we think, is the key; it
doesn't take a lot of money to set up structures for people to work
together and help each other. How do the Chinese do it? Why are their
mental health establishment and their need for mental health facilities
so relatively small? Because social organization solves most of the people's everyday problems without their having to resort to the mental
health establishment.

## MENTAL HEALTH AND COMMUNITY ORGANIZATION

In the cities, neighborhoods are organized into social units by means of
elected committees whose function it is to provide social services in the
area. This organization begins at the building or courtyard level, in which
a leader and sometimes a deputy leader are elected, usually from among
the retired workers. They organize various social services in the building,

including organizing other retired workers to look after the building's children, organizing study groups for the non-workers in the building, performing some health work, and resolving family quarrels.[4] The next level of organization is the street or lane committee, which serves a one-block or several-block area. Members of this committee, also made up mostly of retired workers and housewives, are nominated by residents of the area and approved by the local communist Party officials. The street committee looks after sanitation, health services, and day care. It runs street clinics, which are set up every several blocks within the city. All minor health problems and preventive services are organized by the street clinics, which are also convenient in emergencies. In addition to "physical" health care, the street clinics also handle personal problems that cannot be dealt with adequately by a building leader. Medical workers at the street-clinic level have about the same amount of training as "barefoot doctors." Their training in mental health work is minimal, but a sympathetic ear and a desire to help are often all that are needed. Building leaders and street-clinic medical workers sometimes decide to call together a family, or the residents of an entire building, to discuss a problem, determine who was right and wrong in an argument, and collectively arrive at a solution.[5] Here is how one couple's marital difficulties were handled by one neighborhood committee:

{The wife} belonged to . . . the equivalent of a P.T.A. That meant that she was out many nights of the week doing political work. Her husband, who worked during the day, did not like her not being at home at night. It's a very familiar battle-of-the-sexes story, and he wanted her doing things at home. And she said, "But the work that I'm doing is serving the people, and I want to do it." And he said, "You have to serve your family. You haven't even cooked a meal in a long time." It got to the point where they almost came to blows and were talking divorce.

A member of the neighborhood committee heard about it. . . . Six people went to see the couple and had six meetings with them. . . . They sat down together. They pulled out Chairman Mao. They asked the husband and wife to make self-criticism and then to criticize the other, and through this process they were encouraged to reunite, since obviously there could be no "fundamental contradiction" between them. They were both "the people." Indeed, the problem was resolved. The husband learned to cook, and the wife agreed to do some things differently, and it was a real compromise. She ended the anecdote by saying, "All the people in China are united and I couldn't even unite with my husband. Isn't that ridiculous?"[6]

Mental Health and the Quality of Life

In addition to these means of solving problems, every adult is a member of a study group, either at his or her place of work or in the neighborhood. In the workplace, in addition to the daily discussion of work-related questions, a work unit gets together several times a week to study world affairs and—at least until recently—Marxist writings. Retired workers and housewives study together in the neighborhood, organized by the building leader or street committee.[7] In addition to theoretical study and discussion of world events and local affairs, personal problems can also be raised in the study group. Very few problems can fester and become serious in an atmosphere of regular and open discussion.

Not only personal problems but much petty crime is dealt with on the neighborhood level in China. A minor or first offender is brought before members of the neighborhood committee, the local governing body, and his/her actions discussed and criticized. The committee discusses the crime with the offender, tries to educate the offender as to why the crime was wrong, and hopes that this kind of intervention will suffice to prevent the person from committing further crimes. Of course, serious crimes, which do occur occasionally, are not dealt with in this way. But in the majority of cases, only after repeated discussion, criticism and struggle with a particular individual, only after an individual has shown him/herself unwilling to change the behavior, will they be brought before the official legal system. Most of China's criminal behavior, already very rare compared with our own country, is dealt with in this way, making the actual legal and prison systems infinitesimal compared with ours.

Paul encountered an interesting case on his first trip, in a neighborhood in Beijing. An elderly man was taking a walk in the neighborhood when a young boy on his way to school on his bicycle knocked him to the ground, breaking his leg. After the victim was treated in the hospital and returned home, the neighborhood committee considered what the student should do as compensation to the injured party. The man's medical bills had been paid by the State, but he would not be able to walk for a few months while his leg healed. It was decided that the young man should go to the invalid's house every day to assist him, making meals and cleaning, during the recovery period. This method of a community handling its own problems gives the people who live there a feeling of personal worth and a sense of control over their own lives.

Neighborhood committees perform a wide range of social services, including the establishment of "service stations" for repairs of clothing, shoes, and appliances; laundering, tailoring, and the washing and quilting of padded bedding and clothing.[8] Neighborhood child-care centers, schools, and hospitals are also run by this group. A subcommittee is in charge of rent collection and distribution and maintenance of housing.[9] The neighborhood committee also organizes old people to help each other and to look after children while their parents are at work.

People who want to participate in cultural or recreational activities with others have a wide range of possibilities open to them. A lovely sight in Chinese cities in the early morning is that of thousands of people, from six to ninety, gathered to perform the ancient and graceful exercises of t'ai-ch'i-ch'uan, exercises that formerly were the province of only the rich. Physical fitness is very important to the Chinese, and people participate in sports much more than they do in the U.S., where spectator sports are the norm. The Chinese have a motto, "Friendship first, competition second," which means that it is much more important to enjoy the sports than to win. Indeed, when Chinese people are at a stadium watching a competition, they applaud good plays by both sides, and find our carryings-on and partisan cheering outlandish! Participation is most important; to this end, sports teams of all kinds, from ping-pong to volleyball, are organized in schools, at the workplace, in the neighborhoods. Workers in both factories and fields take exercise breaks to loosen up in the middle of a day's work.

Cultural activities are also widely available. Workers and peasants participate in after-work drama, dance, and singing groups, as well as in arts and crafts. During the Cultural Revolution, when the heavy hand of the Gang of Four was felt particularly in the realm of art and drama, many professional artists and musicians were severely oppressed, often forced out of their fields for years on end. Only a few select operas and ballets with approved "revolutionary" themes could be performed; even traditional works were frowned upon. But even during this time, with these limitations, ordinary people still participated in after-work cultural programs. Now, since the downfall of the Gang of Four, there is a resurgence in all the arts, with performances of formerly outlawed traditional and western works playing a greater role. The issue of freedom of expression in the arts is one that concerns Americans. It seems to us that since the downfall of the Gang of Four there has been a vast increase in free expression and publication of the works of ordinary people. Among leisure-time artists, traditional themes rather than revolutionary themes seem most popular, as people try their hand at age-old art forms.

At the time of Liberation in 1949, many valuable Chinese traditional art and craft forms were on the verge of extinction as master craftspeople, unable to sell their work, resorted to other jobs or to begging to stay alive. Soon after it took power, the Communist Party made a concerted effort to find, support, and often gather together these masters, setting up studios in which they could work and teach their skills to young artisans. The result: China's booming craft industries, many examples of which we are now seeing as Chinese imports become all the rage.

China's cultural heritage has been opened to the majority of her people since 1949, and archeological treasures have been unearthed as part of a project to find and restore much of this now-buried history. As visitors to China attest, these sites are frequented by thousands of Chinese visitors. The history of such places as the Ming Tombs is recounted in detail, with frequent reference to the misery of the working people of the time who built the tombs.

American psychologist Virginia Goldner, after visiting China, contrasted the two societies' ability to deal with the ordinary mental health problems of everyday life this way:

*If I were to ask anybody I might meet to come up with a number that would reflect the number of people that they would consider their social network—the number of people who have a real role in your life—what number would you come up with? There is a psychiatrist named Ross Speck who does a kind of work called Family Network Therapy . . . which is quite interesting. He believes that an active social network of people can do a much better job than any paid professional to get somebody's life back in shape.*

*He puts this belief into practice in a very radical way. When two distressed parents come to see him because their son or daughter has been hospitalized many times and is once again threatening suicide and they don't know what to do and they're at their wits' end, he says to them, "Well, Mr. and Mrs. Smith, if you would like me to help you I can only help you if next week in your living room you pull together 40 people. And this group of 40 people is going to help you because I can't do it alone." Immediately, of course, the family says, "How could we possibly find 40 people. Even if we knew 40 people, how many of them would be willing to come and do this?" Needless to say, under desperate circumstances miraculous things happen, and most people agree to come. Who do they turn out to be? Some combination of people at work and friends and relatives and the butcher, the baker, the candlestick maker, the grocery store man at the corner. They become the social network.*

*For most of us, the concept of 40 people who would be willing to go out of their way for us is quite a large number. I interviewed a fair number of Chinese people closely on this matter to find out what was the size of*

Mental Health and the Quality of Life

*their social network. It is close to a hundred people. These people are really intimately and actively involved in each other's lives. They meet each other's emotional and political needs, and every other kind of need, and in return they gain the right to set limits on each other's behavior. It's a reciprocal thing. Life is part of a very delicate and elaborate set of relationships.*

*Nothing that happens, therefore, is terribly private. In fact, there's really no ideal of privacy anyway. So if something is going wrong in your life or in your relationship with any person, all of the other people in your social network will know about it.*[10]

The question of privacy is one many Americans are interested in, and indeed, as Goldner points out, in China there is not the same concern with privacy as there is in the United States. This is not unique to China by any means. In few developing nations would one find privacy raised to an ideal. In China, given the physical limitations of housing, traditional values about the interrelatedness of family members, and socialist values about working together to achieve the development of the country as a whole, privacy is not a priority for practical as well as philosophical reasons. Ruth Sidel, in the concluding chapter of her book *Families of Fengsheng,* in which she introduces us to the lives of people in an urban neighborhood and the social structures of the neighborhood and workplace, challenges the legitimacy of the American ideal of privacy. She believes, as we do, that some of the "privacy" so sought after by Americans often leads to alienation, loneliness, and the inability to be intimately involved with others' lives.[11] She argues, quoting freely from Philip Slater's *The Pursuit of Loneliness,*[12] that Americans are losing out on the human needs of interrelationship, caring for each other, and being cared for. We agree with Sidel's perspective; the everyday lives of the Chinese people provide a startling contrast in that the Chinese see themselves as contributing to a whole that is larger and more important than their personal concerns. But we believe that the difference is largely structural; Americans are not a collection of privacy-seeking, loneliness-loving individuals, but are forced by the structure of our society into privatized nuclear units in which "looking out for number one" is the basic ethic. Everywhere we turn we see examples of individuals breaking out of that isolation and organizing together to some end, be it social or political or economic, but the structure of American society is so isolating that this kind of uniting, even for the simplest tasks—like car pools—takes great effort. Just imagine, if you think we're exaggerating, how you would respond to a request by a social worker from your local mental health clinic to look in on your neighbor down the hall, who was just released from a mental institution, at six o'clock every evening, and make sure he's taking his medication. This kind of intervention by neighbors is crucial in the aftercare of Chinese mental patients. In America we buy this kind of involvement from other people, in the form of homemakers, sickbed attendants, baby nurses, cleaning persons—and our money, even when we do have it, cannot buy the kind of concern and involvement that we might be giving each other for free, and that the Chinese routinely provide for each other, as in this Beijing courtyard:

*Sun Fu-lun, living at No. 27 in a courtyard of six families, doesn't go out to work because she has a number of children to take care of. All the husbands and wives in the other five families go out to work, and when their children come home from school there is usually no one home. So Sun Fu-lun has boiled water on hand for the children to drink and helps them to do things like prepare meals and buy groceries. Her grateful neighbors do all they can after work to help her with her household chores, and knit sweaters for her children in spare moments. Coming from different places and working at different jobs, the six families did not know each other before, but now they feel very close to each other. Since Sun Fu-lun is always at home, the other families leave their keys with her and she has become the yard's "housekeeper."*[13]

Closely related to the issue of privacy is that of freedom. Americans ask a lot of questions about the lack of freedom in China. They want to know whether the Chinese can really have good lives and good mental health with so little freedom of speech, not much control over their personal lives, and no privacy. Our response as mental health professionals is, first, is freedom to live for oneself alone with little concern for the well-being of others really mentally healthy? And are we Americans as free as we think we are even in the realm of personal choice? We cherish, in our society, the notion of mobility, but what determines most of our moving around? Do we seek other environments in which to express our innermost selves, or do we go where there are jobs? And don't our jobs often uproot us more than we would choose if the choice were really up to us?

How much personal freedom do Chinese people have? In some ways, a good deal less than we have; in a developing country, one cannot have the range of choices and mobility that one can have in a more technologically advanced society. Further, in a society where people are interrelated and where there is much social planning as a whole, the individual's range of choices is constrained by the needs of a planned, developing society. At this point in China's development there are not

Mental Health and the Quality of Life

even enough jobs for graduating middle school (high school) students, although it is hoped that future modernization and increased technology will provide more jobs in years to come. What is more, many urban young people who were sent to work in the countryside during the Cultural Revolution want to move back to the cities they came from, to be near their families and to settle down in a more familiar environment, and their demands are placing further stress on a strained job market. Many city youth have started small, private service enterprises such as cleaning, laundries, and shoemaking. They are answering a need for more of these services without waiting for an overstrained government to set them up, and are thereby providing themselves with a livelihood instead of waiting for state-run industry to provide it. Their efforts have been saluted by the Chinese government.

Given the job situation in general, the ability to change jobs is extremely limited in China. It can be done, but usually a different job will be found within the same workplace. Sometimes economic necessity prevents changing jobs and sometimes dissatisfied workers feel better after discussing their dissatisfaction with their work team. Workers whose health necessitates a change of job—such as pregnant women whose work is physically taxing, or former mental patients—are found less demanding jobs at the same workplace. Given this kind of control over the workplace, the solution is almost never to leave the workplace entirely, but rather to adapt the workplace to the health needs of the workers.

Housing choices are extremely limited in China, too, there being not enough to go around—certainly not enough modern housing—so that it is difficult even to get a home or an apartment when one gets married. To have the luxuries of hot and cold running water, refrigeration, and indoor plumbing, is beyond the expectations of most Chinese people. An American woman visitor told Martha about the time a Chinese woman was proudly demonstrating the luxurious new workers' housing she had just moved into. The Chinese woman pointed proudly to an outdoor water tap and said, "Look, we now have running water." The American woman wanted to know why, since the workers had indeed planned and built this new housing just the way they wanted it, they hadn't installed running water indoors. The Chinese woman looked at the American woman as if she were nuts and pointed to the faucet: "Look, we have running water! Why on earth would we need it indoors?"

What about freedom to be involved in the everyday decisions that affect one's workplace, one's neighborhood, the schools one's children go to? In a real sense the Chinese have a lot more community control than many Americans. As a member of a work team at a commune, factory or other workplace, one participates in decisions about one's work. As a member of a neighborhood, one participates in decisions about maintenance, health care, local services from child care to mending clothes, and community affairs. The community control so often sought here is a reality in China, and in this sense there is a great deal of grass-roots democracy in China.

But things can go wrong, and during the Cultural Revolution these decision-making processes were severely damaged. The Chinese are now coming to grips with the legacy of Confucianism in a much more serious way than they had been able to, because only by understanding this feudal tradition can they understand the destruction of grass-roots democracy all over China that took place during the Cultural Revolution. It was not too much socialism, but too much feudalism that brought an end to free discussion and consensus at many workplaces during these years. Being afraid to speak one's mind is something people are trying to deal with seriously now, but the call for more democracy is by no means universally accepted, as the closing of "Democracy Wall" (a well-known spot where ordinary people could air their grievances and opinions in poster form) shows.

The Chinese have little tradition of expressing dissenting views against authority. For two thousand years they practiced the Confucian rule of obedience, son to father and so on, up to the emperor. Since Liberation the Chinese people have had a small taste of what it is like to speak out; this is a new experience. During the Cultural Revolution, however, a lot of people were persecuted and put in jail for holding views unpopular with followers of the so-called Gang of Four. In the last several years there has been some relaxation of these tight controls; how far this trend will go remains to be seen. Americans have to be careful not to take on a "missionary attitude" that the Chinese should adopt our kind of free speech. When more freedom of expression comes in China, it will flower in a unique Chinese-Marxist way that is hard to predict.

In the United States we guard our freedom of speech jealously; at times like the McCarthy era in the 1950s we learn what it is like to be denied freedom of speech and dissent. In our society, if you have enough money, you can publish and widely distribute your views; but for most of us, freedom of the printed word is a constitutional guarantee but not a fact of life. In China, a socialist country, the government controls the press, and at times this control becomes overbearing and oppressive.

Mental Health and the Quality of Life

The constraints are different, but in both societies there are limits to freedom of speech and expression.

The state of religious freedom in China is of some interest to Americans. Many Americans feel that religion plays an important part in their mental well-being; others feel that religion has damaged their mental health. In China, although tradition has always been and still is very important, religion has little influence today. There has never been an official national religion in China, and we do not know how many people are participating in any religion except Islam, which is practiced by members of the ten-million-strong Moslem minority group. There used to be a common saying that the Chinese were "Confucian in office, Taoist in retirement, and Buddhist as death approaches," and these beliefs still affect the behavior of the Chinese. Confucianism, which is not a religion but an ethical philosophy, has played a major role through the centuries in molding Chinese personality and family relationships, and is still an influence on conduct despite many areas of conflict with Marxist tenets. Religious practice and expression, often suppressed during the Cultural Revolution, are now reemerging as the government once again guarantees freedom of religious expression. What organized religion is not allowed to do, and hasn't been allowed to do since 1949, is to proselytize to win converts.

In vivid contrast to the social isolation and fragmentation found in the United States, a major emphasis in Chinese social life is participation. People are called upon to participate to the best of their ability, in whatever way possible. The system, though poor in resources and finances, is flexible enough to provide ways for almost everyone to contribute to the development of the country. Housewives for whom the responsibility of a full-time job is too great are the backbone of a lot of neighborhood committee work. A mass movement for a number of years has been the development of "housewives' factories," formed both in the neighborhoods and on communes by women who wanted to contribute on a part-time basis. These factories were originally small scale and quite primitive, producing small parts for larger factories nearby or repairing machines. Over the years, many of these factories have grown considerably and involve the labor power of millions of women who would otherwise have had no way of contributing to socialist construction.[14]

Old people are extremely busy and useful in China. Most live on pensions of 70 percent of the salary they made when working. Some supplement their income by doing handicrafts at home. But their main function is as teachers of the young, who have not personally experienced

the horrors of the old society. They do this by giving talks at schools and by telling stories of the "bitter past" while supervising the children's after-school activities.[15] The children, in return, run errands and perform chores for the old people, and in some cases even teach old people to read. Old people also contribute to the running of street and neighborhood activities. Not unusual is the story of seventy-five-year-old Li Shu-fen, who came to Beijing to live with her daughter's family and look after her grandchildren. When the neighborhood set up a nursery, she began looking after the children there. When she was sixty-five years old, not knowing how to read or write, she took a course in acupuncture and became a skilled acupuncturist, working with the neighborhood clinic, making a modest salary which she wanted to refuse but was persuaded to take. In 1979, at the age of seventy-five, she was being taught by her grandchildren to read and write. She concluded her interview, "I'm old in age, but young in spirit. Society is different now and I'm going to keep on studying and working for socialist construction as long as I can."[16]

Most old people either live with their families, who are legally obligated to help look after them, or in their own apartments in the cities. Those who have no family or are too infirm to maintain their own apartment, even with the help of neighbors, live in old-age homes, called "homes of respect for the aged." Even here old people are not isolated from the rest of society; they are frequently visited by schoolchildren to whom they tell stories of the "bitter past," and with whom they form ongoing relationships. Old people in China have been given five guarantees by the government since 1949: food, clothing, shelter, medical care, and a burial place. Even before 1949, Communist organizers in the liberated areas organized old people by promising them these "five guarantees."[17] Here is the story of one older woman's contribution to a commune:

*Weng Feng-chu . . . started taking care of children in 1955 and has always worked with a sense of responsibility. . . .*

*When we asked Weng Feng-chu why she continued working so hard despite her advanced age, she replied: "I myself had several children in the old society, but they all died of sickness and starvation. I regard all the children who come to the creche as my own children and grandchildren. I take good care of them and bring them up so that parents can set their minds at rest while doing production work and can contribute more to socialism. This is what brings me most happiness!"*[18]

Interestingly, Paul was told on his last trip that there is almost no involutional melancholia or senile psychosis in China, whereas these

Mental Health and the Quality of Life

mental illnesses associated with aging are prevalent in our own country. It seems clear that being active and remaining a contributor to one's community keep older people healthier in China.

Children are also given the opportunity to contribute to the building of their society by performing productive labor in their classrooms for a certain amount of time each week. In one school in Shanghai, four- and five-year-olds spend up to an hour a week folding boxes for crayons. For this work, which would otherwise have to be done by factory workers if the children did not do it, they are paid, and the money earned is used to buy equipment for the class.[19] Children are thus given the feeling from very early on that they are contributing members of their society.[20]

The capabilities of handicapped people are also utilized to their fullest—often in regular workplaces, sometimes at home, and occasionally, through the initiative of the handicapped people themselves, in workplaces of their own creation. In one instance a neighborhood factory similar to the housewives' factory concept was started by a group of blind people. The work they set for themselves was mechanized, and they encountered resistance from sighted neighbors who were afraid that they were taking undue risks. But the factory was started, and the blind workers proved the sighted ones wrong. They proudly showed their factory to a visiting group from Vancouver.[21]

"Women hold up half the sky." This is the Chinese motto that expresses their resolve to see to it that Chinese women take their just place in society. Since 1949, when women were the property of their husbands, and crippled, bound feet were a symbol of feminine beauty, Chinese women have made great strides. In the early days, before the entire country had achieved liberation, woman Communist organizers working in the villages would organize "speak bitterness" sessions similar to our consciousness-raising groups. The women of the village would be called together, and one woman would tell the story of her own oppression. In the course of liberating villages, the Communists wanted the women to be liberated from their feudal ties as well; these "speak bitterness" sessions not only raised the consciousness of women to recognize and get angry about their oppression, but enabled them to do something about it. Groups of women would visit one woman's husband and discuss women's equality with him. Confronted by groups of women rather than by their own wives individually, husbands were forced to pay attention to their wives' new demands, and gradually started to remold their thinking. Naturally, this massive change in the role of women did not occur without years and years of struggle. Shortly after the 1949 Liberation, the Marriage Law of 1950 did away with feudal customs surrounding marriage, forbidding arranged marriages and bride prices, and allowing women the right to divorce.

Massive organizing efforts on the part of the Communists and the great influx of women into the workplace, insuring their economic independence, have resulted in an enormous change in the status of women in China since 1949. Comprehensive, well-run child care facilities are almost universal, so that most women workers return to work after an eight-week maternity leave at full pay. Their babies are looked after in creches right in the workplace, and nursing mothers (most Chinese women nurse their babies) are given several nursing breaks during the workday. Day care centers for older preschool children are either at the workplace or in the neighborhood in which the family lives. Preschoolers are sometimes looked after by their retired grandparents, also. The existence of good-quality child care in China makes it possible for 90 percent of Chinese women to work outside the home.

Women workers participate in every sphere of work, including construction, heavy industry, and other physically taxing jobs both in city and country. This participation has not, however, been automatic. Women have had to fight for the right to jobs that were formerly considered too hard for them. And there is persistent sex-role stereotyping about jobs that women can do better than men, although they are not always the same as our stereotypes. For example, almost all crane operators in China are women, because women are said to be more careful than men at this dangerous job. But in the creches and nurseries virtually every child care worker is a woman; in China, as in the U.S., the care of little children is considered woman's work. In this country that notion is occasionally challenged by male child-care workers who are every bit as caring as their female counterparts, but we haven't heard of this happening in China as yet. On Paul's 1975 China trip, he and ten other visiting Americans were allowed to attend a women's committee meeting in Sian where at least one difference in viewpoint between the American women and Chinese women was revealed. The American women visitors asked the Chinese women what they considered a good job for a woman in China. One of the Chinese women said that being a salesperson in a department store was appropriate for women because they were naturally more tactful than men and got along better with customers. This attitude upset the American women, who tried to explain the American feminist view that tact is a learned quality. Stereotyping by traits like this, they felt, could limit women to certain service-oriented jobs instead of allowing them to share equally all kinds of work with men. The Chinese listened to a translation by the Chinese guide, who was a woman, and then exploded into feverish discussion among themselves. Paul's group was never given a translation because their guide became so involved in the heated exchange that she had no time to translate! But the Americans sensed that the Chinese understood the point their guests were making and were troubled by it.

Many of the Chinese women who work find themselves with two jobs—their outside job and their job as sole housekeeper. This is a subject of much ongoing struggle in the households of China; many men do much housework, and the official line is that housework should be shared, but this is still a widespread problem. The existence of women's committees to intervene in cases where they feel women are being abused by their husbands, or even to encourage husbands to be more helpful around the house, is a great help. The fact that many women still have two jobs probably helps explain the relatively small number of women in top leadership positions. Again, this is an area in which the Chinese admit they have a lot of work to do.

Women in China have a long way to go before they will achieve true equality, but in comparing their situation now with their situation a third of a century ago, they have made enormous progress. If we compare their status even to that of American women, they come out ahead in many respects. A Chinese doctor now studying in New York for two years, whose teenage children live with their father in Beijing, told Martha that she had tremendous compassion for American women of childbearing age and could not understand how they could cope virtually alone with the task of raising children.

Whenever we talk to Americans about the mental health of the Chinese, they express concern about the "prudish" Chinese, who are far less open about displaying sexuality than we are in America. Can a nation in which people are encouraged to marry in their late twenties, and in which premarital and extramarital sex are absolutely frowned upon, possibly be mentally healthy? And what did we think about the widely reported story of a mural in Beijing Airport in which a nude figure was ordered covered up by a local official? What we try to explain is that there are vast cultural as well as political differences. Although China is a socialist country, it emerged from a basically feudal culture. Paul was told by a Beijing physician about his experiences in Inner Mongolia at the beginning of the national campaign to wipe out venereal disease. During his first trip to Mongolia on this mission in 1950, shortly after Liberation, the Mongolian women were quite willing to be examined by a male doctor. The physician felt that this reflected a long history during which these women had been considered worth little and had been forced to submit to men in every way, including sexually. On the doctor's second visit, four years later, things had changed considerably. The Mongolian women, having been raised to a position more equal to that of men by the new government, had developed more self-esteem and along with it a "revolutionary modesty," and now felt greatly concerned about revealing their bodies to a male doctor for examination. Public displays of affection between men and women have never been considered proper in Chinese culture, although we have seen many examples to the contrary. A friend of ours reports that he set out, in the early 1970s, to find the lovers of Shanghai, and—official statements to the contrary—he did indeed find couples in the park of an evening behaving much like courting couples the world over.

When thinking about sexuality in China, we try to remember that in the U.S. sex is pushed with every soft drink and pop song. We are overstimulated, whereas the Chinese simply do not have that constant sexual message wherever they turn. Another friend told us that after a month in China, seeing people all dressed in similar blue or gray pantsuits, he left through Hong Kong, where he saw women in gaudy dresses and high heels, and realized that "for the first time in my life, I had spent a month looking at women's faces."

Since the fall of the Gang of Four, when even talking about romantic love was considered counterrevolutionary, there is a new emphasis on romance in newspapers and magazines. Even in the English-language magazines, some love stories—pretty mild stuff, we might add—have been printed. Young people in particular are reacting to the overzealous squelching of romance during the Gang of Four period, when one was supposed to give one's all to the revolution and not care about such bourgeois things as love and marriage. The policy during that time of splitting couples by sending them to jobs in two different cities is now being overturned as fast as possible. This policy visited great hardship on family life in a country where long-distance travel is not very accessible to ordinary people and telephones are few and far between.

Homosexuality is still largely denied by the Chinese as existing in their country since Liberation. In 1980 Paul was in Los Angeles watching the news on television with a psychiatrist from Beijing who was there to attend a mental health conference, when the San Francisco Gay Freedom Day parade flashed on the screen. As the marchers cavorted in their colorful outfits, the Chinese psychiatrist seemed genuinely bewildered. "I wonder why there are so many of them here," he mused, adding that in China, homosexuality was "contrary to the culture and morals." Wondering if this opinion was held by Chinese-Americans, Paul tried to find

Chinese-American homosexuals in California. He discovered several gay Chinese-Americans who told him that homosexuality exists in most Chinese communities outside China, and that Chinese-Americans prefer to over-look homosexuality as long as the gay individual does not let homosex-uality interfere with getting married and having children. This could also be the case in China, but we don't know. We have been told that in pre-Liberation China, in the early years of the twentieth century, there existed several communities of upper-class lesbian women who were educated and financially able to escape male oppression by setting up their own cooperative living arrangements. This was a tiny phenomenon, and no longer exists in China.

The Chinese people are grateful for the progress they've made since 1949. As a man working in the Loyang caterpillar-tractor plant told Paul in 1975, "My mother starved to death. My brother had to go to another family. I started in a factory in Shanghai at age thirteen where they treated me like a slave. When I got sick in 1948, I was thrown out. Fortunately for me, the liberation of Shanghai came in 1949."

Now, working to make China a technologically modern socialist country by the year 2000, the Chinese people are not resting on their laurels. They are pleased with their progress, but want a better standard of living, and are working together to achieve it. Young people in par-ticular are discontented. They do not have the same perspective as their elders on the accomplishments of the Chinese revolution, not having been around before it. Those who have no jobs are very unhappy; those who have jobs in the country and want to be back in the city with their families are also very unhappy. In a country with only 275,000 university places (the U.S. has 2,400,000), many aspire to an education they will not be able to have. Don Porteus, an American teacher of English at Dalian, Liaoning Province, took a survey of his students there in 1980, asking them what were the ten ways in which they expected moderni-zation to improve their lives. Their answers give us a real sense of the standard of living in China today:

1. More good food
2. Better education
3. Better housing
4. Better working conditions
5. Better clothes
6. Better medical care
7. More spare time (for culture, recreation, etc.)
8. A television for every family

9. Washing machines
10. An opportunity to travel.

The answers seem to reflect a desire to improve the lives not only of the individuals and their families, but of all people in the society.

It seems to many Western visitors that China has a lower rate of mental illness than the West. Our colleague, Dr. Phillip Shapiro, an American psychoanalyst and China visitor, speculates that the reason for less mental illness has to do with the lack of disease, drug abuse, poverty and unemployment, competition, violence, racism, and sexism. He noted that the children were treated with great patience by their parents, and that collective child-rearing practices "reduce the intense and conflict-ridden over-attachment to parental figures, which is a factor in much mental illness."[22] We agree with him, but we think that mental health is far more than the absence of mental illness, and the reason the Chinese are so mentally healthy must therefore go beyond the absence of bad things. We think that the life of the Chinese people, owning their own country, poor though they may be, and with the opportunity for each person to contribute to the building of the whole country, produces mental health. Everyone can belong and have a sense of purpose; everyone can feel that he or she is helping to build China. Participation, purpose, belonging: This is why people in China are mentally healthy, despite the fact that they live lives which are very hard in many ways.

# Notes

1. Ruth Sidel, *Families of Fengsheng: Urban Life in China* (Baltimore, Md.: Penguin Books, 1974), p. 73.
2. Ann Masengill, *Letters from Americans in China* (San Francisco: U.S.-China Peoples Friendship Association, Western Region, 1980), pp. 1–2.
3. Jack Scott, personal communication (conversation), 1973.
4. Ruth Sidel and Victor Sidel, "The Human Services in China," *Social Policy,* Vol. 2, No. 6 (1972), pp. 29–30.
5. Ibid.
6. Virginia Goldner, "The Politics of Mental Health in China," *State and Mind* (Spring 1978), p. 16. By permission of Virginia Goldner, Ph.D., Assistant Clinical Professor of Psychiatry, Albert Einstein College of Medicine, New York, N.Y.
7. Liu Ju-chin, "Our Neighborhood: Study Brings a Broader View," *China Reconstructs,* Vol. XXII, No. 8 (1973), p. 7.
8. Lucille Stewart Poo, "Street and Neighborhood Committees in China: First-hand Report," *Far East Reporter* (April 1973), p. 20.
9. Ibid. p. 21.

Mental Health and the Quality of Life

10. Goldner, op. cit. pp. 15–16.
11. Ruth Sidel, op. cit. pp. 156–162.
12. Philip Slater, *The Pursuit of Loneliness* (Boston: Beacon Press, 1970).
13. Liu, loc. cit.
14. "Our Neighborhood: Street Factories," *China Reconstructs,* Vol. XXII, No. 8 (1973), pp. 9–11.
15. Ruth Sidel, *Women and Child Care in China* (New York: Hill & Wang, 1972), pp. 28, 34, 151.
16. "Three Senior Citizens Tell Their Stories," *China Reconstructs,* Vol. XXVIII, No. 7 (1979), pp. 34–35.
17. Ibid. p. 37.
18. Our Correspondents, "A Visit to the Tungting People's Commune (VI)," *Peking Review,* Vol. 16, No. 18 (May 4, 1973), p. 14.
19. Sidel, *Women and Child Care,* pp. 144–145.
20. Ma Chung-lin, "Primary Education: A Lesson from Life," *China Reconstructs,* Vol. XXII, No. 6 (1973), p. 13.
21. Canada-China Friendship Association of Vancouver, personal conversation, 1973.
22. Phillip Shapiro, "Mental Illness: A Social Problem with a Social Cure," *Getting Together,* Vol. 5, No. 3 (February 1–5, 1974), p. 7.

# Chapter 2

# Health Care for the People

*Comrades, syphilis is a disease that was bequeathed to us by the rotten society we have thrown out. It's no fault of yours if you have syphilis and no shame should be attached to it. It's only shameful if you cling to your syphilis when you can easily get rid of it. We've got rid of the landlords and the bloodsucking government that looked after* their *interests and now we have a government that looks after* ours.[1]

One of the most dramatic achievements of the Chinese revolution is the health-care system. It is rational, effective, comprehensive. No one in China goes without health care for lack of resources; the technology may be many years behind our own, but whatever technology there is, it is at the service of anyone in China who needs it. The system avails itself of the "great treasure-house" of Chinese traditional medicine, seeking to integrate this ancient science with modern western medicine, utilizing the best of both systems. How the Sick Man of Asia, as China was known before 1949, became the healthy nation with the excellent health care system it now enjoys is what we would like to talk about now. Of particular interest to us is the way ordinary Chinese people in their millions were brought into the process of dealing with health problems and transforming health in China. This approach, which the Chinese call the "mass line," is something we are very interested in and will focus on below.

We will not present an exhaustive history of work done in health care since 1949, since that job has been undertaken elsewhere.[2] Rather, we would like to provide you with enough information about health care as a whole so that you will be able to understand mental health care as part of that whole, since the Chinese see mental health as a small specialty area in health care.

# BEFORE THE REVOLUTION: THE SICK MAN OF ASIA____

With a population near four hundred fifty million before 1949, China had about twelve thousand to twenty thousand doctors trained in modern western medicine, almost all of whom lived in the big coastal cities. They made their living mostly by treating wealthy patients; the small number of charity patients these doctors took occasionally had barbarous experiments performed on them without their knowledge.[3] Doctors of Chinese traditional medicine were far more numerous; there were several hundred thousand spread throughout China, but their fees made them inaccessible to the masses of Chinese people. Most people were able to afford "treatment" only from the Chinese equivalent of witch doctors. In addition, many peasants were familiar with folk medicine—that is, the curative properties of various herbs—and some even knew some acupuncture. Apart from the lack of medical facilities, sanitation was nonexistent, and many serious diseases were spread because of the lack of sanitation. Between 5 and 10 percent of the urban population of China had venereal disease,[4] and in some rural areas this figure was as high as 48 percent.[5] Thirty-three percent of the population was afflicted with trachoma, an eye infection that often leads to blindness.[6] Entire areas were wiped out by schistosomiasis (snail fever), a disease carried by snails and spread through the use of untreated human excrement as fertilizer; the disease was endemic in some areas of the country. The crude death rate in peacetime was about twenty-five per thousand;[7] the infant mortality rate (before one year of age) was two hundred per thousand live births—one in five.[8] In addition, millions of people died in famines, and additional millions were so weakened by starvation that their resistance to any disease was nil.

This is, of course, the briefest of sketches of the health situation before the Liberation in 1949, but it serves to give us an idea of the enormity of the task that faced the Chinese people at Liberation.

# THE EARLY STRUGGLES:
# THE IMPORTANCE OF THE MASS LINE____

In a country of nearly four hundred fifty million, with so few doctors, there was no way even a dent in the massive medical problems of China could be made by old methods. New ways of getting health care and education to China's masses of people had to be developed, and the initiative of ordinary people had to be utilized. Cadres (political workers) had to be trained to do medical work. Right at the start, many doctors argued that only specialists could properly do medical work, and that training nonmedical personnel would lower the standards of medicine and be irresponsible; but the Communist Party cadres, supporters of the mass-line concept, argued that although the standards in China's few medical colleges were very high, the masses of Chinese people had no health care at all, so what was the use of these standards? At China's First National Health Congress in August, 1950, preparations for a nationwide campaign to cure the Chinese people and clean up the country were made, and a set of guiding principles was laid down which showed a strong emphasis on the mass line:

1. Health work should primarily serve the masses of the laboring people.
2. Chief emphasis should be placed on the prevention of disease.
3. Close unity should be fostered between traditional and modern doctors.
4. Health work should, wherever possible, be conducted by mass campaigns, with active participation of medical workers.[9]

How did these guidelines work in practice? We can find out by examining several of the early health campaigns in China.

## Venereal Disease

This was a delicate problem: how to get sufferers from venereal disease, once they recognized their illness, to come for treatment? Thousands of cadres were trained to recognize the symptoms of venereal disease. After a trial run in one county, which proved overwhelmingly successful, they were armed with medicine, slides, and questionnaires, and sent all over the Chinese countryside. In every village they conducted slide shows and talks about the effects of the disease and discussed the cure. People who thought they might possibly have the disease were urged to come for examination and treatment. During the public meetings, people were urged to think of venereal disease not as a personal shame, but as a relic of the old society; the politics of the disease were spelled out. Joshua Horn, an English doctor who lived and worked in China for fifteen years, tells us that this is what was said at such meetings:

*Comrades, syphilis is a disease that was bequeathed to us by the rotten society we have thrown out. It's no fault of yours if you have syphilis and no shame should be attached to it. It's only shameful if you cling to your syphilis when you can easily get rid of it. We've got rid of the landlords and the bloodsucking government that looked after* their *interests and now we have a government that looks after* ours. *We have a Party that speaks for us and shows us how to go forward. Now it calls on us to get rid of syphilis and we should seize the opportunity. This form asks ten questions and you should answer them honestly. We will be glad to help any of you who can't read or write. If you don't remember the answers to some of the questions, ask your friends and relatives. In fact, there's nothing wrong with friends and relatives jogging your memories even when they're not asked. This is* our *country now and we should all be concerned about the well-being of everyone else.*

*Comrades, we're going forward into Communism and we can't take this rotten disease with us.*[10]

When a few people who had been cured by these medical workers came forward and told the story of their own illness and cure to their neighbors, more and more people came for treatment. Medical workers made house-to-house surveys, getting people to answer the questionnaires, which were guidelines to diagnosis; treatment was conducted, with the result that over 90 percent of the cases were found and treated by the political and medical workers. Doctors, using more orthodox medical methods, found the other 10 percent of the cases and treated these.[11]

But even this political approach would not have been sufficient by itself to control venereal disease at the source—which was, in China, a widespread network of prostitution. Within about a year after the revolution, all brothels were closed, often by local masses who knew without being told that these were an evil of the old society that did not have to come along into socialism. Former prostitutes were treated for venereal disease, with which 80 percent were afflicted.[12]

A 1950 article about the process of rehabilitating some 1,289 former prostitutes in Beijing, of whom only 79 did not suffer from VD, gives us some insight into the quality of treatment and the kind of reeducation the women received:

*[The women} were, in the beginning, not in the least happy about the opportunity for rehabilitation which had been given to them. At first they were frightened and bewildered, and after these sentiments had worn off, they became very bold and complained loudly about the poor living quarters, the simple food, and about being held in the center against their will. They began reciting the rumors previously spread by their one-time master-owners—that they would be sent to the Northeast to marry "laborers," that they would be despatched as "comfort" girls to troops in the front lines. It*

*took great patience and skill on the part of the experienced women workers assigned to the job of re-educating them to calm them and explain that these were groundless rumors. Even then a number of women still believed that the rumors were true. . . .*

*Gradually the tension among the women eased. There was considerable surprise expressed when they returned to their former residences to collect personal belongings and found everything intact. This was the first experience these women had ever had with uniformed men who didn't loot, and they said so. . . .*

*Once the women realized that they were not going to be harmed, that the stories which the brothel keepers had spread were really false and that the institute personnel were genuinely interested in helping them, they were greatly moved. At first with this realization some of the girls could do nothing except lie on their beds and weep, for never before had they been treated as human beings.*

*After a few days the education program was initiated; the greatest emphasis was placed on rousing the consciousness of the women, in helping them realize that the causes of their suffering and former predicament were in no way predetermined by a "cruel fate" or "destiny." The women were invited to drama performances which were carefully selected so that they could identify their lives with those of the people on the stage. One recurring character, for example, would be the peasant girl who has been maltreated by the landlord and who is finally cast out, ending up in a brothel. This was a common occurrence in the villages before liberation.*

*The girls would return from these plays and discuss the stories. They would compare the stage version with their own life stories and in this way they began to see, through discussions, that it was the old social conditions which had been responsible for their hardships. The girls did not talk easily, but as more and more of their number began telling of their own experiences, others opened up. It was not uncommon to have tears interrupt stories. . . .*

*Under the guidance of the women cadres, who worked hard to get at the real reasons why the girls had been forced into prostitution, the informal discussions at which the girls told each other of their backgrounds developed into "air-your-grievance" meetings. . . .*

*In addition to the social and political education which the girls received, they were given very thorough medical treatment, and, later, training for productive work. When the girls first entered the institute, more than 80 percent were illiterate, but today they are all studying characters. . . . Some of the girls are even able to write simple plays about*

Health Care for the People

*their own lives. Peking citizens have attended several such plays, which have been praised for their artistic merit as well as for their social content.*

The article goes on to describe specific work and living arrangements made for the young women, including some marriages and reconnecting with families the women hadn't seen for years, and ends: "All sections of Peking society are watching the progress of these women, who have received many letters and visits from students and workers from local schools and factories."[13] This kind of rehabilitation was carried on all over China. One former prostitute wrote, "The old society made people into devils. The new society makes devils into people."[14]

Thus, not only were the masses of venereal disease sufferers cured, but within a year or so of Liberation it was assured that the Chinese people would not be getting venereal disease anymore. There is no active venereal disease at all in China today[15]; in fact, young medical workers are being trained who have never seen the symptoms of active syphilis because not a single case can be found to demonstrate them.[16] The big venereal disease clinic in Beijing was closed several years ago because it had no more work to do[17]; medical staff were deployed elsewhere. China is the first country in history to have eradicated venereal disease.[18] Before the revolution and shortly thereafter, tertiary syphilis was a major cause of mental illness; there are no more such cases now.

## Opium Addiction

In the nineteenth century the British found themselves in the position of having to drain their silver reserves to pay for Chinese exports. Rather than continue to pay for these—mostly tea, silk, and porcelain—in silver, they started to use opium; from 1800 to 1838, the amount of opium brought into China by the British increased twentyfold. In 1839 the Commissioner of Canton, having written to the British to no avail to have them stop sending opium, ordered a shipment of opium dumped into the harbor. The British responded with the Opium Wars, which lasted from 1839 to 1842. China lost these wars, and was forced, among other indignities, to exchange its goods for opium.

As a result it became a highly narcotized country. By 1850 a fifth of the revenue of the British government of India—the source of opium—came from Chinese consumption of this drug. By the twentieth century China produced its own opium for the profit of urban gangsters, regional warlords, and officials in the government of Chiang Kai-shek. Punishment for addicts was severe, but opium remained ubiquitous and profitable despite prison sentences and executions of addicts. Within a year of the

Liberation of 1949, the Chinese Government instituted a comprehensive program designed to eliminate the use of opium from the nation. The problem at that time was massive, far more common even than our present-day American drug problem. How did the Chinese combat this massive problem? Again, the use of the mass line was essential. The sources of supply of the drug had to be wiped out. Masses of people took part in locating poppy fields and destroying crops, later using the fields to grow badly-needed foodstuffs. The people in different localities fingered the opium traffickers for the new government. Twenty or thirty of the biggest drug dealers were executed; a large number ran off to Taiwan.

Minor pushers and addicts were treated differently. The keynote, again, was patient reeducation, with a strong political emphasis to make addicts aware of the reasons for their addiction. They were treated, mostly at home, in a program of gradual reduction and ultimate withdrawal from the drug over the course of two or three weeks, and given injections of magnesium sulfate, a muscle relaxant. Former addicts were urged to speak about the bitterness of the old society which had driven them to take drugs; they were not only taken off drugs, but were thoroughly rehabilitated and welcomed back into Chinese life without stigma or prejudice. Within several years of Liberation, drug addiction was completely eradicated, and it remains so today. China is the first nation in the world to become drug-free.[19] In contrast, Hong Kong, with a population of four million people, has eighty thousand to a hundred thousand addicts. In eliminating the drug problem, China has eliminated another major source of mental illness.

## Schistosomiasis

This disease is carried by snails, hence the name "snail fever." It is caused, though, by a fluke that lives in the snails. It is spread when untreated, infected human waste is used as fertilizer; but the snails, which inhabit the soil along the edge of rivers, are the source of the disease. Schistosomiasis is a killer. It causes the abdomen to swell with fluid, which is why it is popularly known as "big-belly disease," and causes growth to be stunted; eventually the victim dies. Treatment is not easy; it is long, slow, exhausting, and painful to the sufferer. So in dealing with the disease, there was a twofold reason to use the mass line: People would continue to be plagued with schistosomiasis until the water supply and food chain were decontaminated, and those who did contract it would find the treatment process very difficult. A narrow medical solution, relying only on the expertise of doctors, would not work. First the contaminated waterways had to be cleaned up, a long and hard job; several times a year the same places had to be checked and all snails destroyed. In some places the entire breeding area was buried. This kind of work could only be done by millions of people; the entire nation's waterways had to be examined by people who waded or rowed slowly along the water's edge, spotting and destroying the snails. The second aspect of the attack on schistosomiasis was introduced as part of a mass sanitation drive called the Patriotic Health Campaign, in which treatment bins for human fertilizer, which is still widely used in China, were set up all over the countryside. Treatment of fertilizer is a simple matter, but before it was instituted the disease had become endemic in some areas. Contaminated fertilizer produced contaminated crops, eaten by people who then contracted the disease.

There is still some little incidence of schistosomiasis in China, mainly in one area, but the disease is under control all over the country. In areas where the disease is still found, riverbeds are still inspected and snails destroyed several times yearly, principally in the area along the Yangtze River.[20]

One woman in a village in which Joshua Horn worked told him of her experience with schistosomiasis:

*I married when I was twenty-four years of age and when my belly started to swell, I thought I was pregnant. But it was the God of Plague who had lodged in my belly. After Liberation I got some injections which made me feel very bad. But my disease gradually got better and when I was forty-four my belly started to swell again. This time it was a real pregnancy. I had a lovely little daughter and on her first birthday I had her photo taken and sent it to Chairman Mao. He sent me a nice letter back.[21]*

## The Patriotic Health Campaign

This mass sanitation campaign attacked the sources of disease all over China. It included cleaning streets; setting up sanitary toilet facilities, often in villages which had never had any before; and, as mentioned above, setting up treatment bins for human fertilizer. Part of the campaign was the struggle against the "Four Pests": flies, mosquitoes, bedbugs, and rats. People were urged to kill as many of these pests as they could each day, and each person was urged to kill ten flies a day for the revolution. When five hundred million people are killing ten flies apiece every day, the flies don't last long! People who visit China after spending time in other Asian countries often remark on the absence of the insects so prevalent elsewhere. The campaign also discouraged spitting on the street, although this remains a problem. Streets are swept and washed every morning all over China.

As a result of the early struggles against disease in China, smallpox, venereal disease, cholera, plague, kala-azar, and opium addiction were completely wiped out. Malaria and schistosomiasis are under control everywhere, with a very small number of people still contracting these diseases.[22]

## THE CULTURAL REVOLUTION IN MEDICINE

It would be impossible at this time for us to be able to give our readers a thorough understanding of the Cultural Revolution in health work, to wrap it up in a neat package, and say, "This is what happened; it was good—or bad." To try even to approach such a neat summation of events with the extremely fragmented information and understanding that are available to us now would be a disservice. Not only westerners, but the Chinese themselves, are in the midst of trying to understand what happened in China during the years 1965–75 in all areas of work, not just medical and health work. Probably by the time you read this, we will know more than we do as we write, but that is part of the challenge of studying a society which is still growing, struggling, and changing.

Most of the material coming out of China right now attacks the work of the entire Cultural Revolution, referring to the period as the "ten lost years." But the fact is that both of us, as we said in our Introduction, got turned on to China right in the middle of the Cultural Revolution; and one of the aspects of Chinese life that most excited us was the work being done in health care. To be sure, much of what excited us then and continues to excite us now was work done before the onset of the Cultural Revolution, but much of it was work being done during the Cultural Revolution as well. For years Martha said, "If I were on a desert island and could have only one book about China with me, it would be Joshua Horn's *Away With All Pests*," which describes dramatically the work in health care from the time of Liberation through about 1969. Some of the work enthusiastically reported on by Dr. Horn, an English doctor who lived and participated in health-care work in China for fifteen years, is now being criticized in China. For those of us who are studying this work from afar, with perhaps occasional three-week forays to China, it would be difficult indeed to try to pass judgment. What we'd like to do here, therefore, is to give you some information about the kind of work that was done, and to try to make a start at understanding its positive and negative aspects. The natural place to start is to take a look at the "Instruction on Health Work" of June 26, 1965, written by Chairman Mao Tse-tung, which was a major guideline for all work done in health care during the Cultural Revolution, and which included the statement that was to become the major slogan for the Cultural Revolution in health work: "In medical and health work, put the stress on the rural areas."

*Tell the Minister of Public Health that the Ministry works only for 15 percent of the nation's population, and that of this 15 percent, mainly the lords are served. The broad masses of peasants do not get medical treatment, and they are provided neither with doctors nor with medicine. The Ministry of Public Health is not that of the people and it is better to rename it as the Ministry of Urban Health or the Lords' Health Ministry or the Health Ministry of the Urban Lords.*

*Medical education must be reformed. Basically there is no need to read so many books. How many years were spent by Hua T'o or Li Shih-chen of the Ming Dynasty in school? There is no need for medical education to enroll senior middle school students, those graduates who have spent three years in a junior middle school are good enough. The important thing is to improve themselves through study in practice. Although such doctors sent to the countryside are not very proficient, yet they are at least better than quacks and witchdoctors. Furthermore, the countryside can afford to support them. . . .*

*The present methods of examination and treatment used in hospitals are basically unsuitable for the countryside. The method of training doctors is also for the purpose of serving the cities although there are more than 500 million peasants in China. A vast amount of manpower and material supply has been diverted from mass work for carrying out research in diseases which are not easy to understand and difficult to cure—so-called pinnacles of medicine. But no attention is paid or less manpower is devoted to the prevention and improved treatment of common diseases, recurrent diseases and diseases which are often encountered. It is not that we should ignore the pioneering problems, but less manpower and material supply should be devoted to them, while the bulk of manpower and material supply should be devoted to solving the most urgent problems of the masses.*

*Only some doctors who have been out of college for one or two years and are not very proficient should be kept by hospitals in the cities. All the rest should go to the countryside. . . . In medical and health work, put the stress on the rural areas.*[23]

Health Care for the People

Although we read this statement with enthusiasm a few years ago, it is clear to us now, with hindsight, that some of its intemperate language was the basis for sweeping attacks on all aspects of medical education and research. But let us look first at the aspects of the work that we still believe were valuable.

Mao was pointing, indeed, to the fact that the masses of China's rural population—and 80 percent or more of China's population lives in the countryside—were without adequate health care. Those doctors who did practice in the countryside, in China's vast interior, were at commune and county hospitals or in towns. The difficulty of traveling to see a doctor was a deterrent to many peasants' seeking medical help; in emergencies, lives were lost because of the distance between peasants and even rudimentary emergency care. The mass movement of health workers to the countryside was an exciting project almost unparalleled in its sweeping quality. From every health facility in every city, mobile medical teams were put together and sent to the countryside for six months to a year. These teams consisted of all levels of hospital personnel, from doctors to maintenance staff, and one-third of all city hospital staff was sent to the countryside at any given time. The work they did in the countryside was informed by a guideline called the Six Tasks.[24]

The first was to provide preventive and therapeutic services, with preventive work given priority.

The second was "to train auxiliary medical personnel from among the local people."[25] The people trained in this program became popularly known as barefoot doctors; they were peasants chosen by their own comrades for training by the visiting mobile medical teams. Their training, usually conducted during the winter when agricultural work was not pressing, lasted for several months; the peasant doctors learned to recognize and treat many common ailments. What made them different from workers trained as auxiliary medical personnel in other countries is that they remained peasants—doing agricultural work as they had before training, except when they were needed in their capacity as doctors—and they were paid the same wages as other peasants. The idea was that they should maintain ties to their co-workers, which would help them do their work in a dedicated way.

Barefoot doctors were also trained in birth-control techniques and midwifery, and their training was often continued during the winters of a second and third year, or on a part-time basis all year round. Roughly 90 percent of the medical problems of the people in the countryside are now treated by barefoot doctors; more difficult or specialized work is done at production brigade clinics, commune hospitals, or, in rare cases, city hospitals. Likewise, most births in the countryside are handled by midwives; only complicated deliveries are sent to hospitals. Over a million barefoot doctors have been trained since 1965,[26] and some barefoot doctors have been selected by communes to be sent to medical school to train as full-fledged M.D.'s.

The principle of peasant doctors had been conceived and several thousand personnel trained during the Great Leap Forward in the late 1950s, so the concept did not originate in the Cultural Revolution. As with a number of achievements of post-Liberation China, Cultural Revolution enthusiasts often attributed all progress to work done only after the beginning of the Cultural Revolution. The barefoot doctor movement seems to be a case in point, since the program was begun in the late 1950s, though it became a massive program only after 1965.

The principle of the barefoot doctor was also applied in the cities, where "worker doctors" were trained from among factory workers. Again, they remained factory workers, spending only part of their time in medical work; they received only a month's training, unlike barefoot doctors, since medical facilities are more readily available in the cities. Worker doctors continue to make the rounds in the factories, examining every worker about once a week, treating minor ailments, and dispensing birth-control devices and information. A large part of their job is preventive medicine and education of their fellow workers about medical problems. They also work on problems of occupational health, with which they are intimately familiar.[27]

The third of the Six Tasks was "To make the Party's policy of planned parenthood become a reality in the Chinese countryside."[28] This was one of a number of family-planning campaigns that have been waged since Liberation. In general, in the past, the Chinese policy has been to encourage couples to marry late and to have no more than two children. This policy has always been more difficult to implement in the countryside than in the cities, for a number of reasons. First, there were never enough personnel around to educate people in both the how and the why of family planning. Second, in the rural areas people traditionally had many children because not all of them would survive to adulthood, because children provided for the parents in their old age, and because Confucian tradition made it honorable to have many children. Although Liberation made these reasons for having large families obsolete, it also made it possible for people to provide adequately for large families for the first time, and they wanted them. The job of the mobile medical teams was to discuss with rural people the reasons for limiting the size of families and to introduce them to the various birth-control techniques available. Contraceptive devices are almost all free of charge.

China has fifty-five minority nationalities, and although her population overall is one billion, some nationalities had been so decimated by war and famine in the past that their populations were down to a few thousand. In the case of the minority nationalities, it has been the government's position that the people may want to have large families in an effort to stabilize their nationality's population and ensure its future, and they are encouraged to do so. Of course, birth-control methods are available to any individuals who want them. But the general policy in these areas has been to encourage large families, whereas the general policy among the 94 percent of China's people who are of the Han nationality has been to encourage having no more than two children.

At various times since Liberation, the family-planning campaign has been promoted more or less assiduously. During the late 1950s, there was great political struggle on the question of family planning. The political line which won, and which was put into practice, was that socialism made work available for as many people as there were; that people could produce sufficient quantities of the necessities of life no matter how many of them there were. Family planning was to be made available and encouraged, but under socialism it was incorrect even to visualize an overpopulation problem; such a thing was logically impossible.

The period directly following Liberation itself, eradicating starvation and many deadly diseases, created a vast increase in population in the early years of People's China. Combined with the policy which held sway from the late 1950s through the Cultural Revolution, the result was a "baby boom" of the late 1950s and early 1960s. They are the youth of today's China, and they have a serious unemployment problem. Leaving aside the question of underemployment in China's countryside, urban young people are getting out of middle school and finding that there are no jobs for them. Never having been employed, they are not entitled to unemployment benefits, and the shortage of places in Chinese universities leaves few of these youths any constructive options. As we mentioned in Chapter 1, many are performing small neighborhood service functions. But youthful unemployment in China today is a serious problem.

The Chinese now admit that the combination of at times incorrect population planning policies and the chaotic situation in production during the last years of the reign of the "Gang of Four" have had at least temporarily dreadful results. They have now embarked on a massive birth-control campaign, with couples being urged in no uncertain terms to have only one child.

Since 1949, the Chinese say, the population of China has more than doubled, so that it is now one billion. The "natural increase rate" to 1970 was 25.95 percent; from 1970 to 1979, this rate dropped dramatically, to 11.7 percent. (Which figure suggests to us that family-planning programs undertaken during the Cultural Revolution were to some extent successful.) If the present rate of increase persists, with the average Chinese family having 2.3 children, then the population of China by the year 2000 will be 1.3 billion. With an aggressive campaign throughout China to limit the family of the future to one child, if the average family could be reduced to 1.7 children, the population in the year 2000 would be brought below 1.2 billion.[29]

In order to accomplish this goal, strong measures are being taken. Families with more than two children will in the future be penalized by getting no additional rice rations for additional children, and by having to pay for the schooling of additional children, but families limiting themselves to only one child will receive economic advantages. Several of our Chinese psychiatry and psychology colleagues—such as psychologist C.C. Ching of Beijing University, from whom we obtained these statistics, and T'ao Kuo-t'ai of Nanjing, China's only child psychiatrist— are concerned about the long-term effects of a nation of only children, and are looking for help from us in the United States in setting up child psychiatry programs. They are also concerned that only children will have a hard time looking after elderly parents. Professor Ching suggests increased "social security" guarantees for old people so that couples will not continue to have large families to insure their security in old age. He further suggests that a good deal of education be done to try to eliminate the age-old Chinese patrilineal family structure, in which only a son continues to be a contributing member of his family, and daughters become part of their husbands' families. Only by accomplishing a new understanding that children can continue to play a role in the families into which they are born will the Chinese eliminate the custom that couples must keep having children until a son is born, to insure the continuation of the family and the assistance of a child in one's later years.

However, we digress. Let us return, now, to the fourth of the Six Tasks: "To cooperate with and raise the level of the medical services which existed in the countryside before the mobile teams arrived on the scene."[30] To a large extent, the only locally available medical care before the arrival of the mobile teams and barefoot doctors was provided by doctors of Chinese traditional medicine.

During the Great Leap Forward, in 1958, Chairman Mao issued a directive which said that "Chinese medicine and pharmacology are a great treasure-house, and efforts should be made to explore them and raise them to a higher level."[31] This directive was taken very seriously in a number of areas of work, including mental health work, as we shall see later on. Again, however, we have a case in point of Cultural Revolution propagandists claiming that nothing had been done along these lines until the Cultural Revolution, which was simply not the case. But we feel that it is safe to say that it probably took the mass movement to the countryside during the Cultural Revolution to get Chinese traditional doctors there working with western-trained doctors, who simply were not in the countryside in any numbers before 1965.

Not only in the countryside, but all over China, the "treasure-house" of Chinese traditional herbal medicine continues to be researched, discarding what is not useful and systematizing what is, standardizing dosages and learning what the active ingredients are in the useful medications.

The fifth task was "To cooperate with and assist the Patriotic Health Campaign,"[32] that is, the nationwide sanitation campaign mentioned earlier. Mobile medical teams worked alongside local people setting up night-soil (human fertilizer) treatment where there was none, investigating the water supply and setting up water treatment where necessary, sometimes installing running-water systems and bath-houses, eliminating lice, and sanitizing food. The enthusiasm of the local people has ensured the continuation of these programs after the departure of the mobile medical teams.

The sixth task was that members of the mobile medical team were "to utilize the opportunity of a year [or six months] in the countryside, in close contact with the peasants, to deepen their understanding of the laboring people, and to change their thinking in such a way that they fit better into the new society and become more effective in building socialism."[33] It is difficult for us to describe this kind of process objectively. When we first studied China we thought it was wonderful that elitist doctors were learning how to respect and identify with ordinary working people. There is so much arrogance and aloofness in the medical profession in our country that it was exciting for us to read stories like the one told by Dr. Lin Chiao-shih, a woman obstetrician and one of China's best-known specialists:

Health Care for the People

*I didn't know the first thing about the broad masses of the poor and lower-middle peasants. When they welcomed us as "the medical team sent by Chairman Mao to the countryside," I felt enthusiastic, but that it was only natural that they should show this respect. I thought that it was creditable for a person over 60 to go to the countryside and said to myself, "I've come to save you from your sufferings."*

*Once, I was called to help a woman about to give birth. A local girl, who as medical attendant was learning from me, went along. Upon examining the woman in her home, however, we found her time had not yet come, and I was a little impatient. But not the medical attendant. As if in her own home, she treated the patient like one of her family. Seeing the water vat empty, she went out to fetch water. Then she lighted a fire in the stove and set about washing the woman's clothes, not sitting idle for a minute.*

*Her warmth and manner deeply moved me. Why was she like this? Why was I so cold towards the poor and lower-middle peasants? Although she was not yet my equal professionally, I being more experienced and her teacher, she was head and shoulders above me in service to the people, and a model for me to learn from.*[34]

We have difficulty, when faced with examples like this, in trying to understand once and for all just what took place during the Cultural Revolution. To be sure, struggles against hierarchical relationships in the medical field are close to our hearts, and we continue to be enthusiastic about the possibility of individuals' going through transformation, through criticism and self-criticism, in the course of doing their work. We continue also to be enthusiastic about the possibility of breaking down the contradiction between mental and manual labor, of making it possible through integrating these types of work in everyone's lives for "mind workers" to understand, appreciate, and respect the contribution of manual workers instead of feeling superior to them, as is certainly the case in this country. But we also know, as well as we know anything that happened especially during the later years of the Cultural Revolution, during the reign of the Gang of Four, that thousands of intellectuals and researchers of all kinds were castigated and punished severely. Instead of being allowed the opportunity to learn through their daily work how to appreciate the contributions of both mental and manual labor, many thousands of intellectuals were cut off from making any kind of positive contribution whatever to the task of socialist construction in China.

China's thousands of years of Confucianism have left a deeply-imbedded feudal legacy of veneration for intellectuals and disdain for manual workers, and this legacy has yet to be successfully overturned. But to treat all intellectual workers as enemies, cutting them off from using their skills and ideas in the service of developing China, was clearly not the way to do it. Unfortunately, the excesses of this aspect of the Cultural Revolution make the job harder, not easier, to deal with in the coming few years. And most likely a number of arrogant intellectuals who should have been struggled against will go on thinking the way they always have.

When you have been the victim of a policy, or of its incorrect implementation, it is easy to condemn it entirely, and certainly that has been the case with many hundreds of intellectual workers. There are also a good number, however, who recognize the positive aspects of this campaign, and who have said that they were glad to have had the opportunity to transform their own understanding of the lives of the laboring people of China, but only wished they could have continued doing their own work instead of being completely cut off from making any professional contributions at all for several years. It is clear, though, that although the policy sounded excellent to us a few years back, its implementation was a disaster and a personal tragedy for many decent people.

We need to understand that revolution takes place not in the realm of ideas, but in the real world. Hence, it is possible that for some years it was important to disperse medical personnel throughout the countryside to raise the level of medical care available to the masses. And then, years later, it is possible to say that that particular task is not eternally the only correct thing to do, and that other needs arise as a result of differing conditions at different times. In China's medical work, education and research have been sadly neglected for years, and if not developed will hold back the possibility of good-quality medical care for China's masses for many years to come.

In sum, it was good that at one point medical workers were dispersed throughout China's vast countryside. They improved the quality of health care and gained a better understanding of the health care needs of China's millions. But the task is now different—it is one of concentrating the expertise and resources and providing high-powered training and updating of knowledge. At some time in the future, when the task of modernizing and developing China's medical expertise has been underway for some years, perhaps another campaign to disperse this knowledge to China's rural masses will again be appropriate.

During the Cultural Revolution we learned also about an attempt to break down the hierarchical structure of Chinese hospital staffs. We were told that in the course of treating a case, the doctors, nurses, and support staff who were involved with the particular patient met to discuss the case, the difficulties involved, and the care that the patient would need. Patients, too, were often included in these discussions, because it was felt that patients who had an understanding of their problem and its treatment would be active participants in their own cures rather than passive observers of the medical machinery. Hospital workers who were intimately involved could contribute to the patient's treatment and participate more effectively when they understood the case rather than carrying out orders about which they had no understanding. This kind of cooperative, teamwork approach is something about which we were very excited when we first learned of it. It is our understanding that this kind of team approach still exists today, although in hospital administration there has been a "return to the white coat" in all hospitals. As in all Chinese institutions since the fall of the Gang of Four, administration is no longer by Revolutionary Committee. The traditional plan of management by a superintendent has now returned to China's hospitals, and they are once again controlled by the professionals. We do not know what effects this change will have.

## MEDICAL EDUCATION

The length of time for training doctors has fluctuated in China since the revolution of 1949. At that time, medical school training lasted six years following graduation from middle school (roughly equivalent to our high school). At the start of the Cultural Revolution, medical education was suspended for three years, from 1966 to 1969, and when medical schools reopened, they instituted a three-year curriculum. While the motivation for this reduction in curriculum—to train more doctors more quickly—may have been laudable, it became clear after several years that graduates of the three-year medical programs were simply not adequately prepared. As Dr. Hans Müller, Vice-President of Beijing Union Medical College, explained, with a twinkle in his eye, to a visiting Canadian, many of these doctors have had to be "recalled," just like cars in North America, for more training![35]

Now, since 1978, a five-year program has been established. (As Paul discovered in his talk with Dr. Müller, not everybody agrees with the five-year program. Paul was told, "You know, there are limited facilities to train doctors, and the five-year course means that fewer doctors graduate into the society each year than if the course were four years. I admit that you get a better doctor in five years than four years, but given the great need of the country, doctors should go out and learn on the job." His frankness in disagreeing with public policy revealed a freedom of expression nowadays that Paul did not find earlier in the Chinese medical community.)

Selection criteria for entering medical students have changed markedly since the Cultural Revolution, when political attitude, class background, and recommendations from fellow workers were most important. Examinations have been reinstituted and play a key role. What is more, there are, out of China's ninety medical schools, four which have been selected as "heavy points," or "centers of excellence," and are funded by the central Ministry of Health. Eleven other medical schools are earmarked for future development as "heavy points."

Students who gain admission into these centers of excellence have, on the average, much higher examination marks than those who are accepted into other medical schools. Interestingly, one criterion for admission to a center of excellence is that the applicant be from an area in great need of good-quality doctors.[36] Another change in policy is that many medical students are entering medical school straight out of middle school (high school), rather than being required to work for several years in between. Some people feel that this may foster the development of doctors divorced from the practical lives of the masses. But in years past it was found that students who participated in manual labor for two years before entering medical school had forgotten all their scientific training in the intervening years. In a country so urgently in need of scientific advancement as China, this waste of scientific know-how is unconscionable at this time.

Once in medical school, students concentrate on basic sciences. They study English and spend 30 percent of their time learning Chinese traditional medicine. Students wishing to specialize in psychiatry do so in a year's additional training after graduation, combining this study with hospital work. There are also some medical schools of Chinese traditional medicine; in these schools, students must spend 30 percent of their time studying western medicine. At these schools as well, the curriculum has been expanded from three to five years, and here also, the majority of additional study time is being devoted to basic sciences.

A recent Canadian visitor to the People's Republic provides a revealing example of the continuing integration of Chinese and western medicine within a changing set of medical priorities:

*Perhaps the best symbol of this integration that we encountered was the family of Dr. Chang, a specialist in infectious diseases at the Hunan*

Health Care for the People

*Medical School in Changsha. Dr. Chang has two sons. The elder, aged 25, entered a school of traditional medicine this past fall. The younger, aged 20, undertook western schooling like his father. The older son had spent 5 years in the countryside and had come to appreciate the benefits brought to the people by the traditional physician. He felt that that type of physician practised a medicine that the people understood as part of their culture. The traditional doctor seemed oriented to those things that were most sought by the people. Seeing this, the elder son wanted to make his contribution in the same way. The younger son, fresh out of middle school, was going straight to medical school without his brother's experiences. He is dedicated to scientific medicine and does not share his brother's views.*

*Although he has never been abroad, Dr. Chang Sr. was trained in western medicine before 1949. He has devoted his life to the fight against infectious diseases, especially schistosomiasis, in that southern, rice-growing part of China where this disease has been most stubborn. The older son, a product of the Cultural Revolution, will seek his life among peasants as a traditional doctor. The youngest son, only now coming to manhood, is eagerly embracing the ways of the industrialized world. Thus within two generations of this one family the shifting emphases in medical education in the People's Republic of China are reflected.*[37]

We hope that this chapter has provided enough background for the reader in the development and philosophy of the Chinese health care system so that we can now move on to how that history has affected mental health work. Certainly, many of the themes are the same: involving the Chinese people in their millions in projects designed to improve mental health for everyone; involving mental patients actively in their own treatments; and most important, believing in the ability of human beings to understand their world and, on the basis of that understanding, to transform it.

# Notes

1. Joshua Horn, *Away With All Pests* (New York and London: Monthly Review Press, 1969), p. 91. Copyright © 1969 by Joshua Horn. Reprinted by permission of Monthly Review Press and The Society for Anglo-Chinese Understanding.
2. Particularly useful to readers who want to know more about health care in China are Dr. Joshua Horn's *Away With All Pests,* and Ruth and Victor Sidel's *Serve the People: Observations on Medicine in the People's Republic of China* (New York: Josiah Macy, Jr. Foundation, 1973). Dr. Horn was an

English surgeon who lived and worked in China from 1954 to 1969; his understanding of the rise of health care in China is particularly broad. The Sidels have visited China several times and written extensively about medicine and social services in China.

3. Sidel and Sidel, op. cit. p. 20; Horn, op. cit. p. 70.
4. Horn, op. cit. p. 86; Mark Selden, "China: Revolution and Health," Health Policy Advisory Center *Health-PAC Bulletin*, No. 47, (December 1972), p. 3.
5. Selden, op. cit. p. 4.
6. Ibid. p. 3.
7. Ibid.; Sidel and Sidel, op. cit. p. 18.
8. Selden, op. cit. p. 3.
9. Ibid. p. 4.
10. Horn, op. cit. p. 91.
11. Ibid. p. 92; see also Bibliography: Horn, 1971.
12. Edgar Snow, *Red China Today* (New York: Random House/Vintage Books, 1971), p. 272.
13. "Peking's Former Prostitutes," *China Weekly Review* (July 29, 1950) pp. 148–150.
14. Horn, op. cit. p. 88.
15. Ibid. p. 86.
16. Snow, op. cit. p. 275.
17. Horn, 1971.
18. Selden, op. cit. p. 4; Horn, op. cit. p. 93.
19. Selden, op. cit. p. 5; Sidel and Sidel, op. cit. p. 23; E. Grey Dimond, *More than Herbs and Acupuncture* (New York: W.W. Norton & Co., Inc., 1975), p. 134.
20. Horn, op. cit. pp. 94–106.
21. Ibid. p. 105.
22. Selden, op. cit. p. 5.
23. "Collection of Statements by Mao Tse-tung, 1956–1967," *Current Background* 892 (October 21, 1969), quoted by Selden, op. cit. p. 8, who says, "The full text of Mao's statement has never, to my knowledge, been officially released. The present version was printed by Red Guards."
24. Horn, op. cit. pp. 130–146.
25. Ibid. p. 135.
26. Selden, op. cit. p. 10; "Medical Care for 700 Million: Some Questions Answered," *China Reconstructs*, Vol. XXI, No. 11 (November 1972), p. 14.
27. Sidel and Sidel, op. cit. pp. 68–72.
28. Horn, op. cit. p. 140.
29. Zweig, Michael, "Urban Unemployment in the People's Republic of China," unpublished paper presented at the annual meeting of the Eastern Economics Association, Philadelphia, April 1981. For the statistics, we are grateful to Professor C.C. Ching; they are from an unpublished paper he prepared in 1980 on effects of the one-child family.
30. Horn, op. cit. p. 142.
31. "Directive on Study of Traditional Chinese Medicine," *Chinese Medical Journal*, Vol. 77, No. 12, (December 1958), p. 603.

Health Care for the People

32. Horn, op. cit. p. 142.
33. Ibid. pp. 142–143.
34. Lin Chiao-chih, "The Party Keeps Me Young," *New Women in New China* (Beijing: Foreign Languages Press, 1972), pp. 25–26.
35. D.G. Bates, "Medical Education in China after the Gang of Four," originally published in *Canadian Medical Association Journal,* Vol. 120, No. 12 (June 23, 1979), p. 1578.
36. Ibid.
37. Ibid. pp. 1581–1582.

A quiet moment at the Shanghai Psychiatric Institute (*photo by Marv Miller*)

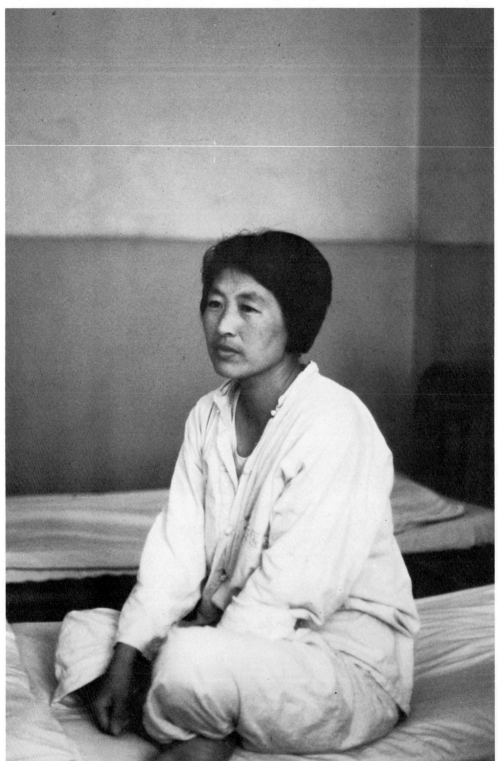

On a visit to Palo Alto, California, 1981: Dr. Wu Chen-i and Dr. Shen Yu-tsun of Beijing's Third Teaching Hospital, and Dr. Hsia Chen-yi, head of the Shanghai Psychiatric Institute (*photo by Margaret Lowinger*)

Doctors Wu and Lowinger (*photo by Paul Lowinger*)

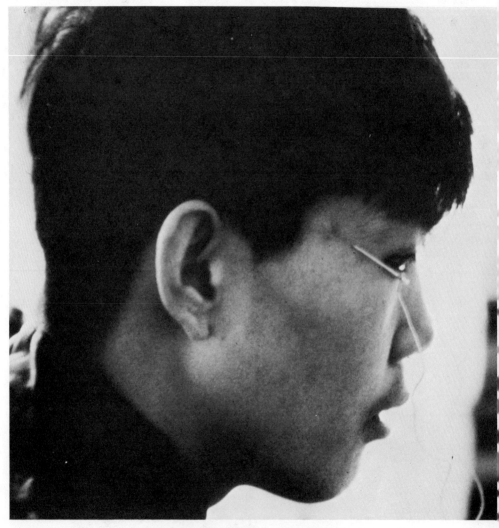

Electro-acupuncture being applied to
a psychiatric patient in Shanghai
(*photo by Marv Miller*)

Dr. T'ao Kuo-t'ai of the
Nanjing Neuropsychiatric Institute
(*photo by Paul Lowinger*)

A ward in the Shanghai Psychiatric Institute (*photo by Marv Miller*)

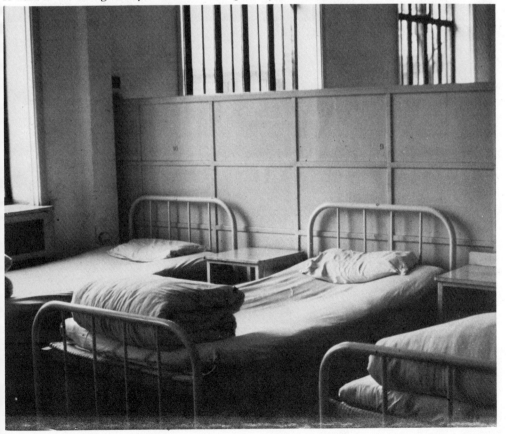

Shanghai Psychiatric Institute patients and staff members singing together
(*photo by Marv Miller*)

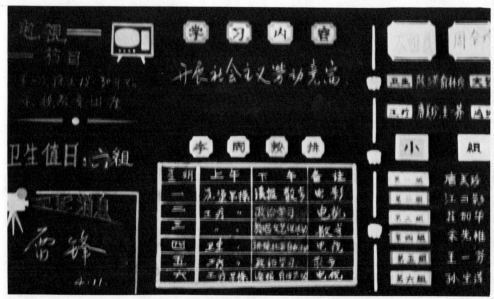

Chart showing patients' daily schedule at the Shanghai Psychiatric Institute
(*photo by Marv Miller*)

Mental and physical well-being:
Workers perform t'ai-ch'i-ch'uan exercises in a Beijing courtyard at 6 A.M.
(*photo by Kathy Chamberlain*)

A display of herbal medication "for
tranquilizing" in Shanghai's Museum of the
School of Chinese Traditional Medicine
(*photo by Marv Miller*)

Patients making boxes at the Shanghai Psychiatric Institute as part of the constructive labor program (*photo by Marv Miller*)

A peaceful interlude in Hangzhou (*photo by Naomi Woronov*)

# Chapter 3

# The Rise of Mental Health Care in New China

*Psychiatry in China has only a short history. The recent war with Japan undoubtedly has created numerous psychiatric problems that demand immediate attention. The prospective changes in the economic life of the Chinese people following post-war reconstruction will make the situation more complicated. It is high time to develop psychiatry in China.*

—Ling Ming-yu, 1946[1]

In order to understand the rise of psychiatry in New China, we really need to know how it began and developed in pre-Liberation China. Psychiatry as we know it did not develop as a specialty of medicine anywhere in the world until the eighteenth century, and modern psychiatry did not arrive in China until western missionaries brought it there in the late nineteenth century. But China's medical tradition is three thousand years old, and it abounds with references to psychiatric problems.

## PSYCHIATRIC THOUGHT IN TRADITIONAL CHINESE MEDICINE

As early as the fourteenth century B.C., a carved "oracle bone" referred to "wind maladies."[2] Disorders of wind were commonly thought to cause psychiatric problems. And in a document called the *Kuan Tzu*, from the eighth century B.C., it was written that

> *. . . in the capital, there are institutions where the deaf, the blind, the dumb, the lame, the paralyzed, the deformed and the insane are received when ill and where they are cared for until they recover.*[3]

Throughout traditional Chinese medical writings there are references to treatments of mental disorders. Earlier writings refer to specific acupuncture treatments for various symptoms such as hallucinations, overexcitement, and amnesia,[4] while later writings—that is, as "late" as the seventh and twelfth centuries A.D., record drug as well as acupuncture treatments. A Chinese writer quoted this major work, *Standards for Diagnosis and Treatment* by Wang K'en-t'ang, written in 1608:

> *It divides nervous and mental disorders into the following three kinds: a. Insanity. "The insane person is sometimes violent, sometimes stupid, singing and laughing or sad and weeping. He gets no better even after months and years. The common name for this disorder is wind in the mind. Those with frustrated ambition are liable to be so affected." Dementia praecox or schizophrenia was probably the chief disease in this group. b. Mania. "The patient is boisterous, garrulous, raving, stubborn, and violent. He abuses everyone indiscriminately—friends, relatives and strangers. He may even climb any eminence at hand, sing at the top of his voice, take off his clothes and run away, climbing over the wall or onto the roof in a way that no normal person would be able to do. He may tell of things that were never seen." c. Fits. "The person subject to fits becomes dizzy and cannot recognize people. He falls to the ground, having convulsions and suffering from jerks over which he has no control."*[5]

Traditional Chinese medical thought is very much a balance model, in which disease—including psychiatric disorders—is caused by a lack or overabundance, and in which moderation in emotional life is to be striven for. Balance and moderation led to health; excess or lack led to disease. In this model, the Chinese have had a holistic approach to medicine for centuries, and their understanding of the interrelationship of mind and body has a long tradition as well.

Coexisting throughout Chinese history with the "Great" tradition of Chinese medical and psychiatric thought was the "Lesser," or folk tradition, involving demonology, spirit possession, exorcism, and so forth. Most Chinese people afflicted with mental disorders throughout Chinese history were likely to be treated, if at all, in this folk tradition. Numerous

The Rise of Mental Health Care in New China

gruesome exorcism rites have been described, often involving the departure of the patients as well as of the devils they were possessed with.[6] These rituals and methods of "treatment" existed well into the twentieth century, and it was into this situation that the missionaries brought their western psychiatry in the latter half of the nineteenth century.

## WESTERN PSYCHIATRY COMES TO CHINA

In 1899 the first psychiatric hospital which attempted to provide modern psychiatric care was opened with thirty beds by Dr. John Kerr in Guangzhou (Canton).[7] Forced to close by "labor problems" in 1937, it had at that time five hundred beds.[8] The Beijing Refuge for the Insane was established in 1906, and is reported to have had two hundred beds in 1933, when it was reorganized by the staff of Beijing University Medical College into the Beijing City Psychopathic Hospital. The staff conducted research on the patients there, which culminated in the publication, in 1939, of "Social and Psychological Studies of Neuropsychiatry in China."[9] In Suzhou (Soochow), a psychopathic ward was set up at the Elizabeth Blake Hospital, but was forced to close in 1937 during the Sino-Japanese War[10]; and Mercy Hospital, in Shanghai, a five-hundred-bed facility, was opened in 1935. In 1939 a Buddhist charitable organization founded the Therapeutic Institute for Nervous Diseases in Shanghai.[11] An attempt to open a psychiatric facility in Nanjing (Nanking) in 1937 was abandoned because of the Japanese occupation; its founder went instead to Chengdu, and established a mental hospital and child-guidance clinic, and returned to Nanjing in 1947 to open the psychiatric hospital.[12]

The care given at these early institutions was uneven. At the best, the John Kerr Refuge, the treatment available was about as good as one could get anywhere at that time; it included freedom for the patient, medication, occupational therapy, and kind treatment by doctors and staff. It was run by Presbyterian missionaries, and patients got a large dose of Christianity with their treatment. Other institutions did not provide such decent care: at the Shanghai Municipal Psychiatric Hospital, a two-hundred-bed facility established with the help of the Kuomintang in 1934, there were four classes of patient care. These ranged from first class, which cost the patient's family $1,500 a month (this ward was almost vacant, and was later converted to staff quarters); second class, for $1,000 a month; and two wards of charity patients, always overcrowded, in which 30 percent of the patients died each year, and which were staffed sometimes by one nurse alone, with a doctor visiting twice a week.[13] At such

The Rise of Mental Health Care in New China

institutions patients were often isolated, confined, chained, and beaten; they received little real psychiatric care.

Most mental patients were kept in isolation and restrained by their families, who feared their doing injuries to themselves and others; they were chained and caged, or actually built into dark little rooms with no doors, only openings through which food could be passed.[14] Many were disowned by their families, or left to wander the streets by families who could not afford to look after them in economically disastrous, famine-ridden times. Such people were often ridiculed and stoned by the public, and were sometimes put on exhibition at the Spring Festival. The Kuomintang Army conscripted the mentally ill off the streets,[15] and mentally ill people whose behavior came to the attention of the police were often jailed.

In 1910, Dr. Andrew Wood, an American psychiatrist who later became Head of Psychiatry at the University of Iowa, began lecturing on psychiatry in Guangzhou (Canton). In 1919, he became Professor of Psychiatry and Neurology at the Beijing Union Medical College, initiating the first Western psychiatric education in China.[16] Later, psychiatric training was undertaken at the National Medical College of Shanghai, under the auspices of Dr. Richard S. Lyman, a graduate of Johns Hopkins, and Dr. Fanny G. Halpern, a neuropsychiatrist from the University of Vienna. Dr. Halpern made a number of contributions; apart from helping organize Mercy Hospital in Shanghai and training psychiatrists at the National Medical College, she helped establish a nursing school which trained psychiatric nurses, and was instrumental in the formation of the Mental Hygiene Association of Shanghai in 1940. This organization folded during the Japanese occupation in 1943, but was re-established on a national basis as the National Mental Hygiene Association in 1947. The psychiatric hospital in Nanjing, affiliated with the Central University there, began to provide psychiatric education in 1947.[17]

In a 1946 article, Chinese psychiatrist Ling Ming-yu described what he saw as the psychiatric needs of the people of China, and suggested directions for the work to take. He described traditional Chinese family life as sheltering individuals with mental problems, and suggested that since there were so few psychiatric beds in China anyway, much care could be given at home. He listed major causes of mental illness at that time as drug-related, VD-related, and related to the enormous difficulties sustained by the population during the anti-Japanese war of 1937–45:

*Millions have been killed or wounded, hundreds of thousands of homes have been broken up, and a vast amount of property has been destroyed. There*

_____The Rise of Mental Health Care in New China

*has also been mass migration of people from the eastern to the western part of the country in the face of almost unbelievable difficulties. In many communities scattered throughout China the normal social structure has been uprooted to such an extent that not a single native soul was left. City inhabitants had to stand the terror of aerial bombing for years. Millions of soldiers had to fight under the most unfavorable conditions. The amount of emotional shock sustained by the whole nation therefore is almost beyond imagination.*[18]

Dr. Ling also forecast difficulties caused by the postwar reconstruction and modernization:

*In a word, the industrialization of China will require so much readjustment in the lives of the Chinese people that the psychiatric profession will be called on for much intelligent planning for the prevention and cure of such personality difficulties as are sure to arise.*[19]

A student of Dr. Richard S. Lyman, Dr. Ling believed that China's American friends would provide much assistance in reopening closed facilities and developing modern psychiatric work in postwar China.

Based on the best information available, and adding up beds institution by institution, it would appear that there were one thousand to fifteen hundred beds in existence for mental patients at the time of Liberation, 1949. Although other estimates have been as high as six thousand beds for this period,[20] the smaller figure is more widely accepted.[21] This for a population of 400 million or more, in which the incidence of mental illness requiring hospitalization was estimated, by various missionary psychiatrists, to be in the neighborhood of one million cases.[22]

And so we find, at the time of Liberation in 1949, a nation with a three-thousand-year "Great Tradition" of medical and psychiatric thought; as long a folk tradition of exorcism and demonology in the treatment of most of those who were mentally ill; and a young, small, western-trained psychiatric discipline, which had been interrupted by years of war, in a huge nation with pressing mental health care needs. Now let us look at the work done in mental health after Liberation.

## MENTAL HEALTH WORK IN THE EARLY YEARS AFTER LIBERATION

*The ignorance and prejudice of the people towards mental patients, the indifference of the authorities to this class of sufferers and the lack of*

The Rise of Mental Health Care in New China

*trained medical and nursing personnel in psychiatry are some of the difficulties confronting workers in this field. A lot of spade work has still to be done. With the advent of a new era there are bright prospects of greater emphasis on psychiatry and mental hygiene work in China in future.*[23]

So wrote Dr. K. C. Wong of the Chinese Medical History Society in an article published within weeks of the Liberation of 1949. Yet, because other health problems facing the Chinese in 1949 were so pressing and epidemic in nature, mental health work was not a major focus of work in the early years of Liberation. As we have seen in the previous chapter, two major causes of mental health problems, drug addiction and VD,[24] were eliminated during the mass campaigns of the early 1950s.

And even though mental health work was not a focus in the early years, much important work was done. According to Wu Chen-i,[25] by 1958 there were sixty-two new psychiatric hospitals in the twenty-one provinces and autonomous regions, as well as a number of psychiatric sanitariums for the chronically ill.[26] An Australian visitor reported the number of beds in 1955 to be five thousand.[27] By 1958 there were fourteen[28] to nineteen[29] times more psychiatric beds than in 1949, for an estimated total of twenty thousand beds.[30] The number of psychiatrists increased sixteenfold, and there were twenty times the number of psychiatric nurses.[31] Kao[32] converts these figures to mean a total of 5,700 medical professionals, including 900 doctors; Cerny says there were 100 neuropsychiatrists in 1952, and 436 by 1957.[33] In Shanghai and Nanjing alone, 375 psychiatrists of "high and medium level" were graduated between 1953 and 1958.[34] Twenty times as many patients were being treated in 1958 as in 1949.[35] In 1949, psychiatric beds accounted for 1.1 percent of the total number of hospital beds; in 1958, this figure had increased to 3.6 percent.[36] Kao[37] converts these percentages into the figures 1,100 beds (1949) and 11,000 beds (1957). Finally, psychiatric admissions, reported to be 6.8 percent of all hospital admissions from 1949 to 1952, were up to 21 percent for the years 1952–1957, though down to 12 percent for the years 1958–1965.[38]

By 1958, for the first time, the Chinese had become self-sufficient in all hospital equipment, medical supplies, and drugs needed in mental health work; previously, almost everything had had to be imported.[39] As a result of the gains of these early years, recovery rates for Guangzhou and Shanghai in 1958 were given as 80 percent, contrasting with a 40–50 percent recovery rate of 1950.[40]

The array of treatment techniques broadened in the early years, so that in addition to insulin and electric shock treatment and "heat treat-

_____The Rise of Mental Health Care in New China

ments," hypnotherapy, drugs (including herbal medications), acupuncture, "stimulation of the nerves," and psychotherapy were all being used, as was a combination of these methods.[41] The first work on childhood mental illness was started in Nanjing in the early 1950s.

The Shanghai Municipal Psychiatric Hospital, mentioned earlier, was taken over by the state in 1952; by 1957 it had grown from two hundred to nine hundred beds, and by 1965, it was reported to have twenty-five hundred beds. Gregorio Bermann, an Argentine doctor who visited the hospital in the 1950s, described the changes following state takeover:

*The conduct of the personnel toward the patients changed radically: isolation, confinement, punishment, and repression were abolished. It was decided that the personnel should live, eat, and sleep together in friendship and solidarity with the patients. After four years of this new treatment of the majority of patients, forty-four of the worst cases with more than fifteen years hospitalization, among whom more than 70 percent exhibited destructive psychoses, were chosen to be treated by these new methods. The results were very encouraging. Four were discharged, four worked well, many others looked after their personal cleanliness and participated in community life. In the beginning, twenty-five male nurses and servants were assigned to the forty-four patients. Now fifteen watch over seventy. The wards are now regulated, the sick are clean, they are not destructive or aggressive, and community life is smooth and productive.[42]*

Although it was not until the Great Leap Forward that mental health work was coordinated nationwide, early research work was carried on. In 1955 a neurology and psychiatry society was organized under the Chinese Medical Association, and began publishing *The Chinese Journal of Neurology and Psychiatry*.[43] In 1953 a conference on Pavlov was held in Beijing.[44] Clinical studies included experimentation with hypnotherapy, started in 1951, reporting effective rates of 80 percent with drug-induced hypnotherapy in cases of "diseases of the nerves," and 61.5 percent effectiveness in "split-personality."[45] Electric hypnotherapy was reported "more effective for psychasthenia [neurasthenia] and hysteria, and poorer with diseases of the split-personality."[46]

Insulin treatment of schizophrenia was widely studied, reporting an effectiveness rate around 75 percent.[47] A nonconvulsive electric stimulus method developed in 1955—different from other, non-Chinese varieties of electrical stimulation—was reported to be "not only quickly effective, but . . . not painful or frightening." Its effectiveness rate in 220 cases of hysteria was reported to be 83.6 percent.[48]

The Rise of Mental Health Care in New China

Group psychotherapy was first tried at the Graduate School of Psychiatry in the Beijing College of Medicine in 1953, and all twenty-nine patients were reported to show "definite improvement." At the Nanjing Mental Health Institute, group psychotherapy combined with "a small amount of drugs" had "very good" results.[49]

In the field of psychology, the Soviet Union was taken as a model in the early years after Liberation. Soviet texts were translated into Chinese and used as the basic texts; Soviet psychologists visited and lectured in China, and Chinese psychologists traveled from all over the country to hear them. When the Soviet Academy of Medical Sciences in 1950 passed a resolution making Pavlov's theory of conditioned reflexes the basic foundation of psychology, biology, and medicine, this had a profound effect on the development of psychology in China. And since Western psychology was considered by the Soviet Union to be idealist, Chinese psychologists adopted this view as well. In particular, social psychology and psychological testing were considered reactionary by the Soviets, and the Chinese followed suit, with the result that social psychology and testing have received little attention in China since 1949.

In 1955 the Chinese Psychological Society was reinstituted; in 1956 the Institute of Psychology, which had been planned since 1950, was founded; and in 1956 the Chinese journal *Acta Psychologica Sinica* began publication.[50]

## THE GREAT LEAP FORWARD IN MENTAL HEALTH WORK

### All-China Congress

The Great Leap Forward was a period of innovation throughout Chinese life and society; millions of people participated in making steel in "back-yard steel plants," and the cooperative farms were organized into the People's Communes. Along with the rest of society, mental health work took a great leap. In June of 1958 the Ministry of Health organized the first National Conference on Mental Health,[51] bringing together in Nanjing psychiatric workers from all over China to sum up the work that they had been doing since 1949 and to chart a course for future work to be coordinated on a national scale. "Mental health," it was said, "is listed as one of the three largest subjects for scientific research."[52]

The Conference resolved, among other things, to strengthen research work in order to formulate a better program of prevention; to

The Rise of Mental Health Care in New China

improve the quality of care and treatment so as to "raise the rate of complete recovery, and reduce recurrence"[53]; to train a large number of mental health workers; to continue and increase basic research into mental health, incorporating work in biology, pathology, physiology, and anatomy; and finally,

*In order to fulfill all of our responsibilities, we must diligently learn the philosophy of Marxism-Leninism and the ideas of Mao Tse-tung. We must arm ourselves with dialectical materialism. We should learn the advanced experience of the socialist countries, among which the first is the Soviet Union. We should also learn and study our own medical legacy, and absorb from all these sources treasures of experience and theory to enrich our own specialized knowledge, so as to do our work well.[54]*

### National Mental Illness Prevention Work Plan
In order to implement the decisions arrived at during the Conference, the first Five Year Plan for mental health work in the People's Republic was written on July 15, 1958, and circulated nationwide on September 15, 1958, with the following covering letter from the Ministry of Health:

*The National Mental Illness Prevention Work Plan (1958–1962) has already been revised in accordance with the views of the Mental Illness Prevention Work Conference convened in Nanjing. It is hereby issued to you, and we hope you will thoroughly implement it.[55]*

The Five Year Plan included setting up mental illness prevention centers or hospitals in every province or locality which had none within one to two years; in areas which already had some facilities, more were to be established according to local needs.[56] Many medium-grade personnel were to be trained.[57] Administratively, the nation was to be divided into five "collaborative areas," with Beijing, Shanghai, Nanjing, Chengdu, and Changsha serving as centers. Beijing's An Ding Hospital and other facilities were to serve as centers for the Northeast, Inner Mongolia, Hebei, and Ningxia; the Nanjing Nervous and Mental Illnesses Center as the resource center for Jiangsu, Anhui, Shanxi, and Shaanxi Provinces; the psychiatric staff of Sichuan Medical College for Xinjiang, Qinghai, Tibet, Sichuan, and Gansu; similar staff of Hunan Medical College for Hunan, Guangxi, Guizhou, and Yunnan; the Shanghai Municipal Mental Hospital and the Shanghai First Medical College's mental illness staff for Jiangxi, Zhejiang, Fujian, and Hubei; and the Guangzhou Municipal Mental Hospital for Guangdong Province. The Plan reported, but said that they were incomplete, the following statistics:

The Rise of Mental Health Care in New China

that as of 1958 there were 46 mental hospitals and clinics with 11,000 beds in 21 provinces and municipalities; that 5,000 "or more" professional personnel had been trained since 1949, including 400 doctors, of whom 30 were practitioners of traditional Chinese medicine; that in 1957, 73,000 mental patients had been treated, resulting in complete cure for 27,000, and that China had an estimated 1 million mentally ill people.[58] These statistics were later revised in the 1959 article by Wu Chen-i summing up the Conference and China's first ten years of mental health work[59]; the more complete statistics have been cited earlier in this chapter.

## Results of the Work Plan
## and the National Conference

One of the first results of the National Conference and the Work Plan was the undertaking of a nationwide survey to locate and treat the mentally ill. By late 1959 eighteen million people had been surveyed in Shanghai, Nanjing, Beijing, Hunan, Siping, and Chengdu; in all except Shanghai, the surrounding farm villages were included in the survey. Techniques for conducting the survey and educating people about mental illness resembled the mass-line techniques employed during the anti-VD and anti-drug campaigns of earlier years:

*The doctors . . . nurses and mental health social workers organized themselves into small groups. They checked with the local police offices, the resident councils, and block committees to gain some knowledge of the condition of mental diseases in the area. Then they made door-to-door visits, and collected information concerning each patient (including potential patients). They gave these patients mental and physical check-ups, made diagnoses, and kept the files. . . . The groups organized the masses, families of the patients, and the Red Cross Committee of the block. Meetings were held and informative literature was distributed. They began a program of mental health education, and helped the residents to correct their past misgivings about mental diseases, so that all of them may not only take good care of the afflicted, but also report new cases quickly.[60]*

As a result of the survey, outpatient mental health clinics were set up in a number of cities, including thirteen in Beijing and eighteen in Shanghai; sometimes the clinics were housed in the same buildings as birth-control clinics.[61] Some of these clinics expanded to include a few inpatient beds, and in Nanjing, in addition to setting up mental health clinics, over two hundred homes were equipped with sickbeds. Dr. Wu wrote in 1959, "We are very earnestly carrying out this program, and hope that a mental health network will be established all over the country."[62]

During the Great Leap Forward a slogan was adopted: "No shrieking in the adults' wards and no crying in the children's wards."[63] The principle that treatments that were either painful or frightening were not to be permitted was formulated as nationwide policy after the National Conference and in the Work Plan. Lobotomy was outlawed:

*The frontal lobotomy or other clinical methods that can injure the lives and health of the patients should not be used. We must implement the system of protective treatment and resolutely oppose the binding or imprisoning of patients.*[64]

That lobotomy was still being practiced at the time of Liberation is not in question. An article published in the *Chinese Medical Journal* in 1950 reports on thirty-three cases of lobotomy in Tianjin (Tientsin), Sian and Nanjing during the 1940s, where three different psychiatrists were using the treatment. One of these psychosurgeons, in reporting his data, spoke harshly of colleagues' criticisms:

*I met criticism from a few established and leading surgeons. Some expressed the opinion that the operation of prefrontal lobotomy was "mutilating and inhuman."* . . . *However, I was not at all moved by such emotional criticisms and continued my work on the subject.* . . .[65]

The caution with which the Chinese regarded electroshock treatment, then still in use, was stated by Dr. Wu:

*In this country, specialists are divided in their opinions about electric shock treatment. They are generally quite cautious in its use. In recent years, hydergine has shown obvious effectiveness, and the use of shock treatment has been greatly reduced. It seldom is used alone, and if it is used at all, it is in combination with other methods.*[66]

In addition to surveying mental health facilities nationwide, adding to them, and enunciating principles for the conduct of mental health work, mental health institutions had to be rehabilitated if they had not been cleaned up since Liberation, and personnel in these institutions had to be reeducated. The Work Plan criticized some mental health workers for treating mental patients incorrectly, for "despising" them and not listening to what they had to say, and urged that "it is necessary to . . . establish the ideology and working style of love for patients."[67]

In cleaning up entire institutions, the call from Mao Tse-tung to "rescue the dying, heal the wounded; practice revolutionary humanitarianism"[68] was used as a guideline. The Shanghai Convalescent Home provides a dramatic example of this kind of work. It had been privately owned until 1956, when the owner turned it over to the state and continued to work there.

*It housed about fifty-five women who entered it in a state of severe chronic dementia, all of whom had a history of from four to fifteen years' illness; all had been in other mental hospitals. When they arrived, they were disheveled, dirty, incapable of personal care, and in a state of deep mental and frequently also physical prostration.*

*The treatment was divided into four stages:*

*1. To start these human residues moving, these remains with hardly a mental glimmer, to rescue them from their deep autism, it was decided to begin with one of the most deep-rooted vital elements, rhythm. They were thus first given music therapy. The patients were divided into groups of ten to twelve led by assistants. They heard music every day for one to two hours. This was not just any music; it consisted essentially of stimulating, exciting songs, full of vitality and capable of arousing enthusiasm, revolutionary songs in particular. In the beginning the patients did not seem interested, but it did not matter whether or not they responded to the music. Most, if not all, started to react after ten to twenty days; they followed the songs with their hands and feet, gestured, and accompanied the music with head movements. This was continued for a month and a half to two months until the patients sang the songs themselves. I myself was impressed to see these patients, earlier so demented, sing about ten songs in my presence. Three to four months passed in this way to verify whether there was true improvement corresponding to the degree in which they cooperated in these music sessions. At the end of that stage, they started to participate in group activities, always under the direction of an aide.*

*2. Now they had to acquire new habits; this was the rehabilitation which is part of any therapy for chronic cases. It required patience from the physician, nurse, or group leader, infinite, as that of a mother for her child. The patients got up at six o'clock in the morning, washed, took care of their personal hygiene, brushed their teeth, made their beds, and straightened their rooms. In the beginning they were taken by the hand and shown step by step how to perform those activities. After a time, both the patients and their surroundings, earlier so deteriorated and dirty, adopted norms of cleanliness and became orderly. For main meals or breakfast they stood in line and were taught how to eat and what manners to adopt.*

*In the beginning, twenty-five persons had been required for the care of forty patients. Now only six nurses were needed for fifty-five patients.*

The Rise of Mental Health Care in New China

*3. The third stage aimed at restoring intelligence. The patients had forgotten almost everything and now had to be shown things and acts in every detail. At the start, one person told stories and encouraged responses and conversation. The patients were taken to exhibitions and for walks. Their interest in other activities of daily life was stimulated. Four times a week there were sessions using TV, radio, movies, and readings from journals and magazines. When their condition permitted, they attended classes one or several times weekly to learn arithmetic, their Chinese idiom, and other subjects. Then they were taught mental hygiene. They listened to talks on the meaning of mental disease, were told that this is not a disgrace, and were taught ways to get rid of their illness.*

*At this stage, the patients began to take note of each other, and learned to organize their daily lives. They were encouraged to write about their own experiences and to report their impressions. Sometimes self-education is more effective than that offered by the physicians. This stage takes three or four months.*

*4. When the patients were able to occupy themselves, relationship with their families and environment was reestablished. The patients were permitted to go home on visits for one to three days. It was then determined whether their condition was such as to enable them to stay with their families. If such was the case, they were discharged from the hospital. However, the nurse always visited their homes every two days and then every four, five or more days. In the meantime, the social worker who had visited the family gave them instructions and suggestions on their life, study, and work.*

*These four periods together usually take one year. . . . About 80 percent of the patients recover or show considerable improvement. They are at least not destructive, aggressive, or dirty, and they can take care of themselves. . . . They usually return to the work they did before. No change is seen in 10 to 15 percent of the cases.*

*Prior to entering the Home, these patients had been subjected to highly diverse therapies: Insulin shock, electroshock, and neuroleptics. During the course of their reeducation they occasionally had to take neuroleptics, hypnotics, or other medication, usually up to 150 mg. chlorpromazine or at most 200 mg.*[69]

The psychiatrist at this institution who developed this treatment said that he had used dialectical materialism in developing it, and that

*. . . he began to think about the possibility of applying this method after reading Mao's work* On Contradiction. *Each thing in the world has its opposite. If the patient has features of abnormality he must have other*

The Rise of Mental Health Care in New China

*features of normality. The patient himself is a contradiction. Those features may be exchanged, one against the other. Mental patients suffer greatly in their innermost self. They feel despised, they live in isolation. Accordingly, the first and foremost treatment is that physician and hospital personnel be the patients' friends and show them their sympathy. They must share their lives at meals, work, and recreation and even sleep nearby. This is done by the staff in the required degree. The patients must be restored to life, and therefore, they must be accompanied without uniforms, without white aprons, without the exercise of rigid authority. . . .*

*Music and songs are important, but they are not the sole treatment and sometimes not even its most important part. The physicians' and staff's devotion play a great role. Nothing is more important in the therapy of neurotics or psychotics than the therapist himself, the human element, the warm solidarity shown in attending to the patients.*[70]

The Work Plan also directed institutions to remove chronic cases from the acute-care facilities and place them in sanitariums.[71] Several years later, one neurologist was to report that

*The organization, administration and medical treatment of chronic cases have virtually undergone a revolution in some places by the establishment of sanatory villages in which the medical workers eat, live and work with the patients and give necessary instructions. They also discuss with the patients medical and administrative problems. They organize and guide the collective recreational, occupational and physical activities in a manner of mutual assistance and as a result, a definitely speedier and higher percentage of recovery has been attained.*[72]

## AFTER THE GREAT LEAP: BASIC RESEARCH

*In actual practice, the great multitude of the masses have created and accumulated many a precious experience in psychology. It is the responsibility of the psychological workers to generalize and elevate them in a much better way to guide practice, and simultaneously to enrich the content of psychology.*[73]

In the early years, Chinese researchers in psychology and psychiatry, trying to formulate a dialectical materialist psychology and following in the footsteps of their Soviet counterparts, rejected Freud's work. He was, they said, a bourgeois idealist: idealist because his theories were undemonstrable; bourgeois because they mirrored the social realities of middle-class nineteenth century Vienna, but claimed to be valid for all classes at all times in all societies.[74] In so rejecting this claim, the psychologists were guided by Mao Tse-tung's 1942 writing on human nature:

*Is there such a thing as human nature? Of course there is. But there is only human nature in the concrete, no human nature in the abstract. In class society there is only human nature of a class character; there is no human nature above classes. We uphold the human nature of the proletariat and of the masses of the people, while the landlord and bourgeois classes uphold the human nature of their own classes, only they do not say so but make it out to be the only human nature in existence.*[75]

At a meeting held in Sian by the Shansi branch of the Chinese Psychological Society in April 1959, the question of the class nature of consciousness was hotly debated. Was there a class character to behavior patterns? To consciousness? The functioning of the brain, some said, was independent of either racial or class character; others said, however, that

*... The relation of practice to nervous activity and the mind should be: practice (existence) determines nervous activity (behavior pattern), and nervous activity produces psychic consciousness which reflects practice (existence).*[76]

A 1959 article urged Chinese medical psychologists to pursue the study of psychosomatic medicine, neglected by medicine as a whole. The author clearly saw the need for investigation into the psychogenic nature of some illnesses, mentioning hypertension and ulcers, and proposed working with gynecologists, pediatricians, and dermatologists on psychogenic factors in their work.[77] But in proposing research in psychosomatic medicine, he vigorously rejected Freudian-based Western approaches:

*They refer all the psychic factors in all the diseases to what is known as "subconscious" in psycho-analysis. This so-called subconsciousness cannot be objectively verified. . . . The emergence of the American "psychosomatic medicine" has not given any aid to modern medicine, except this objective fact of explaining the need for the aid of psychology in modern medicine.*[78]

A theory of the human mind which regards people as passive victims of an unconscious over which they have no control was simply not acceptable in a society engaged in the transformation of human relations; rather, what began to develop at this time was a theory stressing the

The Rise of Mental Health Care in New China

primacy of an active, conscious will which makes it possible for people to struggle against psychological problems and transform themselves into healthy and productive people.[79] Accordingly, one psychologist described in 1959 the "psychological therapy" being developed by psychologists and medical workers at this time as comprising three elements:

1. The introduction of knowledge concerning neurasthenia to reduce the patient's worries about the disease and to increase his confidence in rapid treatment.
2. To teach the patient concrete ways of conquering the disease and increase his courage to fight it.
3. To analyse the specific causes of the disease of each patient and help him change his incorrect attitude toward these causes and form the proper attitude of dealing with them.[80]

As important, perhaps, as these theoretical reasons why Freudian psychology was rejected by Chinese psychiatric workers is the simple fact that there was no Freudian tradition in pre-Liberation Chinese psychiatry. Chinese psychiatrists were familiar with neither psychoanalysis nor other western psychotherapies, having been educated in a strictly medical-psychiatric tradition. It seems to us that the simple historical absence of these strains of a psychological tradition accounts as much as the ideological explanations for the lack of a Freudian-based strain in post-Liberation Chinese psychiatric thinking. In our own country as well as in other Western countries, Marxists who are interested in psychology have tried—albeit with less than great success until now—to integrate the psychological understanding of Freud, the neo-Freudians, and other psychological thinkers with Marxist political understanding. Had there been a Freudian and psychotherapeutic tradition in China, we believe that at least some attempt to do this kind of study would be found in the Chinese psychiatric work since Liberation. The utter lack of it, and the lack of sophistication in the anti-Freudian papers which do exist, speak more of a lack of exposure than a thoroughgoing ideological critique of the Freudian approach. David Ho, a well-known Hong Kong psychologist, feels that Freudian psychology and Maoist thought are not necessarily antagonistic:

*In contrast to the psychoanalytic tradition, Mao's view of cognition is focused on consciousness, not on the unconscious. Mao spoke of raising the level of class consciousness—which seems analogous to expanding the ego's sphere of consciousness. The unconscious is not mentioned in Mao Tse-tung Thought; nevertheless, there appears to be no compelling reason or logical*

The Rise of Mental Health Care in New China

*necessity for its exclusion. Both psychoanalysis and Mao speak of conflicts and view personality growth as a process of conflict resolution. However, they differ in their conceptualization of the nature of both these conflicts and their resolution. Mao sees class antagonism, not sex and aggression, as the main driving force behind human action; to be sure, sex and aggression are common to all men—but not without class character in any concrete instance of their expression. In psychoanalysis, conflicts are internal, and their resolution is a matter of struggle within the individual. In Mao Tse-tung Thought, internal conflicts are but reflections of external conditions, the resolution of which is dialectically related to external class struggle; furthermore, each individual's struggle is linked to those of others and of human society as a whole. Psychoanalytic theory dwells on the intrapsychic life of individuals; in Mao Tse-tung Thought, a man's character is defined in terms of what he does in relation to society.*[81]

Psychoanalyst and Duke University Professor Emeritus Bingham Dai, born and trained in China and still practicing, commented in a letter to Paul,

*When I began to teach and practice my sociologically oriented version of psychoanalysis in the Peking Union Medical College from 1935 to 1939, I actually started to give personal therapy to a number of our staff, including psychiatrists, social workers and psychologists, with the serious intention of forming a society of psychoanalytically oriented psychotherapists. But this plan was abruptly interrupted by the Japanese occupation of Peking in 1937, and I had to return to this country in 1939. . . .*

*Actually, there is a great deal of affinity between the Chinese traditional emphasis on self cultivation and the psychoanalytic methods of self study.*[82]

In our opinion, whether or not a synthesis can ever be made between a Freudian (or neo-Freudian) understanding of individuals and a Marxist-Leninist analysis of human history, is not the issue. The issue for the Chinese is that it has not been tried. And further, a materialist understanding of mental illness would seem to require a more vigorous examination of personal psychological history than the Chinese have yet made in their treatment of mental patients. As we write this, in 1982, the expanded relations between the psychiatrists and psychologists of our two countries seem to make this kind of research and treatment more possible than ever, and that is a very exciting prospect.

But let's return to the academic psychology of twenty years ago. Some psychologists at this time were discussing "the nature of psychology," trying to decide whether it was a natural science or a social science, or both.[83] Others tried to define the object of psychological research: was it "response," "man" as the "agent of response," or the relationship between the "brain," "objective reality," and "response," one author wanted to know, as he discussed the debate going on in his "psychology circle."[84] Another author lists the legitimate area of study as

*... three problems relating to consciousness: (1) The origin, occurrence and development of consciousness. . . . (2) The process of human response to objective reality. . . . (3) The characteristics of man's conscious activities.*[85]

Another psychologist described psychology's place in the development of socialism, citing as legitimate areas of applied research the study of "labor psychology," involving improvement of production and lessening of work intensity and workplace accidents; "educational psychology," to understand better when and how children learn certain types of concepts so as to improve teacher training; and medical psychology.[86] And at another symposium on psychology, this one held at Taiyuan in 1961, psychologists argued over the question of "the material nature of psychological phenomena," the various positions being (1) the phenomenon-substance theory; (2) the quantitative-change-to-qualitative-change theory and (3) the theory that the brain, high-level nervous activity, and psychological phenomena must be distinguished from one another.[87]

Dr. C.C. Ching, a Beijing psychologist who recently spent six months studying in the U.S., describes the struggle in psychology at this time as being between two lines, one which held that psychological functions were nothing more than "higher nervous activity." This line was called reductionist by those holding the view that human psychological activity is "far more sophisticated than and qualitatively different from that of animals."[88] This group was accused of dualism by the other group. Further, he tells us that in 1958 the emphasis on physiological study in psychology was criticized by a group that said psychologists had ignored the

*... "class nature" of people by one-sidedly emphasizing the mind as a function of the brain, a view that was said to violate Marx's principle that a person is a social being involved in class struggle. This trend was called the "biologizing" of mental phenomena.*[89]

Research psychologists were trying, at this time, to define the subject matter of psychology, a field in its infancy in China, as well as to develop a dialectical materialist approach to the field.

The Rise of Mental Health Care in New China

The period between 1958 and 1965 in psychology is recalled by Dr. Ching, who works at the Institute of Psychology in Beijing, as a period of growth and development. Between 1960 and 1965 five hundred papers in many areas of psychology were published, and the Chinese Psychological Society's membership was at an all-time high of 1,087 in 1965. Dr. Ching sums up the period in this way:

*It should be noted that research work in this period was no longer confined to the Soviet tradition and developed in a more independent atmosphere, freely borrowing useful ideas from both East and West. Some of the studies of this period, the selection of problems, and the approaches to problems were truly international and of rather high standards. Thus, on the eve of the Cultural Revolution in 1966, after fifteen years of toil, psychology at last had a strong foothold in the ranks of science.*[90]

## After the Great Leap: Clinical Research

In both theoretical and practical work, the Chinese relied heavily on Pavlov's study of the nervous system, the brain, and "higher nervous activity." The concepts of neurological excitation and inhibition played an important role in their understanding of neuroses and psychoses. Using this Pavlovian framework, a number of new treatments were developed during this period.

Medical psychologists and psychiatrists worked together for the first time to develop the "Rapid Combined Treatment of Neurasthenia." This area of work was very popular in the late 1950s, and much research was done to develop a fast, efficient, humane method of treatment of "neurasthenics." (This term is used by the Chinese to describe most of the different kinds of neuroses, and includes symptoms such as fatigue, insomnia, anxiety, and lack of energy.)[91] Chinese psychiatrists described how they arrived at a diagnosis of neurasthenia:

*We used Pavlov's theory of psychasthenia {neurasthenia} and the symptomatic descriptions of V.A. Gilyarovsky and E.A. Popov, as a diagnostic basis. We considered the following aspects: (1) When objective reasons for exhaustion were eliminated, and the pathological symptoms persisted, and even became more severe for over a month, we diagnosed the symptoms as psychasthenia {neurasthenia}, otherwise not. (2) When other physical disorders were present (tuberculosis, high blood pressure, rheumatism, syphilis, stomach or duodenal ulcers, over-active thyroids, severe anemia or malnutrition, and chronic diseases of the eye, ear, nose or throat), we did not diagnose the patient to be suffering from psychasthenia. (3)*

## The Rise of Mental Health Care in New China

*Although there was no clear indication of emotional causes, and yet the typical symptoms of psychasthenia were present, and no physical disorders were discovered, we diagnosed the illness as psychasthenia. (4) If a patient complained about headache or other organic malfunction without suffering from other general symptoms of a weak suppressing process (such as extreme irritability, lack of patience and reduced self-control, inability to concentrate, lack of memory, and insomnia) we did not diagnose the trouble as psychasthenia. (5) When symptoms of other mental diseases, such as compulsion or hysteria, were present along with the characteristics of psychasthenia, we did not diagnose it as psychasthenia.*[92]

These investigators interviewed 25,471 persons[93] and discovered that 86.7 percent of the neurasthenics among them came from a group of "mind workers," while the rest came from "manual laborers," and hypothesized that

*The work of the mind is more likely than physical labor to cause too much tension of the cerebrospinal nervous system. {But} when we discovered that those who work with their minds have a more frequent occurrence of psychasthenia, it does not mean that they use their minds too much. It is rather due to the fact that they do too little physical labor.*[94]

Physical fatigue caused by heavy manual work did not cause neurasthenia, the authors said, and they did a further study of different types of factory work to determine what kinds of work were more or less likely to produce the kind of strain that would lead to neurasthenia. They said that neurasthenia was a psychosomatic illness, and that emotional elements were the major causes, but that "people's mental state is closely related to the nature and condition of their work and their living routines."[95]

The combination of treatments used in the rapid combined treatment of neurasthenia included drugs, physical therapy, physical exercise, and psychotherapy, and took about a month. The drugs used were "Pavlov's mixture": bromides and caffeine; insulin, which lowers blood sugar; and Novocaine (procaine, an antidepressant). The physical therapy was Gilyarovsky's nonconvulsive electric-stimulus treatment, in which mild electric currents were applied to the temples for half an hour each day.[96] The particular drug or drugs used, and whether or not a patient received the electrical-stimulation therapy, were determined case by case. The other treatment components, physical exercise and psychotherapy, were received by all patients. The physical exercise was based on traditional Chinese exercises such as t'ai-ch'i-ch'uan. Psychotherapy was done both individually and in group sessions, and there were also lectures describing

_____The Rise of Mental Health Care in New China

the illness, and conferences among all the patients. The psychotherapy was conducted

> . . . according to the principle of education in our country, and Pavlov's theory of the activities of the cerebrospinal nervous systems. The basic content of our psychotherapy includes the following three aspects:
>
> A. Help the patient to regard his illness with a correct attitude, and to establish a spirit of revolution and optimism. Help the patient to be cheerful, lively and spirited. Help the patient to dispel fears and worries about his illness, and establish his confidence in complete recovery and his determination to fight against the disease. In order to inspire the patient's will to struggle against his illness, we must solve the problem of motivation. We think the sense of responsibility toward socialism is the only unlimited source of motivating power.
>
> B. Hand over to the patient the knowledge of his illness. We emphasize the fact that there is an objective regularity regarding the occurrence, development, worsening, or recovery of the disease. When the patient understands these regularities, he may take an active position. Instead of passively enduring his sufferings, he may actively hasten his own recovery.
>
> C. Try to encourage the patient to develop his subjective activeness which is the positive subjectiveness and creativeness with which he may fight against his illness. We want the patient to combine the objective regularities of the illness with the special conditions of his environment and himself to formulate a concrete and practical method to fight against his illness. This is very large in scope. It includes reasonable organization of his work and study, to stress planning, and to improve methods. He should arrange his life rationally. He must participate in a suitable amount of recreation, and cultural activities, as well as physical exercise. He must, on his own initiative, correct his own bad temperamental characteristics, and raise his level of ideas and cultivation. In this manner, many of the negative elements in the patient's environment which were harmful to his (her) health may be changed into positive elements to promote his health.[97]

The treatment was conducted at an outpatient clinic at the workplace, for those patients who were comfortable living at home; for others, there was a sort of "halfway house" arrangement set up in a school dormitory or rest center at the factory.[98] The researchers noted that the percentage of patients cured or "apparently better" was 79.4 percent, including 41.2 percent cured or "basically cured,"[99] but they were cautious in their evaluation of the method because it had been used for only ten months at the time they wrote the article. Although they felt that all the treatment components were important and that they could not single out any particular aspect as being most important, they concluded by saying:

*To elevate the idea of developing the patient's subjective activeness to the prominent position where it rightly belongs is the element of our quick combination treatment that we would very much like to make a special note of. This is a worthy subject of study in psychotherapy.*[100]

As we shall see, although the Pavlovian language is no longer used, many aspects of the rapid combined treatment that were first devised at this time are still in use in China.

Research into the causes and treatment of schizophrenia was undertaken at this time as well. Some schizophrenics were said to have a "weak type of central nervous system"[101]; other studies pointed to biochemical and metabolic problems,[102] and research showed some hereditary tendency to the disease based on higher incidence of schizophrenia in the families of schizophrenic patients.[103] Some of the treatments of schizophrenia and other serious mental illness investigated were:

*1. Artificial hibernation.* Described as being more effective than insulin shock therapy or drugs alone, especially for schizophrenics, the treatment was said to cause the cerebrospinal nervous system to

*. . . produce a strong suppression which in turn erases or prevents the body's defensive reflex. . . . The meaning of the process of defensive response in the treatment of nervous activities has been made clear by the theory of Pavlov.*[104]

In a study done at the Beijing College of Medicine, the treatment consisted of medicating the patients with both chlorpromazine (Thorazine) and pethidine (meperidine, a synthetic narcotic), and placing them on a mattress of ice bags, lowering their temperature over the course of several hours to about 34°C for one or two weeks. Patients slept deeply for seventeen to nineteen hours a day during the first five days of the treatment, and then for twelve to fifteen hours a day. In the view of researchers and patients alike, there was improvement. The researchers contrasted the rapidity of improvement with the slower gains made using drugs alone, and believed the hibernation method better also because it relied on smaller dosages of the medications. The method was of interest to many psychiatrists, who tried it out in various parts of the country, but it was said that "the durability of its effect, its way of improvement, and its function remain to be studied."[105]

*2. Insulin shock treatment.* A 1959 article summed up the work of the first few years after Liberation with insulin used by itself or in conjunction with electric-shock treatment or drugs, and using different dosages that rendered the patient unconscious or semiconscious for the duration of the treatment. Also discussed was the innovation of bringing the patient out of shock by feeding him or her fried rice powder or fried flour instead of sugar water; it was said that these substitutes caused fewer cases of nausea. Again using Pavlovian terminology, the theory behind this form of treatment was that

*When low blood sugar caused excess suppression, and gradually extended from the surface of the cerebrum to the sub-surface, . . . the vegetative nervous system began to have increased activity. . . . Activities of the 2nd signal series, the activities of the 1st signal series, the food reflex, and the defensive reflex, all gradually became suppressed.* [106]

3. *Electric stimulus.* A Chinese researcher, Wang Ching-hsiang, developed a nonconvulsive electric-stimulus treatment which was described as different from others in that it was "not painful or frightening," and was said to be effective in 83.6 percent of 220 cases of hysteria. [107]

4. *Hypnotherapy.* Both drug-induced and electric hypnotherapy (the induction of sleep) were tried; their efficacy was said to be good for neurasthenia and hysteria, not as good in other illnesses. The fact that the treatment did not cause pain was noted, with suggestions for further research. [108]

5. *Herbal medications.* These medications were investigated and began to be used very early on in the treatment of psychiatric disorders; little specific information about their use during these years is available, however.

6. *Acupuncture.* At the time of the Great Leap, acupuncture was being used at many different hospitals in many cities. It was described as having "quick and obvious results" in the treatment of hysteria. [109] In addition, a "nerve stimulation method" was mentioned as being helpful in the treatment of neurasthenia; no further details were given.

A 1965 article describing treatment of schizophrenia said that immediate results in treating the acute illness were good, but that maintaining the results and preventing a recurrence were problems, urging follow-up for at least a year after discharge from the hospital to enable the patient to get over the "period of peak recurrence." [110] The author describes measures taken to prevent recurrence:

*(a) energetic and thorough treatment in the acute stage, (b) psychotherapy before discharge from the hospital to enable the patient to understand the nature of his own illness and the method of combating it, (c) proper arrangement of the surroundings and requirements for living, education and*

The Rise of Mental Health Care in New China

*working after discharge from the hospital, (d) suitable measures for the maintenance of the therapeutic result, (e) close follow-up to find out and help to settle the problems of each patient.*[111]

The Chinese approach to investigating treatments for schizophrenia and other serious mental disorders at this time was strongly influenced by the Soviet practice of the period. In addition, attempts were made to incorporate features of traditional Chinese medicine such as acupuncture and herbal medications. And mass-line educational methods which had been successful in other early health campaigns were used both with mental patients themselves and the population at large.

## WORK ON CHILDHOOD MENTAL ILLNESS

Nanjing seems to have been the center of research and treatment of childhood mental illness. In March, 1955 an outpatient department designed especially for the treatment of children's mental problems was opened at Nanjing Hospital,[112] and in March, 1956 ten inpatient beds were made available for children. In April, 1958 a twenty-four-bed children's ward was opened there.[113] An article describing the work done at the Nanjing Hospital was published after the National Conference in 1959. The approach taken by mental health workers was a three-pronged one, utilizing both inpatient and outpatient facilities in coordination with a preventive health survey in which both parents and teachers were asked to help identify children with problems. Mental health workers surveyed thirty-two kindergartens and elementary schools, and conducted research in one. In observing children with suspected mental disorders, researchers used toys, pictures, books, colored chess boards, and "common-sense problems," as well as direct questioning of the child, and often visited the child's home to observe the family situation. Visits to the children's schools were also made. In treating 573 children on an outpatient basis from 1955 to 1959, the children were found to be suffering from a variety of conditions, some of which were the aftereffects of physical illnesses such as spinal meningitis. The majority of children had "underdeveloped nervous functions" (37.5 percent), which were treated with hydergine and small doses of thyroid extract, as well as chlorpromazine for "excited and restless" children; and "functional nervous disorders," (21 percent), which were treated with bromides, caffeine, and luminal with "electric hypnotherapy" used in cases of insomnia. The researchers were cautious in their use of drugs, starting out with very small doses and watching closely for adverse reactions. Insulin could not be used to induce unconsciousness, and electroshock treatment was not allowed for children under the age of ten. Acupuncture was used to treat bed-wetting and nervous vomiting. In working with the children, researchers involved both the family and school personnel so that they would understand the nature of the illness and be able to help in the course of the treatment.[114]

From March, 1956 to February, 1959, 140 children were admitted to the hospital for inpatient treatment; information about treatment is available for 128 children. The attitude toward the needs of hospitalized children was summed up this way:

*Since children are growing and maturing, they need not only medical help, but also nurture and education so that they may continuously develop morally, intellectually, and physically. The healing and prevention of mental disease are very closely related to the development in these respects. Based upon the difference in their age and in their pathological symptoms, we proceeded with our work of combining healing with education. This was their school as well as their hospital.*[115]

While in the hospital, the children were divided into three groups: preschoolers, older children, and "the critically ill group (confused, or otherwise uncooperative)."[116] Each group was assigned special staff members, and programs were designed to meet the needs of the different groups. Older children spent their mornings in classes of no more than forty minutes' length, in which involvement and "self-awakening," and not achievement or standards, were stressed.[117] In the afternoons children were involved in "work therapy" and recreation, and activities were varied according to the problems and needs of the children. For example,

*The violently excited and depressed type carried dirt, weeded the grass, and played ball games so as to develop their positiveness. Hysterical children are usually sympathetic and enthusiastic about serving others. They were encouraged to fix up the rooms, and to take care of the little ones. The schizophrenics tend to retreat into their own dreams, and we tried to induce them to develop an interest in the world around them. They were assigned to make toys, to feed little animals, and to stage plays.*[118]

In addition to medication, acupuncture, recreational therapy, and education, older children engaged in one-to-one or group therapy, although the methods are not described. Children were also instilled with "communist virtues" such as patriotism and responsibility to the collective.[119]

The Rise of Mental Health Care in New China

One case study illustrates the use of this combination of treatment techniques:

*Another 10-year-old girl vomited regularly. She stayed in bed all day, and was very fearful of everything, even loud conversation or the noise made by a rooster. She was sent to our hospital when her vomiting could not be stopped. After we stopped her vomiting with drugs, we were all careful not to mention the word vomit. One of the workers was made responsible for playing with her, and gradually induced her to get up from her bed. We encouraged her to participate in the games, and gave her the job of taking care of the record player. We gradually helped her gain courage and be more cooperative, while we treated her with the insulin low blood sugar method. She progressed nicely for two years, and has now entered a regular elementary school.*[120]

Of the 128 patients admitted during these four years, 58.6 percent were "cured or apparently better." After the children were discharged from the hospital, contact was maintained with them and their parents and teachers. Six of ten cured schizophrenics had relapses, as did three of the manic-depressives, but patients cured of other illnesses were said to have "recovered very well and are continuously improving."[121]

Both in describing childhood and treating childhood mental illnesses, the Nanjing researchers used a Pavlovian model, describing one treatment as helping to "increase the suppressing process of the nervous system."[122] Pavlov's mixture of bromides and caffeine, and insulin and artificial hibernation techniques, were widely used. At the same time, the "rapid combined treatment" method in use in treating adults was used with children, and Chinese methods such as acupuncture were used a great deal. Very important, too, was the development of a network of cooperation among hospital staff, parents, and teachers.

Outside of Nanjing, little work specifically on childhood mental problems was reported. A Canadian visitor reported in 1964 that in the late 1950s a Shanghai mental hospital had established a twenty-bed children's unit, but found that in two years only eight children had been admitted. This ward was converted back to adult use.[123] An Australian psychiatrist visiting China in 1957 was told that the only children's mental facility was the one in Nanjing, which he was unable to arrange to visit. In other locations, discussions with psychiatrists as to the treatment of various childhood mental disorders met with "an almost complete blank."[124] This doctor wondered whether defective children died early due to the harshness of life in China, whether schizophrenia went unnoticed or undiagnosed in a more rural society, or whether the nature of Chinese society actually caused a lesser degree of childhood mental illness.[125] The Canadian psychiatrist, Denis Lazure, concluded from his visits that the latter was the case.

We tend to agree with Dr. Lazure that the noncompetitive and more closely-knit nature of Chinese society produces children with fewer emotional problems. But we also believe that the Chinese are relatively unsophisticated in recognizing and treating some kinds of difficulties which Chinese children may encounter. We know that in the last few years, since communication between Chinese and American psychologists and psychiatrists has increased, the Chinese are asking for help in this area as well as in the area of education.

## THE CULTURAL REVOLUTION
## IN MENTAL HEALTH WORK

Almost nothing was written by the Chinese about psychology or mental health during the Cultural Revolution; publication of all of the relevant professional journals ceased in 1966. Our major source of information about the work of the Chinese before the Cultural Revolution was U.S. government translations of Chinese material. But during the Cultural Revolution there was nothing to translate. Basic research in psychology was curtailed; the Chinese Psychological Association was abolished.[126] Psychology departments in the universities were closed, and those psychologists who remained at the universities (and were not sent to the countryside or to May 7th cadre schools) worked in other departments, such as philosophy or education.[127] Between 1969 and 1972 the Institute of Psychology was closed. Dr. Ching[128] says that between 1966 and 1973 psychology was "completely liquidated," and that teaching and research were practically nonexistent for almost ten years, the years between 1966 and 1976. The one area of psychology that seemed always to remain of interest was educational/developmental, since the Chinese have always felt that these areas have tremendous practical significance for their educational system.

The kind of attack that psychological research experienced during the Cultural Revolution was recounted by Dr. Ching.[129] In 1965 a Dr. Chen Li of Hangchow University did a routine study of color/form preference in small children, replicating a standard experiment. The study was picked up and attacked by a then-obscure intellectual, Yao Wen-yuan, writing under the pseudonym "Revolutionary Man" in a Beijing newspaper. Yao was later to be catapulted into the leadership of China

The Rise of Mental Health Care in New China

as one of the Gang of Four. He attacked the experiment because it isolated color and form as abstractions, and Yao argued that color and form do not exist except in concrete objects. Therefore, he said, the psychologist was studying a problem that did not exist in the real world. He further argued that preferences are always related to the class background and position in society of the person, even the small child, doing the preferring. In sum, psychology was a pseudo-science which did not study the laws of nature in accordance with Marxism.

In this atmosphere it is not surprising that little theoretical work was done in medical psychology or psychiatry during the years of the Cultural Revolution. So Chinese psychiatry was left, going into this dry period, still with a Pavlov-based understanding of mental illness as an "imbalance" between the nervous system's two states, excitation and inhibition, the role of the psychiatrist being somehow to bring the nervous system back into balance through various forms of treatment. This approach can be called "mechanical materialist"; it certainly is not dialectical. We have come across one interesting example of an attempt by a neurologist in the People's Liberation Army to use dialectical materialism in his treatment of an insomniac:

*Chairman Mao teaches us: "Of the two contradictory aspects, one must be principal and the other secondary. The principal aspect is the one playing the leading role in the contradiction. The nature of a thing is determined mainly by the principal aspect of a contradiction, the aspect which has gained the dominant position." This thought came to my mind: It is a normal phenomenon of excitation and inhibition of the cerebral cortex that a person is full of spirit in the daytime and falls asleep at night. The problem of a neurasthenic is that his cerebral cortex is not excited in the daytime when it should be and not inhibited at night, thus disturbing the normal functioning of the nervous system.*

*Excitation and inhibition are the two aspects of a contradiction. One must play the leading role. But which? We take a rest in order to work well, but not vice versa. Excitation thus plays the leading role, and in curing this kind of ailment emphasis should be put on the aspect of excitation. But the old textbooks on nervous diseases said tonics or hypnotics should be prescribed for neurasthenia to quiet the patient down. That is, emphasis was placed on the aspect of inhibition. But practice shows that this kind of treatment cannot solve the problem fundamentally. It often results in the patient's needing an increasing dose of medicine, while the disorder still remains.*

*In line with Chairman Mao's teaching: "When the principal aspect*

The Rise of Mental Health Care in New China

*which has gained predominance changes, the nature of a thing changes accordingly," I decided to change the old, traditional way of treatment. I concentrated on the aspect of excitation which plays the leading role, to help increase the excitation of the patient in the daytime. Sufficient excitation will naturally induce appropriate inhibition.*

*With the assistance of the fraternal hospitals and comrades, I studied and adopted a new way of treatment, that is, increasing the degree of excitation of the patient in the daytime. After repeated experiments on animals and on myself until I was sure that this method of treatment brought no harm to the human body, I tried it out on a patient who had suffered from neurasthenia for more than 20 years. I treated him once each day before noon, one minute each time. After three days the patient felt drowsy between 8 and 9 in the evening, and since then he has been full of spirit in the daytime and able to sleep normally at night. Thus his nervous disorder was cured without a tablet or an injection.*

*To date, we have treated over 500 neurasthenics who suffered from headache and insomnia. The efficacy rate exceeds 80 percent.*[130]

Had more psychiatrists and psychologists been able to conduct research that attempted to apply dialectical materialist concepts, we think we would have seen more work of this kind. What was so frustrating about the Cultural Revolution was that some people were studying dialectical materialism, but many scientists and intellectuals were treated as enemies, and sent to May 7th cadre schools for years to do manual labor, cut off from any opportunity to apply dialectical materialism to their research areas.

In the realm of clinical work as well, almost nothing was written by the Chinese themselves during the years of the Cultural Revolution. One exception is an interesting and lengthy piece that can be thought of as an abstract for a textbook on neurology and psychiatry. It was given—in Chinese—to the first American medical delegation to visit China in 1972, after the "thaw" in relations between our two countries following Nixon's visit, and was translated here. It would be wrong, however, to call this work a product of the Cultural Revolution, as we are told that it was first published in 1959, revised in 1965, and again revised in 1970. We suspect that the 1970 update grafted political language onto the medical "meat" of the piece, with such sentences as "When people's mental activities are being observed, the medical workers must use the class viewpoint to treat everything and analyze everything."[131] The translation of this text is very poor, unfortunately, and the translator saw fit to edit the chapter on psychiatry because it contained "a significant amount of political indoctrination"; nonetheless, we thought that some readers might want to browse through the chapter on psychiatry, which we have included in the Appendix.

One article about mental health workers[132]—psychiatrists, nurses, and others—going to the countryside as part of that overall movement, shows that these workers saw themselves as part of the medical field as a whole; the kind of work they did in the countryside was the same as that done by any other team sent from an urban hospital to the countryside, except that they also treated mental illnesses. They built their own hospital themselves, and produced vegetables to help feed staff and patients. They traveled around the county, treating large numbers of people in their own production brigades, and participated in the local sanitation campaign. Hospitalized patients who were able to do so were encouraged to care for themselves and to serve meals and do mending and gardening. Trying to solve their problems in accordance with prevailing political policies, the workers redivided tasks and trained themselves in many different aspects of hospital work, so that

*. . . our doctors, in their spare time, also did nursing work and the nurses helped with the treatment, answering calls, etc. The druggist helped with the work of registration and bookkeeping and also acted as cashier, while the accountant attended also to the duties of general management. In a word, all positive factors were brought into full play. Everybody got moving and took an active hand in the work, with courage and no fear of fatigue, including such tasks as household cleanliness, laundering and haircuts for our patients and ourselves.*[133]

Foreign visitors report that workers in the lower echelons at mental hospitals were given increased training in mental health work during this period.[134] And, like all other hospitals and workplaces, the administrative structure of mental hospitals was changed to conform with the prevailing Revolutionary Committee structure, in which the facility was run by a team consisting of workers from the hospital, Communist Party cadres, and People's Liberation Army members.[135]

The only other available article written by the Chinese during the Cultural Revolution is a very short piece from *China Pictorial,* a popular picture magazine, in November 1971, called "New Treatment for the Insane:"

*Recently we paid a visit to the Mental Hospital of Chenchow Prefecture, Hunan Province. We saw the patients leading a normal, orderly life. They read newspapers and books, participate in light manual labor, join in physical and recreational activities, and cooperate in their treatment. This is an unprecedented achievement.*

The Rise of Mental Health Care in New China

*One of the personnel explained that a medical group had been sent by the No. 165 Hospital of the People's Liberation Army to popularize a new acupuncture therapy. It arrived in April, 1969. The PLA comrades were inspired by Chairman Mao's instruction, "Human knowledge can in no way be separated from practice." Together with the institution's own doctors, they made extensive investigations and gained a great deal of experience in clinical treatment. They came to understand their patients better. Although the cause of illness was different in each case, most of the patients were in the grip of an intense mental struggle or had lapsed into melancholia for a prolonged period owing to their inability to deal with the objective world correctly. Failure to free themselves of it caused the cerebrum to lose part of its functions. Therefore only careful, deep-going ideological work, and persistent education with Mao Tse-tung Thought, could help the insane adopt a correct attitude. Only thus could the disease be cured.*

*Still, a mental disease is different from an ordinary "ideological illness." And to restore the function of the cerebrum to normal, medicinal treatment is necessary. Electric and insulin shock treatments, large doses of chlorpromazine and restrictive methods such as locking and tying-up, have been abolished for more than two years. Medical workers have combined the advantages of Western and traditional Chinese medicine to create a treatment which includes the new acupuncture, herbal medicines and small doses of chlorpromazine.*

*A woman patient became insane on six occasions and had electric shock treatment some 20 times. Instead of being cured, she suffered great pain, both physically and mentally. Once while out of her mind during her stay at the asylum, she tore a quilt cover to pieces. The cotton was held in place by a web of red threads. These she pulled out and tried to embroider a red flag. Seeing this, the medical workers realized that she was not completely out of her mind. After that, they studied with her often and had heart-to-heart talks to help solve her mental problems. With repeated education from the medical personnel plus medicinal treatment, she returned to normal in only a little over three months.*

*Over the past two years, 79.2 percent of the mentally ill interned at the hospital were cured. Improvement was seen in 98.8 percent of the patients, some of whom had been deranged for more than 20 years and had been hospitalized several times without relief. Those restored to health left the hospital in high spirits and went back to their work.*[136]

Reading this article, we get a capsule "what's wrong with this picture" of the Cultural Revolution in mental health work. First of all, it attributes the positive change in this institution to the coming of the

People's Liberation Army medical workers, giving no credit to the hospital's own doctors or staff. Abusive treatments such as locking- and tying-up are said to have been abolished for "more than two years," implying that these changes took place only after the onset of the Cultural Revolution; in fact, as we have seen earlier, these practices were done away with shortly after Liberation wherever possible, and were abolished nationwide after the 1958 Nanjing Conference. It is true that electroconvulsive therapy (ECT) was abolished during the Cultural Revolution. The article does allow, in passing, that "a mental disease is different from an ordinary 'ideological illness.' " We are then treated to a "case study" in which a woman's attempt to embroider a red flag after she tears a quilt cover apart is seen as an indication that she is not totally out of her mind, a kind of Cultural Revolution soap opera, the red flag being—next to Chairman Mao—the major icon of the time. Finally, the article's concluding statistics are unbelievable, and no Chinese psychiatric worker today would quote such figures. In fact, most western visitors to Chinese psychiatric facilities even during the height of the Cultural Revolution were not told such statistics.

Fortunately for our ability to understand Chinese mental health work, the Cultural Revolution (1966–1976), with its dry spell in publishing, coincided with renewed relations from 1970 on between China and the west, so that much of what we know of recent mental health work in China comes to us from western visitors.

Paul is one of these Western visitors, and here is his account of the first of his trips to the People's Republic.

## PAUL'S FIRST TRIP

I was finally able to secure an invitation to visit China in 1975, and so it was on a hot June day that I arrived in Beijing with twenty-four other excited Americans. Our group had diverse interests. As a psychiatrist, I wanted particularly to discover how the Chinese felt about Freud, schizophrenia, neurosis, and all things psychiatric. Since the tour was not psychiatrically oriented, I decided to find out as much as I could about mental health in China by interviewing people of all kinds, as many as possible, during our six-city tour.

I worked on this project with five other tour members whose interests were similar. All across China we dauntlessly questioned citizens about anxieties, marital and sexual problems, and family discord. We probed into absenteeism from work, alienation, antisocial behavior, and

The Rise of Mental Health Care in New China

any other subjects we could think of that might cast some light on the general state of mental health in the People's Republic.

The Chinese were very cooperative. When our guides explained to them that we were quite sympathetic to the Chinese people, all the workers, peasants, soldiers, women's groups, students, teachers, and physicians were extremely open in their answers to our rather personal questions. As we spoke with more and more people, it became evident that the Chinese were relatively free from psychoneurotic and personality disorders. In other words, there was very little depression, anxiety, fear, or alienation in China, especially when compared with Western society or with other emerging nations. (On my second trip to China in 1979, I learned that the responses I got to these questions were more guarded than I knew at the time because of the atmosphere of fear created by the Gang of Four and the Cultural Revolution. In any case, it is still my impression that the Chinese are less afflicted by psychoneuroses and personality disorders than are people in the United States and Western Europe. Comparison of the amount of mental illness in the two countries is still difficult. During 1980, Dr. Liu Xiehe, a research professor of psychiatry at the medical school in Chengdu, reported epidemiologic surveys of Sichuan [Szechuan] showing a prevalence of 4.6 cases of schizophrenia per 1000 people in this province of 100 million.[137] Also, in 1980, Dr. Hsia Chen-yi, head of the Department of Psychiatry at Shanghai First Medical College and Psychiatric Hospital, reported epidemiologic surveys of his city showing a prevalence of 4.2 cases of schizophrenia per 1000 people.[138, 139] A similar prevalence survey reported in 1981 by Dr. Shen Yu-tsun, head of the Department of Psychiatry of Beijing Medical College and the Third Teaching Hospital, found 1.8 cases of schizophrenia per 1000, or 341 out of a population of 187,126 in an agricultural district, Haidian near Beijing.[140] Recent surveys in the United States, Canada and Western Europe show a prevalence of 5 to 30 cases of schizophrenia per 1000 population, pointing up the wide range in the estimate of this illness even among Western surveys. So although one is tempted to compare these western and eastern surveys of schizophrenia, there are significant differences in methodology and diagnostic standards that make this quite hazardous.)

During the interviews, I was most interested in information concerning absenteeism from work. I felt this indicated the kind of alienation that is often seen in personality disorders. In talking with people, we learned that it is virtually unknown for Chinese workers to be absent from their jobs unless they are physically ill and in treatment at a clinic or hospital. (The Chinese admitted on my second visit that in the cities,

The Rise of Mental Health Care in New China

absenteeism brought on by factional struggles was common during the decade of the Cultural Revolution. Absenteeism from work was less common in rural areas during this period because the forces of the Gang of Four had less impact on the countryside.) Of course, they told us, they do have vacations and take pregnancy leaves, but they go to work consistently and like their work. When I pressed him, however, one of our guides was finally able to recall someone he knew who had been discontented with his job and changed from hotel employment to factory work. The general feeling seemed to be that if one is unsuited to a particular job, co-workers and leaders should recognize that fact before it becomes a problem for the person himself. (The discontent felt by young people who were sent from the cities to work in the countryside was a fact I did not hear about until later.)

In conversation, it became obvious that the general availability of and participation in criticism/self-criticism sessions is used as a Chinese mental health device. These sessions, involving all concerned, take place two or three times a week both at work and in a residential setting. Not only are political decisions discussed, but many important controversial and personal problems are raised as well. (The use of criticism/self-criticism had declined by 1979.)

One of the doctors we spoke to was a general practitioner of medicine in a rural commune in Daqai (Tachai), in northwestern China. He was trained before Liberation in the late 1940s, and now functioned as one of ten physicians, a number of barefoot doctors, and other health workers who served the medical and health needs of the thirty thousand people in the commune. Most of the patients he saw had been sent on to him by barefoot doctors. Of the sixty patients he saw each day, he said, two or three might have an emotional illness. (In 1979 I learned from Chinese doctors that general practitioners there usually found a much higher proportion, about 20 to 25 percent, in their patients.) These patients are often given tranquilizers. I noted with interest that Chinese doctors have access to—and use—Western tranquilizers such as Librium, Valium, and meprobamate, as well as traditional herbal remedies and acupuncture. This commune physician said that he felt that interpersonal stress played a significant role in the sickness of his emotionally ill patients, and that he therefore recommended that these patients be treated through the criticism/self-criticism session. (Many patients with stress-related symptoms were treated with herbs and acupuncture by barefoot doctors or by Chinese traditional-medicine clinics in the cities.)

When we spoke to school administrators and teachers, we wanted to find out about behavioral problems among young children and ado-

*psychiatry is a sensitive political issue, hard to be*

lescents. The consensus was that behavior problems are uncommon, although some children do learn more slowly than others. The teachers said it was rare for a child to be so disruptive that he had to leave the classroom. One teacher did recall a student who had behavior difficulty because of problems in the home. At this time child psychiatry had been abolished in China; it has since been reestablished.

After talking to the people for two and a half weeks, three of us from the tour were unexpectedly allowed to pay one of the first visits by Americans to a mental hospital in Beijing, and we directly questioned two psychiatrists there about their diagnosis and treatment of mental illness. We considered ourselves very fortunate to get inside this hospital, an acute-treatment center in a pleasantly landscaped section of the city. We spent three hours with the psychiatrists, asking questions of every conceivable kind. Dr. Wu Chen-i was a distinguished-looking older man, a medical school teacher who had taken part of his training at the Langley Porter Clinic in California. The other physician was Dr. Shen Yu-tsun, a knowledgeable and intense middle-aged woman who was in charge of patient care at the hospital. Both spoke English and helped our interpreter with translation problems, but always answered our questions in Chinese. I assume this was done so that the Revolutionary Committee member who accompanied us could understand what was said. The hospital we saw was affiliated with the Beijing Medical School, had about eighty beds equally divided between men and women, and offered both inpatient and outpatient services. (There is, in addition, in Beijing, the An Ding Hospital, a fifteen-hundred-bed facility for acute and chronic mental patients.) Dr. Wu told me that besides the patients in the hospital, the staff also cares for five hundred mental patients in their own homes, an unusual arrangement for treatment practiced by some hospitals in China. These "home bed" patients are visited every day by doctors or nurses and receive the same treatment as hospital patients. The Chinese say this treatment method is less expensive than building more hospitals and is very effective.

A separate hospital, Beijing Chronic Sanatorium, with fifteen hundred beds, exists for mental patients who need long-term hospitalization because they have not been successful in resuming life with their families when they return after treatment in one of the other hospitals. This is an active institution, not just a caretaking facility, with a staff of doctors and nurses. Not having visited this hospital, there really isn't any more I can say about it; perhaps this gap will be filled on a future trip. Patients who improve and are sent back into the community are served by district

The Rise of Mental Health Care in New China

medical centers, which treat patients and emphasize prevention of re-currence of illness.

I asked the two doctors about the differences in the type of mental illness seen in China before and after Liberation. One fortunate differ-ence, they said, was the disappearance of syphilis of the brain and nervous system. Before Liberation, they said, neurosyphilis accounted for 10 percent of their cases. But they had seen only one additional case in the last ten years. Senile psychosis and other problems of the elderly were described by doctors as minimal: "In our society," they said, "old people can live useful lives." Other problems they claimed were eradicated were cases arising from malnutrition, unemployment, and opium addiction, about which we spoke in Chapter 2.

Some questions came up about homosexuality, another thing the Chinese claimed they never encounter. "Right after Liberation we saw two or three cases," they admitted, "but we don't anymore because we educate people from the time they are very young in communist theory." (The Chinese now admit that there is some homosexuality, although they still say it is uncommon and "against the state.")

Since stress is blamed for many of our mental problems in the West, we were interested to know what role stress plays in the new China. There was stress, but not the same kind as before Liberation, when

_. . . people had to struggle just to stay alive, working so hard for the capitalists and landlords. Now, people are working for themselves. Because they are masters of the country, they want to work conscientiously, spontaneously. They are not forced to do their jobs._

Stress in China, I was told, is of a different origin and quality:

_In our country everyone would like to do their best to build the socialist revolution, but sometimes a person cannot live up to this ideal because of actual conditions. In such a case, he may feel depressed and think he has let down the Party and the people by not living up to their expectations. For instance, a teacher may find his students, in spite of all he can do, having difficulty learning. This teacher might feel that he is not qualified to be a teacher in our country. You must remember that we, the workers, are now masters of the country, and some, therefore, place a very high demand on themselves. If their level of ability is limited and they are unable to meet their own very high standards, they feel anxious about that . . . but that is not to say that they did not do a good job._

(Later, in 1979, I found out that there had been another kind of stress during this time that was very common, brought on by the attacks

_____The Rise of Mental Health Care in New China

and criticism of the Gang of Four and their followers. This variety of stress was especially acute among intellectuals and cadres—people in leadership roles.)

We wanted to know how neurosis caused by this kind of stress was treated. The Chinese responded that treatment of this sort was relatively easy:

*We use a combination of Western and herbal medicine. First, we give the patients and their families lectures on the causes of these diseases. We tell them the cause of their illness and give suggestions to the school or the department where the patient works. If necessary, the doctors will tell the factory or unit to transfer the patient to a more suitable job. We also give the patient whatever medical treatment he needs.*

Psychoneurotic disorders are often treated in the outpatient departments of the psychiatric hospital. The Shanghai Psychiatric Institute sees four to five hundred outpatients a day, while the psychiatric hospital in Nanjing sees fifty a day. About half of these outpatients have psychoneurotic conditions defined, for me, by the Chinese psychiatrists, as neurasthenia, hysteria, and phobia. The other half are former hospital patients who have schizophrenia and psychotic depression. We were then told:

*When medicine is required, the doctors will tell the patient what it is for and how to take it so he will be aware of its effects. We use Chinese and Western drugs and psychotherapy. Acupuncture, using ear points, has also given very good results in treating neurosis. Acupuncture is especially good for treating insomnia. We also use Chinese herbal medicines, as we find combining treatments to be better than a single method.*

Next, we asked what theory of therapy the Chinese favored. We were told that the basis for their therapy is Marxist dialectical materialism. "We organize small discussion groups," they explained. "The staff and the patients have heart-to-heart chats. The doctors must have an attitude of serving the people wholeheartedly. If this is the case, the patients will be willing to tell the doctor what they are thinking about." A close working relationship among doctors, nurses, and patients was possible, we were told, because all are "brothers and sisters of the same class."

Another aspect of therapy they mentioned was the education of the patient in the theories of "revolutionary optimism." This is accomplished by telling patients the stories of revolutionary heroes' success in overcoming their own difficulties and illnesses. The physicians felt that this education was an important therapeutic technique.

The Rise of Mental Health Care in New China

So that we could more fully understand their emphasis, the Chinese physicians urged us to read an article by Mao Tse-tung entitled, "Where Do Correct Ideas Come From?"[141] They said this article had greatly influenced their psychiatric philosophy.

At this point it hardly seemed necessary to inquire about Chinese attitudes toward Freud, but we did. "According to Freud," they replied,

*. . . one of the causes of disease is sex disorder. In our society, it is totally different because when children are really young, they are told to study for the revolution. They have a clear purpose in study and in work. We educate children in the theory of revolutionary optimism.*

This, the physicians emphasized, meant that the people give little thought to themselves or their individual problems. "As you know," the doctors explained,

*. . . hundreds and hundreds of martyrs have given their lives to the revolutionary cause. This is to say that they were not bothered too much by their personal problems or individual things like love and marriage. We educate our young people in the proletarian world outlook, completely different from the bourgeois outlook. It is one of the fundamental differences between us and the Freudians.*

Pavlov is looked on with more favor in China, as we have seen earlier in the chapter. "Part of his theory is correct," we were told. "But it is not sufficient to explain the entire cause of mental disease. In our view, science is developing forward, so we cannot say that any theory is complete."

In our little remaining time with the doctors, we found that the two most common diseases seen in the hospital are psychotic depression and schizophrenia. The Chinese use the International Classification of Disease (ICD-8), a nomenclature of medical and psychiatric diagnosis similar to that employed in the United States and most other countries. They told us that they were involved in research on schizophrenia, which they suspected

*. . . may have something to do with the endocrine. Factors might include an inflammation or a high fever, or something very serious that happened in the past. Or, a factor might be a great difficulty at work that a person cannot overcome. There may be some biochemical causes for schizophrenia. So far, we haven't discovered them with certainty. In Shanghai, we have investigated about one thousand families in which there are schizophrenic members. We found that these families have a higher incidence of*

The Rise of Mental Health Care in New China

*schizophrenia than others. Perhaps one of the factors is genetic, but we also found that about 50 percent of the schizophrenic patients have no relatives who have ever suffered this illness.*

We shall see in the next chapter how these same psychiatrists' outlook had changed by the time I was able to visit them again in 1979, and what effect, if any, the change in political climate had on the treatment of mental patients.

# Notes

1. Ling Ming-yu, "Psychiatry in China Today," *National Reconstruction Journal,* Vol. 6, No. 3 (1946), p. 30.
2. Lee T'ao, Ch'eng Chih-fan, and Chang Ch'i-shan, "Some Early Records of Nervous and Mental Diseases in Traditional Chinese Medicine," *Chinese Medical Journal,* Vol. 81 (1962), p. 55.
3. K.C. Wong, "Chinese Hospitals in Ancient Times," *Chinese Medical Journal,* cited in John J. Kao, *Three Millenia of Chinese Psychiatry* (New York: The Institute for Advanced Research in Asian Science and Medicine Monograph Series, 1979), p. 9.
4. Kao, p. 10.
5. Lee T'ao et al., op. cit. pp. 58–59.
6. L. McCartney, "Neuropsychiatry in China: A Preliminary Observation," *Chinese Medical Journal,* Vol. 40 (1926), pp. 617–626.
7. K.C. Wong, "A Short History of Psychiatry and Mental Hygiene in China," *Chinese Medical Journal,* Vol. 68 (Jan.–Feb. 1950), p. 44.
8. Ibid.
9. Ibid. p. 45.
10. C.H. Westbrook, "Psychiatry and Mental Hygiene in Shanghai," *American Journal of Psychiatry,* Vol. 110 (1953), pp. 301–305; Wong, "A Short History," p. 45.
11. Wong, "A Short History," p. 46.
12. Ibid. pp. 47–48.
13. Gregorio Bermann, "Mental Health in China," ed. A. Kiev, *Psychiatry in the Communist World* (New York: Science House, 1968), pp. 233–234.
14. Kao, op. cit. pp. 21–22.
15. Eve Sheringham, "Visit to a Mental Hospital in China," unpublished manuscript, 1974.
16. Xia Zhenyi (Hsia Chen-yi) and Zhang Mingyuan, "History and Present Status of Modern Psychiatry in China," *Chinese Medical Journal,* Vol. 94, No. 5 (1981), pp. 277–282.
17. Wong, "A Short History," pp. 47–48.
18. Ling Ming-yu, op. cit. pp. 25–26.
19. Ibid. p. 26.
20. Bermann, op. cit. p. 227.

The Rise of Mental Health Care in New China

21. Jan Cerny, "Chinese Psychiatry," *International Journal of Psychiatry,* Vol. 1, No. 2 (1965), p. 229.
22. Kao, op. cit. p. 20.
23. Wong, "A Short History," p. 48.
24. Ling, op. cit. p. 25.
25. Wu Chen-i, "New China's Achievements in Psychiatry," *Collection of Theses on Achievements in the Medical Sciences in Commemoration of the 10th National Foundation Day of China,* Vol. II (Beijing, 1959). Translated by U.S. Joint Publications Research Service, No. 14,829, p. 596.
26. Ibid.
27. John Williams, "Child Health and Psychiatry in China Today," *The Medical Journal of Australia,* Vol. 44 (October 26, 1957), p. 630.
28. Wu, op. cit. p. 595.
29. Bermann, op. cit. p. 230.
30. Reproduced, by permission, from Victor Sidel and Ruth Sidel, *Serve the People: Observations on Medicine in the People's Republic of China* (New York: Josiah Macy, Jr. Foundation, 1973), p. 161; Cerny, op cit. p. 230; Ilkka and Vappu Taipale, "Chinese Psychiatry: A Visit to a Chinese Mental Hospital," *Archives of General Psychiatry,* Vol. 29 (1973), p. 214. Copyright 1973, American Medical Association.
31. Wu, op. cit. p. 596.
32. Kao, op. cit. p. 49.
33. Cerny, op. cit. p. 230.
34. Wu, op. cit. p. 596.
35. Bermann, op. cit. p. 233.
36. Wu, op. cit. p. 595.
37. Kao, loc. cit.
38. Bermann, op. cit. p. 235.
39. Wu, op. cit. p. 596.
40. Ibid. p. 597. Recovery rate comparisons given here are internally consistent with each other, but we cannot use these figures to contrast them with those of other countries.
41. Ibid. p. 596.
42. Bermann, op. cit. p. 234.
43. Chao Yi-ch'eng, "Neurology, Neurosurgery and Psychiatry in New China," *Chinese Medical Journal,* Vol. 84 (1965), p. 714.
44. Wu, op. cit. p. 599.
45. Ibid. p. 611.
46. Ibid.
47. Ibid. p. 612.
48. Ibid. p. 610.
49. Ibid. p. 605.
50. C.C. Ching, "Psychology in the People's Republic of China," *American Psychologist,* Vol. 35, No. 12 (December 1980), pp. 1085–1086.
51. Ting Tsan, "How to Develop Medical Psychology in China," *Articles on Psychology in Communist China,* translation of selected articles from *Hsin-li Hsueh-pao,* (July–Sept. 1959). U.S. Joint Publications Research Service No. 3424, p. 15; Robert and Ai-li S. Chin, *Psychological Research in Com-*

*munist China: 1949–1966* (Cambridge, Mass. and London: The M.I.T. Press, 1969), p. 66.

52. Wu, op. cit. p. 614.
53. Ibid. p. 617.
54. Ibid.
55. "The National Mental Illnesses Prevention Work Plan (1958–1962)," *Compendium of Laws and Regulations of the People's Republic of China,* translated in U.S. Joint Publications Research Service No. 14,335, p. 562.
56. Ibid. p. 569.
57. Ibid. p. 571.
58. Ibid. p. 563.
59. Wu, op. cit. pp. 594–617.
60. Ibid. pp. 615–616.
61. Ibid. p. 616.
62. Ibid.
63. Cerny, op. cit. p. 230.
64. "National Mental Illnesses Prevention Plan," p. 568.
65. F.E. Wan and T.H. Chang, "Psychosurgery," *Chinese Medical Journal,* Vol. 68 (Sept.–Oct. 1950), p. 273.
66. Wu, op. cit. p. 601.
67. "National Mental Illnesses Prevention Plan," p. 574.
68. Phillip Shapiro, "Mental Illness: A Social Problem with a Social Cure," *Getting Together,* Vol. 5, No. 3 (February 1–5, 1974), p. 7.
69. Bermann, op. cit. pp. 254–255.
70. Ibid. p. 256.
71. "National Mental Illnesses Prevention Plan," p. 569.
72. Chao, op. cit. p. 734.
73. Chen Ta-jou, "How Psychology Can Be of Service to Socialist Construction," *Articles on Psychology in Communist China,* translation of selected articles from *Hsin-li Hsueh-pao,* July-Sept. 1959. U.S. Joint Publication Research Service No. 3424, p. 9. This article was also translated, in U.S. Joint Publications Research Service No. 1932-NY, as "How Does Psychology Serve Socialist Construction?," with the author's name spelled *Ch'en Ta-jao,* pp. 31–40. See reference 80.
74. Taipale and Taipale, op. cit. p. 313.
75. Mao Tse-tung, "Talks at the Yenan Forum on Literature and Art," (May 1942). *Selected Readings from the Works of Mao Tse-tung* (Beijing: Foreign Languages Press, 1967), p. 225; italics added.
76. "Theoretical Problems of Psychology in the Realization of Class Struggle," *Articles on Psychology in Communist China,* pp. 1–2.
77. Ting, op. cit. p. 16.
78. Ibid. pp. 12–13.
79. Chin and Chin, op. cit. p. 87.
80. Ch'en Ta-jao, "How Does Psychology Serve Socialist Construction?," *Translations from Communist China's Political and Sociological Publications: The Movement in Psychology,* U.S. Joint Publications Research Service No. 1932-NY, p. 36.
81. Donald Y.F. Ho, "The Conception of Man in Mao Tse-tung Thought,"

*Psychiatry,* Vol. 41, No. 4 (Nov. 1978), p. 398. Copyright © 1978 by The William Alanson White Psychiatric Foundation, Inc.

82. Bingham Dai, letter to Paul Lowinger, December 12, 1980.
83. Ts'ao Jih-ch'ang, "Why Should We Discuss the Nature of Psychology?", *Selections from Kuang-ming Jih-pao,* U.S. Joint Publications Research Service No. 4937, 31 August 1961, pp. 29–33.
84. Chu Chi-hsien, "Some Views on the Problem of the Object of Study of Psychology," *Translations from Communist China's Political and Sociological Publications,* U.S. Joint Publications Research Service No. 1932 -NY, p. 17.
85. Ts'ao Jih-ch'ang, "What Does Psychology Study?," *Translations from Communist China's Political and Sociological Publications,* p. 1. This is *not* a different translation of the article referred to in reference 83, but a different article by the same author.
86. Ch'en Ta'jao, op. cit. pp. 31–40.
87. "A Symposium on Psychology Was Held at T'ai-yuan," *Translations from Kuang-ming Jih-pao,* U.S. Joint Publications Research Service No. 12524, 14 February 1962, pp. 106–107.
88. Ching, op. cit. p. 1085.
89. Ibid. p. 1086.
90. Ibid.
91. Bermann, op. cit. p. 236.
92. Li Ch'ung-p'ei et al., "Some Problems Concerning the Cause of Psychasthenia and Attempts to Find Quick Treatments," *Collection of Theses . . .,* Vol. II,pp. 654–655.
93. Ibid. p. 655.
94. Ibid. p. 661.
95. Ibid. pp. 653–662.
96. Ibid. p. 664.
97. Ibid. pp. 665–666.
98. Ibid. p. 666.
99. Ibid. p. 668.
100. Ibid. p. 669.
101. Wu, op. cit. p. 602.
102. Chao, op. cit. p. 738.
103. Ibid. p. 733; Wu, loc. cit.
104. Shen Yu-tsun, "Application of Artificial Hibernation in Practice," *Collection of Theses . . .,* Vol. II, p. 618.
105. Wu, op. cit. p. 609.
106. Wang Ching-hsiang, "Insulin Treatment," *Collection of Theses . . .,* Vol. II, p. 681.
107. Wu, op. cit. p. 610.
108. Ibid. p. 611.
109. Ibid. p. 614.
110. Chao, op. cit. p. 735.
111. Ibid. p. 734.
112. T'ao Kuo-t'ai, "Healing and Preventive Work in the Field of Childhood Mental Diseases," *Collection of Theses . . .,* Vol. II, p. 684.
113. Ibid. p. 688.

114. Ibid. pp. 685–692.
115. Ibid. p. 689.
116. Ibid.
117. Ibid. p. 690.
118. Ibid.
119. Ibid. p. 691.
120. Ibid. pp. 691–692.
121. Ibid. p. 692.
122. Ibid. p. 690.
123. Denis Lazure, "Politics and Mental Health in New China," *American Journal of Orthopsychiatry,* Vol. XXXIV (1964), pp. 930–931.
124. Williams, loc. cit.
125. Ibid. pp. 630–631.
126. Albert H. Yee, "Psychology in China Bows to the Cultural Revolution," *APA Monitor,* Vol. 4, No. 3 (1973), p. 1.
127. Ibid. pp. 1, 4.
128. Ching, op. cit. p. 1087.
129. Ibid. pp. 1086–1087.
130. Kuo Shu-su, "Using Materialist Dialectics to Cure Common Diseases," *Selected Essays on the Study of Philosophy by Workers, Peasants and Soldiers* (Beijing: Foreign Languages Press, 1971), pp. 77–78.
131. *Neurology-Psychiatry in the People's Republic of China,* 1971, translated, Bethesda, Maryland, 1973. DHEW (NIH) Publication No. 74-56, p. 75.
132. Fuyu Medical Team, Provincial Hospital for Mental Diseases, Beian, Heilungkiang, "How We Operated a Small Hospital in the Countryside," *China's Medicine,* Vol. 6 (1968), pp. 347–349.
133. Ibid. p. 348.
134. Taipale and Taipale, op. cit. p. 314.
135. Sidel and Sidel, op. cit. p. 162.
136. "New Treatment for the Insane," *China Pictorial,* Vol. 11 (November 1971), pp. 13–15.
137. Liu Xiehe, "Mental Health Work in Sichuan," *British Journal of Psychiatry,* Vol. 137 (1980), p. 376.
138. Xia Zhenyi (Hsia Chen-yi), Yan Heqin and Wong Changhua, "Mental Health Work in Shanghai," *Chinese Medical Journal,* Vol. 93, No. 2 (1980), p. 127.
139. Lin Yang, "Medical and Health Service," *Beijing Review* (1980), Vol. 23, No. 25, p. 24.
140. Shen Yucun (Shen Yu-tsun), Zhang Weixi, Shu Liang, Yang Xiaoling, Cui Yuhua, Zhou Dongfeng, Shi Hengyao, and Su Entao, "Investigation of Mental Disorders in Beijing Suburban District," *Chinese Medical Journal,* Vol. 94, No. 3 (1981), pp. 153–156.
141. Mao Tse-tung, "Where Do Correct Ideas Come From?" (1957), *Selected Readings from the Works of Mao Tse-tung* (Beijing, Foreign Languages Press, 1967), pp. 405–406.

The Rise of Mental Health Care in New China

# Chapter 4

# Mental Health Care in China Today

*When I arrived at the hospital, I thought it was a place dealing with mental illness and I was afraid, because I didn't believe I suffered from mental illness. After a week of acupuncture treatment I no longer heard any sound in my ears. I had been unable to sleep, but after a week I could sleep. In the old society I would have disappeared; in the new society I can recover.*[1]

**W**hat is it like to be a mental patient in China today? Remarkably enough, clinical practice has changed little during the recent years of political turmoil. In fact, we can go one step further and say that even since the early writings during the Great Leap Forward, clinical practice has not changed all that much. The ultra-"leftists" of the Cultural Revolution would have us believe that the humanitarian advances in Chinese mental health work all had their roots in the Cultural Revolution, but that simply isn't the case. To be sure, the emphasis was more physiological before the Cultural Revolution, and more political during the Cultural Revolution, and now the pendulum is swinging away from the political again. But patient care has not been affected very much. Why not? Because two things stand out as a continuity in Chinese clinical practice. First, the Chinese believe in the "medical model"; when people are seriously disturbed, they are called "mentally ill." And in schizophrenia, the Chinese believe that the disorder has a biochemical basis. Second, the "medical model" notwithstanding, the patients have been treated from the early years on with "revolutionary humanitarianism," and whatever kinds of treatments are used, their aim is to put patients into a functional enough mental state that they can begin to struggle actively against the disease with the help of medical workers. Said one group of American visitors,

*The patients, although cooperative, did look somewhat "off balance." (It was clear that we were in a mental hospital.) Some were bouncing their feet in a kind of jittery way, as hospitalized patients often do; others looked vague, though not "vacant"; and some looked at us suspiciously. (With good reason—who were we anyway?) But it was usually easy to make contact with them; a smile and a nod always evoked a similar response.[2]*

During the Great Leap years, patients were mobilized to fight against their own illnesses, and during the Cultural Revolution patients did this fighting in a more explicitly political way, studying Chairman Mao's writings and applying political philosophy and terminology to their personal mental problems, as in this example of a patient whose paranoid distrust of his wife landed him in a mental institution:

*I had a quarrel with my wife. . . . We quarrelled a lot because I insisted that she wanted to divorce me and she said that she did not.*

*During my early period of admission to the hospital I did not know that I had mental trouble. Gradually I recognized that something was wrong in my mentality and I . . . recognized that I had to make a class analysis of the causes of my disease in order to facilitate treatment and prevention.*

*My trouble was that I had subjective thinking which was not objectively correct. . . . I was concerned with the individual person; I was self-interested. I haven't put revolutionary interests in the first place, but if I can put the public interest first and my own interest second, I can solve the contradictions and my mind will be in the correct way. From now on I will study Chairman Mao and apply his writings.[3]*

Now, since the downfall of the Gang of Four and the advent of the modernization period, with political rhetoric at its lowest ebb in modern Chinese history, patients are still being treated with revolutionary humanitarianism, though perhaps describing their problems less politically and more personally than they did during the Cultural Revolution. Although their terminology is different now from what it was during the height of the Cultural Revolution, treatment components remain almost exactly the same, so we can examine mental health care in the recent period as a whole, synthesizing information gleaned by western visitors during the last ten years. The only recent change of which we are aware is the renewed use of ECT (electroshock treatment) in a very few cases

Mental Health Care in China Today

where psychiatrists say they are afraid that the patients will commit suicide and are looking for a faster improvement than they feel they can get with medication alone.[4] Shock treatment was banned during the Cultural Revolution; indeed, it is being used very infrequently even today. The use of ECT is a controversial question, and we would like to remind readers that Dr. Wu Chen-i, who told us on his recent visit to the United States that the Chinese are using ECT again in a select few cases where suicide is a real danger, is the same man who wrote in 1959 that the Chinese

*are generally quite cautious in its use. In recent years, hydergine has shown obvious effectiveness, and the use of shock treatment has been greatly reduced. It seldom is used alone, and if it is used at all, it is in combination with other methods.*[5]

## MENTAL HOSPITALS IN CHINA

People in China are rarely committed involuntarily. If a person appears, to his or her family, co-workers, or neighbors, to have severe emotional problems which are interfering with his or her functioning, the person will be talked to, encouraged to see a doctor, and finally, if all agree that a stay in the hospital is the best form of treatment, the person goes in. The method used to get people to agree to this treatment is patient discussion of the nature of the illness and the fact that it is not a personal shame. People who are close to the patient assure him or her of their concern.[6] Perhaps more important, patients are assured that their jobs will be waiting for them when they leave the hospital, and they receive full pay while hospitalized[7] so that they need feel no anxiety about their own or their families' livelihoods.[8] If a person whom the doctors feel needs hospitalization does not want to go because s/he is suspicious, fearful, or does not believe that s/he is ill, an appeal is made to the family or co-workers to try to get the patient to agree to be admitted. In some cases the doctors will try to persuade the patient to visit the hospital for a simple physical checkup and then try to convince him/her to stay on. There are, of course, some patients who are in such an excited state that the process of persuading them to enter the hospital cannot be carried on; generally, their families or co-workers have them admitted, they are given medication or other treatment to calm them, and at this point, generally within a couple of days of admission, medical workers will discuss their illness and the benefits of hospitalization with them.[9] The

Mental Health Care in China Today

average length of a hospital stay is two or three months, with seventy days being typical; a stay of as long as a year is most unusual, though not unheard of.[10] We are here not describing chronic-care facilities, sanatoria which exist solely for people who cannot go home again.

Upon arrival at the mental hospital, the patient is greeted by mental health workers, one or two of whom will be assigned to his or her case alone, and is also paired with a patient who has been in the hospital for some time and is familiar with hospital routine. This patient, who is generally in better shape than the new arrival, having been there longer, shows the new arrival where he or she will sleep and eat, where recreation facilities are, and the two will discuss what the daily routine of the hospital is like. The daily routine at the Shanghai Mental Hospital as reported in 1973 was[11]:

| | |
|---|---|
| 5:00–5:30 A.M. | Get up and make beds |
| 5:30–6:00 | Breakfast |
| 6:00–7:30 | Occupational therapy |
| 6:30–7:00 (Fri.) | Military training |
| 7:30–8:30 | Study Chairman Mao's work |
| 8:30–10:00 (Mon., Wed., Fri.) | Heart-to-heart talks |
| 8:30–10:00 (Tues., Thurs., Sat.) | Study class |
| 10:00–10:30 | Treatment (such as acupuncture) |
| 10:30–11:30 | Lunch, free time |
| 12:00–1:30 P.M. | Nap |
| 1:30–2:00 | News |
| 2:30–3:30 | Study class |
| 3:30–4:15 (Mon., Wed., Fri.) | Physical activities |
| 3:30–6:30 (Tues., Thurs., Sat.) | Visits from relatives |
| 4:30 | Supper |
| Evening | Television |
| 9:30 | Bed |

Another visitor reported the following list of hospital rules, which were posted on the wall of a recreation room. These rules indicate clearly what is expected of patients:

1. Read the [news]paper every day and study Marx, Lenin and Mao thought.
2. Observe discipline—never hit, swear, take other people's things. Never waste food or other things. Don't fiddle [sic] around when we study.

Mental Health Care in China Today

3. Pay attention to personal hygiene. Do cleaning up jobs every day.

4. We must cooperate with doctors and nurses. Take medicine on time. Don't hide or spill any medicine.

5. Take part in the OT [occupational therapy] actively. Take part in the competitive drive for social emulation to guarantee the quality of the product.[12]

Shortly after arriving at the hospital, the patient will engage in long discussions of what his or her problems are with medical workers, to ascertain the nature of the problem and the course of treatment to be undertaken. Both at this point and throughout the course of therapy the medical workers undertake social investigation by going into the community the patient is from; they discuss the case with family members and friends, and also with co-workers, all of whom contribute information and take part in education about the patient's illness.[13] In one instance, the patient's illness was intimately related to his job.

*A worker . . . was assigned to make technical innovations on a machine. He determined to do a good job, and sometimes worked very late. When a setback occurred in the improvement of the machine, he felt that he had failed to accomplish the task entrusted to him, that he was not worthy of the hope placed in him by the Party and the revolution, and that his comrades would laugh at him. He continued to work hard at the job during the day, but at night suffered from insomnia. He became ill, suspecting the leaders and his comrades of not trusting him and of always gossiping about him. He was diagnosed as a schizophrenic and treated by medication, acupuncture. He was assigned study of Mao's essay, "Serve the People," to deal with petit-bourgeois vanity, the man's main problem. Through study of this essay, he learned that we are to innovate for the revolution, that we work not for ourselves, not for fame or gain, but for the revolution. The leadership and comrades of his original unit came to praise him for his activism and enthusiasm, and at the same time to point out his non-proletarian ideas—his subjective deflection from his main tasks. They told him that they trusted him, that they were not gossiping and laughing about him. He pledged to study Mao and to remold his ideology . . . and to be a good worker wholeheartedly working for the revolution. Not worrying about himself and his own performance, he would put aside his vanity and his distrust of his co-workers.[14]*

Would that we in the U.S. could carry out this kind of social investigation, involving the patient's co-workers. In this case, their very presence and participation showed the patient that they cared about him.

Mental Health Care in China Today

## COMPONENTS OF THE TREATMENT PROCESS

Chinese health workers try to use their understanding of dialectical materialist philosophy in their treatment of mental patients. Whereas we in the United States often find ourselves on opposing sides of the "medical model" controversy, the Chinese have no problem using both physical and mental forms of treatment together. But unlike the eclectic, pragmatic approach used here—"If it works, use it"—the Chinese are clear that physical treatments such as medication and acupuncture are used in order to enable patients to be calm and rational enough to participate in meaningful, rational discussion of their problems. Unlike American mental patients, who are seen as objects upon whom treatments are performed, Chinese patients are responsible for getting better so that they may once more contribute to the development of China. The chief psychiatrist at Beijing Hospital No. 3, Dr. Shen Yu-tsun, puts it this way:

*We employ various medicines in our treatment but the active participation of the patient in the therapy is very important. The majority of the patients are soon able to participate in the study of the philosophical works of Chairman Mao, such as "On Practice" and "On Contradiction." We also give lectures to instruct the patients on the nature of their illness. In this way the patients are enabled to actively criticize their abnormal and distorted thinking processes.*[15]

Patients are frequently treated with a combination of both western and traditional herbal medications and acupuncture to relieve the physical symptoms they suffer from.[16] Although both the Chinese and many western visitors reported that both electroshock therapy (ECT) and insulin shock therapy were banned during the Cultural Revolution,[17] an Australian medical team visiting in 1973 reported seeing patients in one institution, either in Beijing or Shanghai, "emerging from an insulin coma,"[18] and a visiting American team reported insulin in use both at Beijing No. 3 Hospital and in Nanjing, where ECT was also said to be used "if regular measures fail in a given case" of schizophrenia.[19] And although Pavlovian explanations and treatments fell out of favor in the early 1960s with the cooling of relations between China and the Soviet Union, the Australian team as well as other visitors reported that "in Peking it was not unusual to employ 'artificial hibernation' for a few days for disturbed patients."[20] And other visitors reported the experimental use of insulin injected at acupuncture points in very small dosages.[21]

One medication that is in widespread use is chlorpromazine (Thorazine); whereas this medication is frequently used in the West to keep patients in a state of semi-stupor for much of the time, western visitors report that virtually all patients they see in visits to various Chinese mental hospitals are alert and active.[22] Their standard dosage, to a maximum of about 400 mg. a day, is much lower than in the West; its purpose is to calm patients sufficiently so that they can begin to study the causes of their problems.[23] Western drugs now in use include other antipsychotics, perphenazine, trifluoperazine, chlorprothixine, haloperidol, and the antidepressants.[24] The use of lithium carbonate has been reported by many visitors,[25] but it was brand new during the early 1970s, and one American visitor was asked by his Chinese psychiatrist host what his experience with it had been.[26]

Traditional herbal medications are now widely used. Generally speaking, they are said to produce results similar to those of western medications without the undesirable side effects. Sometimes they are used in conjunction with western medications, enabling the Chinese to reduce the dosage of the western medications, thereby running less risk of side effects such as tardive dyskinesia. At the Shanghai Institute there is a ward where the primary emphasis is on traditional medicine, including pulse diagnosis, a rather rarely practiced technique. In Xinjiang (Singkiang), at Ulumushi Fourth People's Psychiatric Hospital, a form of herbal medicine named *Kazakh,* after a local ethnic minority, is practiced along with Chinese and Western medicine.

Acupuncture treatment is widely used; it is efficacious in calming anxious, overexcited patients and enlivening depressed ones. A series of treatments is said to have permanent curative effects. For depressed patients the acupuncture needles are twirled rapidly, for stimulation; for overexcited patients they are twirled slowly, for a calming effect. A recent innovation is the introduction of electro-acupuncture; instead of the needles' being twirled manually, a slight current of one to eight volts is sent through the needles. Once the needles are implanted, the patient can control the flow of current, and does not require the constant supervision of an acupuncturist.[27] These treatments last from five to twenty minutes, and are given twice a day over the course of twenty days to a month, although individual cases may vary from this average.[28]

Physical exercise is considered an integral part of treatment, reflecting the value placed on exercise throughout Chinese society, and also again indicating an analysis of the person as a whole consisting of mind and body.

Chinese mental patients generally spend at least an hour a day engaged in manual, productive labor. This work helps patients feel that they are not out of touch with the rest of Chinese society, and that they are still contributing even from inside the hospital.[29] Often patients work growing vegetables in a garden outside the hospital, which are then used to defray the cost of maintaining the patients. Since many factories also have such gardens which are worked by the factory workers and their families, this gardening is not exclusive to hospitals. Other forms of manual labor that have been mentioned by western visitors are handicrafts; folding bandages; assembling matchboxes, souvenirs, and paper lanterns[30]; preparing medications; and making toothpaste tube covers for use by a nearby factory.[31] Funds obtained from patients' labor go into a patients' welfare fund and are used to purchase recreational materials.[32]

The methods described above are necessary adjuncts to the main focus of mental health work, which is therapy and reeducation. Let's look at the example of a young woman mental patient to help us visualize this relationship between the various physical techniques and the reeducation used, and see which aspect is principal, and also see the goal of the therapy—reintegration with the social whole:

*I was a graduate of junior middle school and in 1969 was sent out to work in an outlying province. I was admitted five months ago to this hospital but I am getting alright {sic} now. My main trouble is auditory hallucinations. I hear something in my ear saying, "What is below your pillow?" I found old magazines on the subject of a biological radio apparatus and I came to the ridiculous conclusion that a special agent is investigating me by means of this biological radio apparatus. I became agitated and heard loud speeches in my mind which gave me a very bad headache. During the midst of my torture I was sent to the hospital and received medication. My headache is much better but I still have hallucinations.*

*The doctors organized a study class of Chairman Mao's works and I joined the class and studied the five works. I studied my hallucinations and gradually recognized that they were nonexistent. I found that investigation is like a pregnancy, and solving problems is like delivering a baby. As I investigated my problem I gradually recognized that the biological radio was nonexistent. Now I still have some hallucinations but after ten minutes I recognize that they are not real. Now whenever I have hallucinations, I study the works of Chairman Mao and attract {sic} my mind and my heart so I will get rid of my trouble.*

*My treatments consist of acupuncture, medicine, herb medicine, and study. Also I am considering what happens in the whole world. I talk with doctors and patients; I do physical exercises; I have not completely recovered yet but I have faith I will get better and will win the struggle.*[33]

Mental Health Care in China Today

This patient is receiving a range of treatments, from drugs to acupuncture to physical exercise to study sessions. Is it just that a little of everything is thrown together here? No, clearly it was first necessary to rid the patient of her severe headaches before she could begin to think about the nature of her illness. The acupuncture is for a similar purpose—to relax an overexcited patient. The physical exercise is for her general well-being. But these treatments are adjuncts to the main focus of work with this patient, which is to examine the nature of her illness and to understand that the hallucinations do not originate in the real world even while she is still suffering from them. She is overcoming the hallucinations by learning the difference between her subjective feelings, which produce the hallucinations, and the objective world. This patient is also being kept up to date on events outside of the hospital, to facilitate her reintegration into society.

What is the character of the therapeutic work that is done? How is it done? What techniques do the Chinese use? We would call Chinese psychotherapy rational-directive if we wanted a familiar label to attach to it, because it simply consists of straightforward discussion either on a one-to-one basis, in which case it is called "heart-to-heart talks," or in small groups. Here is a western visitor's account of a small group session:

*There were twelve male paranoid schizophrenic patients with three therapists who played a "supporting-leading role," sitting among the patients around a table. Each patient in this meeting reported to the group his own symptoms and problems. Then these symptoms and problems were commented on and analyzed by other patients in this group. From time to time, when the situation required, the therapists helped patients to lead the discussion or commented on the patients' statements; but discussion was mainly carried by patients themselves. At the beginning of the group meeting, I was surprised to hear patients casually using psychiatric terms and concepts such as visual and auditory hallucinations, delusions and ideas of reference. Later I learned that before a small group discussion took place, patients were given lectures on psychiatry. This process is called "transmitting psychiatric knowledge to patients." The existence of such classes is an indication that patients are considered to have an important role in their own treatment. In this study group, I found the patients articulate, frank and ready to speak their minds. After the rest of the patients analyzed a patient's symptoms and problems, or offered "criticisms," the patient defended his own position vigorously. This back-and-forth debate on one patient's problem continued for a while before turning to the next patient. Occasionally, the positions of some patients were somewhat modified after the debates, but they generally tried hard to defend themselves. I was amazed at how easily patients handled the criticisms of others. When they did not agree with others' statements they did not appear offended. This imperturbability may come from the training the Chinese receive from childhood on criticism, self-criticism and transformation sessions.*

*While patients in the small group discussion might be blind to evidence of their own delusions and problems, their analysis of their fellow patients' problems and delusions seemed quite reasonable. . . .* [34]

Why do the Chinese use a medical model when dealing with psychological problems? Why are people labelled mentally ill? It is because they have made a mistake in perceiving reality, and in order to correct that mistake it must be so labelled. It is not really the label "mentally ill" that we in the west are concerned with, but rather the consequences of being so labelled here. To be labelled mentally ill means to be shut out of the social whole, to be isolated, to be treated as an enemy; it is to be locked out and locked up. It is not the medical model *per se,* but its consequences that we object to here in this country. Take acupuncture, for example. Acupuncture is definitely a physiological treatment, but it is not seen as abusive because patients undergoing acupuncture treatment are conscious and in control. Behavior modification, on the other hand, is not, strictly speaking, a physiological treatment, but some of us find it objectionable because the patient may not be in control of the treatment. Thus, the issue is not the medical model itself, but *its consequences* for the people labelled mentally ill. In China the goal of mental health treatment is at every step to reconnect patients with the social whole from which they are temporarily estranged by virtue of their confusion about reality. It may be useful to visualize mental health problems, as the Chinese do, as "contradictions among the people," which are by nature non-antagonistic. The mentally ill person has a problem that needs to be solved, but it can be dealt with in a comradely manner, the way that non-antagonistic contradictions are dealt with.

Virginia Goldner describes her understanding of the Chinese use of the medical model this way:

*The Chinese think there is something called "mental illness." They do not share, with the anti-psychiatry movement here, the notion that mental illness is a myth. They think it's an illness, which is to say "illness" in the literal, medical sense. They think it ought to be treated in a hospital by people called doctors, who wear white coats. There's no soft-pedalling of the medical model in China. Mental health workers look and act like mental health workers. . . .*

Mental Health Care in China Today⎯⎯⎯⎯⎯⎯⎯⎯⎯⎯

*The Chinese describe the "illness" that mental patients have in Western terms. . . . This is where one of the interesting contradictions begins. While on the one hand they believe in "mental illness" and call these illnesses by their Western name, at the same time they explain antecedent conditions which led to this situation, as well as the conditions which determine its treatment, in entirely political terms. They seem to use the medical model to describe it, and a political model to explain it.*

*At the beginning I had . . . a contemptuous explanation for this. I thought that the Chinese were rather naïve. . . . How can you mix the medical model with a political explanation? They are like apples and oranges. . . .*

*It turns out, I think, that this interesting mix of politics, biology and psychology . . . really reaches back to very traditional, very old ideas in Chinese medicine.*

*In Western terms there are illnesses of the body, illnesses of the mind, and then there is society. In China, a person's illness is understood to be the product of spiritual, ethical, social, biological and psychological factors. It was always a very beautiful mix, a very holistic theory, as opposed to our very dualistic and mechanistic theory. What I thought was a very naïve contradiction turns out to be a very advanced synthesis.*

*Mental illness, the Chinese believe, is caused by biological, constitutional and what they call psychogenic factors. By psychogenic factors, they are referring to a person's difficulties in handling the contradictions of his or her life. . . . Contradictions in your daily life (which they see in political terms), when laid on top of some constitutional and biological base, could produce what they call "mental illness."*[35]

Chinese psychotherapy is grounded in dialectical materialism. It is dialectical because it sees the mind of the mental patient as containing two aspects, the rational and the irrational, and contends that the irrational aspect has for the moment taken over as the principal aspect of the contradiction. The job of psychotherapy is to enable the rational, temporarily in the secondary position, to assume its principal position once again. The therapy is materialist because it is grounded in the belief that there is a real world, that can be understood, and that the problem of mentally ill people is that they have made a mistake in their perception of that real world. They are confused as to the nature of that world, and study and therapy will help them clear up this confusion.

There is a real world, and we want to get you back in it. This is the message of Chinese therapy and reeducation, and this materialism plays a vital role in the treatment process, as in the case of this young woman:

Mental Health Care in China Today

*She thought her food was poisoned, and had not eaten for a week at the point at which she was admitted to the hospital. A nurse had a heart-to-heart talk with her, telling her that not eating was bad for her health and that if she did eat she would contribute to the revolution. The patient was then willing to touch the food, but would not swallow it. The nurse decided to continue her propaganda work by setting an example. She ate the food herself, eating what the patient had refused to eat. After this example, the patient ate her first meal in the hospital.*[36]

Another simple demonstration of efforts to reconnect patients to the real world was noted at the Shanghai Psychiatric Hospital, where five patients, said to be "severely disturbed" and recently out of isolation, sat around a table with three staff members. The staff members were turning the pages of several colorful picture magazines, pointing out various things in the pictures and chatting with the patients about what they were looking at, in order to bring the patients out of themselves and back in touch with everyday events.[37]

The mobilization of patients' "positive aspects" to defeat their "negative aspects," and the encouraging spirit with which their treatment is imbued—revolutionary optimism—were taken one step further even than the individual patients during the Cultural Revolution. In one hospital, patients were mobilized into four "divisions," after the model of the People's Liberation Army, and they then constituted a "collective fighting group instead of a ward."[38] A psychiatrist at this hospital explained, "It is not enough to have the doctors or nurses use initiative; we need the patients' initiative to work together against the disease."[39] We don't know whether this imagery is still being employed, but we suspect not.

## THE USE OF MAO'S THOUGHT IN CHINESE PSYCHOTHERAPY

As we see in the illustrative case histories from that period, the writings of Mao Tse-tung were of central importance to the reeducation of mental patients during the Cultural Revolution. At first glance, this seems strange and out of place because we think of Mao as a "political" writer and cannot see the relationship between political writings and psychotherapy. To understand this phenomenon better, there are two things we need to realize: first, that Chairman Mao has always been regarded with immense love and respect by the masses of Chinese people. He played a central role in their liberation, and is revered not only as a political leader, but as a teacher and philosopher who applied the teachings of Marx and Lenin to China and expanded on their philosophy. And second, dialectical materialism, as it is used in China, helps patients to figure out how the world, and their minds work; it can be applied to problems which seem, on their face, to be the most "personal." Mao's lengthy essay "On Contradiction,"[40] for example, helps patients to understand the contradiction in their own minds between the rational and irrational components. Another writing popular in mental health work, mentioned to Paul in his first visit to a Chinese mental institution, is "Where Do Correct Ideas Come From?" In this essay it is said that correct ideas come from "social practice, and from it alone,"[41] specifically from three kinds of social practice: class struggle, the struggle for production, and scientific experiment. "It is man's social being that determines his thinking," it continues. Certainly this is in great contrast to western psychiatric philosophy, which starts with what's inside our heads.

Two case histories from the early 1970s, collected at the Third Beijing Teaching Hospital, illustrate the use of Mao Tse-tung's philosophical works in therapy. The first was a mental patient examined in 1972 at the Third Beijing Teaching Hospital by Dr. Phillip Shapiro, an American psychiatrist. Dr. Shapiro's opportunity to interview this patient was arranged by Dr. Wu Chen-i, who was at that time the head of the Third Teaching Hospital. Before introducing the patient, Dr. Wu had told Dr. Shapiro something about the case. The patient, a man in his thirties, was a teacher of physics at Beijing University. He had been admitted to the hospital because he was plagued by the unfounded conviction that he was being spied upon. He was also experiencing other paranoid delusions. In the hospital he had been diagnosed as schizophrenic. When Dr. Shapiro met him, the patient had been in the hospital for two months. During this time he had attended criticism/self-criticism sessions, which included study and discussions of Mao's essays. There were also heart-to-heart talks with the staff and treatment with chlorpromazine (Thorazine).

The patient told Dr. Shapiro that he felt much better after his two months in the hospital and was looking forward to returning to his job at the university. His fellow teachers had written him that they, as well, were looking forward to his return. He felt that an important factor in his improvement was his study of Mao, in particular, "Where Do Correct Ideas Come From?"[42] This article gave him insight into his paranoia, and as an example of this he described an incident that had occurred some time after his arrival at the hospital. One morning he saw a man whom he recognized as an electronics technician from the medical school where he worked. At once he concluded, "Aha! They have sent him here to spy on me." Later, however, when he saw this man engaged in repairing the electroencephalographic equipment, he realized—mindful of Mao's admonition to investigate what is happening in the real world before jumping to conclusions based on subjective thinking—that the man was there not to spy on him but to keep the hospital equipment working.

As it happened, Paul was able to get an update on this patient in 1979 when he talked with Dr. Wu at the Third Teaching Hospital in Beijing. "He is working very well now at his old position in the University," Dr. Wu told Paul when Paul inquired after him, adding that the teacher comes for treatment every month or two. On these visits he gets low doses of tranquilizing medication and talks to a psychiatrist. Dr. Wu feels that the prompt treatment of his first episode of schizophrenia in 1972 kept him from becoming a chronic hospital patient.

Another patient, at the Shanghai Psychiatric Hospital, described her problem this way:

*"During the Cultural Revolution I had a lot of difficulty handling criticism. I took it much too personally, and this had a lot to do with making me sick, and I want to work on that problem." She made this comment by making reference to a line in one of Mao's most famous articles called "Serve the People" which says, "Communists are not afraid of criticism. Criticism is designed to help us serve others and we should not take it personally."*[43]

Yet another patient reported that her problems stemmed from her confusion between "contradictions among the people," which can be solved amicably, and "contradictions between the people and the enemy," which are antagonistic by nature, and in which no compromise is possible. She'd clearly been reading Mao's "On the Correct Handling of Contradictions among the People,"[44] in which these distinctions are made. She said she had been seeing herself as surrounded by enemies, and had fought her enemies with both "words and gestures," but that because of her experiences in the hospital, where staff and patients both had shown themselves to be friends, and because of her reading of Mao,

*she came to see that the people around her were friends, and that the real "enemy" was the false ideas in her mind. She was not afraid any more, and looked forward to leaving the hospital.*[45]

Another patient, a man of thirty-eight, explained his use of Mao's writings:

Mental Health Care in China Today

*My main trouble is suspicion. I think my ceiling is going to fall down;
when big character posters are up I think it is criticism of myself; and
when somebody is gossiping I think they are talking about me.*

*After I was admitted to this hospital I gradually recognized my
illness. As Chairman Mao says, when we face a problem we have to face it
thoroughly, not only from one side. When I am discharged from the
hospital, the doctors have said that I should have some problem of
investigation in my mind. When I am in touch with people they have
suggested that I make conclusions in my mind after investigation, not before
investigation, in order to see if what I suspect to be true is just subjective
thinking or is objectively correct. By studying Chairman Mao we can treat
and cure disease.*[46]

Patients use Mao's writings not only to understand their problems,
but to change and get well. This use of study is in keeping with Mao's
teaching that

*Marxist philosophy holds that the most important problem does not lie in
understanding the laws of the objective world and thus being able to explain
it, but in applying the knowledge of these laws actively to change the
world.*[47]

## FOLLOW-UP CARE

Social organization and the participation of family, friends, neighbors,
and co-workers are extremely important in helping patients readjust to
the outside world upon leaving the hospital. As the doctors told Paul in
1979,

*Since ours is a socialist country, we have a strong sense of social
responsibility. When people leave the hospital, we ask them to come back once
a week for reexamination and medical information. If they do not come, we
will write a letter or make a phone call to their home. We have a small
group in the hospital that takes care of discharged patients. We also send
mobile medical teams to the countryside to give the clinics, the barefoot
doctors and the people in the communes information on mental disease, and
we bring medicine to the door of the patient.*

In addition to regular follow-up care by medical workers, the patient
is made the object of "great concern" by family, friends, neighbors, and
co-workers.[48] At the workplace, a less stressful job may be found within

Mental Health Care in China Today

the same work unit for a former patient, if it is thought necessary or beneficial.[49] Here are two examples of the salutary results of the work unit's working together with the hospital:

*In conversations with a patient before he was released from the hospital, doctors discovered he was afraid of taking the medication prescribed. He was a shop assistant who dealt with money every day, and he feared the medicine was affecting his memory. The doctors convinced him he should "take a rest" from work for a while, take the medicine, and come back for regular checkups. They also explained the situation to the store manager. After a few months, the patient seemed somewhat better, and was very anxious to return to work. So the doctors arranged with the store manager for the patient to transfer temporarily to a job in the warehouse department, where he wouldn't have to rely on his memory. They also arranged a memory training course for the patient, to help restore his confidence. After six months, the patient happily transferred back to his old job.[50]*

*After a patient left our hospital and went back to his working unit, the authorities of that unit, in consideration of his health, shifted him to another workshop to do another kind of job. However, he took this in the wrong way. He thought that the administrator of his work unit might have some kind of prejudice against him, and he became very disappointed and returned to the hospital to ask the doctor's help. The doctor went to the working unit to learn about the whole process and to explain to the patient. The man gradually understood why his work was shifted, his disappointment disappeared, and he worked very well and was very pleasant.[51]*

Mental health workers play an important role in the aftercare of patients. Not only do patients continue to see a mental health worker at the hospital on an outpatient basis for some time after discharge, but mental health workers also routinely visit a patient's home or work place before discharge to prepare the community and the family for his/her arrival.[52] These people are educated as to the nature of the disorder, how they can help, and what medication the patient should continue to take.[53] One observer noted that

*When needed, groups can be organized at work or at home and in the neighborhood to help patients return to society and maintain their health after leaving the hospital. There is no need to conceal the fact that a patient has been in a mental hospital . . . and the patient can work according to his capacity.[54]*

Mental Health Care in China Today_____

Just how the involvement of the community can prevent readmissions is made clear in the following example:

*A young man released from the hospital lived alone with his elderly mother, and needed regular medication. At the time of his release, the doctor had talked to the mother, and she had promised to see that her son took his medicine at the proper times. But a mobile team had discovered he was not taking the medicine regularly. The problem was that his mother was going blind, and found it difficult to keep track of the time. Team members made arrangements with a neighbor to take charge of the young man's medication, and the problem was now solved.*[55]

Mental health workers also perform needed tasks such as finding accommodation for a patient to be discharged, when necessary.[56]

Former patients, in turn, often serve the useful purpose of going back to the hospital for visits and talks with patients about their own former problems and course of treatment and reeducation, which must provide a tremendous boost in morale and a positive role-model for the hospitalized patients.[57]

## SCOPE OF MENTAL HEALTH FACILITIES: SIZE OF THE MENTAL HEALTH PROBLEM

Just what is the scope of mental health facilities in China today, and what is the amount of mental illness experienced by the Chinese people? Many westerners, including Paul when he went to China in 1975 during the Cultural Revolution, got the impression that there was very little mental illness or stress in China. Paul was told by Chinese psychiatrists while visiting the Third Beijing Teaching Hospital, "among a thousand people, only one will have schizophrenia. . . . This rate is much lower than in some western countries."[58] A more realistic view of the frequency of illness in China is now available. On the other hand, others who have been critical of China's approach to mental health have presented the mistaken view that the mentally ill in the People's Republic are regarded as "class enemies and malingerers"[59] rather than as sick people. We hope that this work will correct such ideas.

As to the scope of mental health facilities, we mentioned earlier that at the time of Liberation, psychiatric beds accounted for only 1.1 percent of the total of hospital beds, and that there was close to a twenty-fold increase by the era of the Great Leap Forward, at which time psychiatric beds accounted for 3.6 percent of the total.[60] In 1980, there were 1,900,000 hospital beds, and with three to four percent of these for psychiatric patients, there were 60,000 to 75,000 psychiatric beds.[61] (The United States, with about one quarter the population of China, had 1,400,000 hospital beds with 261,000 for psychiatric patients in 1980.) Dr. Xia Zhenyi (Hsia Chen-yi), President of the Chinese Society of Neurology and Psychiatry, estimated that in 1981 there were 36,000 doctors and nurses in psychiatric services in China.[62] Although he did not say how many of this group were fully trained psychiatrists, their number is probably about 10 percent, or 3,600. Seven or eight thousand would be middle level doctors with less medical and psychiatric training, and the others are nurses and technicians.

A visitor in the early 1960s reported that at that time, psychiatric beds accounted for 4 percent of the total beds,[63] and contrasted this figure with that of 50 percent for North America; according to this observer, this vast difference was because the Chinese have less need for inpatient facilities than we have in the West. But this seems paradoxical; if facilities were so sadly lacking at the time of Liberation, and are so scanty compared to those in North America, might we not interpret this difference to mean a continued shortage of facilities? One indication that facilities are not lacking, but abundant, was given by a visitor who was proudly shown a mental hospital in Beijing which was three-fifths empty; three of its five floors were no longer in use, she was told, because they were no longer needed.[64]

Although some of our Chinese colleagues now say that there is a need for more facilities in China, we still believe that social organization in China makes it possible for people to get help before their problems become serious enough to warrant hospitalization. In 1981, Paul was told by Dr. Shen Yu-tsun, a visiting psychiatrist from China, that this is because of the active role of the family in people's lives. If a person is having problems, he or she gets support from the family.[65]

## PAUL'S SECOND VISIT: CHANGES IN CHINESE MENTAL HEALTH CARE SINCE THE CULTURAL REVOLUTION

When I returned to China in 1979, I found that the Chinese were much more willing to talk openly and seemed anxious to clear up false impressions that might have been created during the period of the Gang of Four. When I had interviewed Chinese psychiatrists during that period,

Mental Health Care in China Today

in 1975, there was a definite lack of spontaneity—I didn't realize how great a lack until I returned after the fall of the Gang of Four and talked to some of the same people again. I was told by psychiatrists and others in 1979 that the Cultural Revolution had created an atmosphere that had caused some people to become mentally ill as a result of anxiety created by false accusations made against them by followers of the Gang of Four. I heard, for instance, about the case of an older woman, a schoolteacher who had never married and had always lived a quiet life in a small town in Northeast China. This self-effacing teacher was persecuted by followers of the Gang of Four because of a friendship she had had as a young girl, many years before, with a man who had emigrated to Canada. He had been sympathetic to the revolution and had returned from time to time, but the teacher probably never saw him again after their youth. Nevertheless, during the Cultural Revolution, her early relationship with this man was unearthed and she was accused of conspiring with an enemy of the country. These denunciations caused her such stress that she became mentally ill and spent several months in the hospital. Recently, the fall of the Gang of Four, bringing reminders of all the suffering she had endured, precipitated the return of her illness. During this period when I was in China many stories of other victims of this kind of oppression were in the news.

Since the end of the Cultural Revolution in 1976, a new spirit of modernization and open communication has been growing which affects mental health as well as other aspects of life. In mental health activities this recent state is reflected in changes that have taken place in the philosophy of patient treatment, which now allows more consideration of underlying personal, family, and sexual factors in mental illness. In Nanjing I was told about a patient whose treatment program reflects these new attitudes by Dr. T'ao Kuo-t'ai, a psychiatrist who is head of the mental hospital there. The man Dr. T'ao described to me was a teacher. He had already been seen in a Chinese traditional medicine clinic, where he had complained of severe headaches accompanied by dizziness, insomnia, irritability, anxiety, and difficulty in concentrating on his teaching. Many people in China with stress symptoms are treated in clinics such as this, specializing in Chinese traditional medicine— acupuncture and herbs. In these clinics patients receive both western and traditional Chinese diagnostic evaluations. Many of them are cured at the clinics and never enter the psychiatric system at all. This patient's symptoms did not respond to treatment at the traditional clinic, however, and he was sent to the hospital psychiatric clinic. Dr. T'ao told me that the patient had felt that his headaches were caused by his demanding schedule and the heavy workload he had to fulfill. He had complained that he had to teach seven or eight hours a day and prepare in the evening for the next day's classes. The psychiatrist felt that there was an underlying problem which had brought on his symptoms. After asking him to describe his family relationships, Dr. T'ao decided that the basic problem this patient had was conflict with his wife. She was ten years younger than he and liked to go out and visit friends, spend time in the parks and listen to music, while he preferred to read and stay at home. Also, the man had a sexual problem, that of premature ejaculation. After deciding that his illness had a "hidden origin," Dr. T'ao saw the patient and his wife together and helped them explore their marriage. The psychiatrist saw the couple five or six times together, and they developed a better relationship. The patient's symptoms gradually decreased. He felt better about his career, and his family life improved because he had a clearer understanding of what was causing his headaches. His only treatment besides Dr. T'ao's psychotherapy was a small dose of Valium at bedtime.

One can certainly see a difference in the approach to treatment for this man from that of patients treated during the Cultural Revolution. In the earlier approach to curing the patient, emphasis was put on the study of the teachings of Mao, and the therapeutic powers of revolutionary optimism and criticism/self-criticism sessions with the support of tranquilizing drugs. In the 1979 case we see the return to a more introspective treatment. As Dr. T'ao remarked, "Nowadays, if I understand the patient's behavior better by Freudian theory than Pavlovian or other theory, I can use Freudian." This option did not exist during the Cultural Revolution.

### Criticism/Self-Criticism

I found that revolutionary optimism, indeed, remains a mainstay of a patient's treatment. This technique is still considered therapeutic; however, another technique, criticism/self-criticism, is used somewhat differently in mental hospitals now. I was told by Professor Wu Chen-i, a psychiatrist in Beijing, that during the Cultural Revolution this device was "badly used" with "too much rhetoric." Implying that there had been too much criticism previously, he said, "Now there is more self-criticism in the sessions." He also said that the technique was still being used in 1979 at his hospital, and that he himself attended criticism/self-criticism sessions with other staff members.

A number of other Chinese people felt that this technique had been less frequently used since 1977 because of the terrible damage its misapplication had inflicted on people during the Cultural Revolution. Struggle sessions during the Cultural Revolution often involved attacks on a group member and occasionally, we are told, culminated in physical abuse.

The more traditional criticism/self-criticism group consists of five to fifteen citizens who meet at work or in their neighborhood twice a week to talk together about political material they are studying and to try to apply what they learn to their own work and family life. Sometimes, because there is such a close link between political and personal life in China, family and emotional problems are discussed in the group in relationship to political education or work problems. Often there is a leader who plans the sessions but remains in the background. The participants may try to make use of critical judgments about themselves or the others during the meetings in light of the issues being discussed.

The criticism/self-criticism groups originally came into being during the period of 1942–44 in Yan'an, where the Communists settled after the Long March. The groups were used for political education of party members and also for the people who lived in this area. As early as 1939 Liu Shao-chi described the importance of self-criticism in his essay, "How to Be a Good Communist." In 1957, Mao, in his essay "On the Correct Handling of Contradictions Among the People," describes unity-struggle-unity, another name for the process, as a method already used for many years.

The Soviet Communist Party had preceded the Chinese in this field, holding regular study and criticism sessions for its members before and after the Russian Revolution. The Russians, however, never extended the technique to the broad mass of people outside the party as the Chinese did. The reason the Chinese have woven this device so thoroughly into the fabric of their society may be that it resonates with some ancient Confucian ideas of moral behavior. Lowell Dittmer[66] says that it may reflect a Confucian idea of educating and transforming the wrongdoer instead of punishing him—as when, during criticism/self-criticism sessions, an individual, after criticizing his own behavior, is comforted by the group and told that they will help him to improve. Another reason for the widespread use of the criticism/self-criticism practice might be that in a society already so traditionally family-oriented, the criticism/self-criticism group may be accepted as an extended family. According to Martin Whyte, the groups are "supposed to provide a forum for bringing personal disputes into the open and resolving them, creating a warm and supportive atmosphere for participants," as well as to "contribute to effective communications, to getting official ideas down to ordinary citizens," and "to get people to work harder and to volunteer for new and difficult tasks." He says also that they are "expected to contribute to preventing deviance and maintaining social control."[67] Many important mass campaigns have been won, in part, with the use of the innumerable small criticism/self-criticism groups used for education and action. Although it has recently been downplayed, criticism/self-criticism is an integral part of the structure of Chinese communism and will continue to be part of life in China. I feel that there may be a pendulum swing toward greater use of this practice again, although it is possible it may change in form.

### Further Examples of a New Openness

There is no longer an attempt to conceal the fact that some people in China commit suicide. In 1975 I had been led to understand that suicide was nonexistent, or at least very rare. In 1979 I saw three patients in a ward in the psychiatric hospital in Shanghai who, I was told, had attempted suicide. Dr. Wu of Beijing said he treats some cases of attempted suicide in his hospital among patients who were schizophrenic or depressed. Dr. T'ao said that he treats about ten or twenty attempted suicides a year in his hospital in Nanjing. From what I could conclude, even with this new openness about suicide in China, self-destruction is not a problem of anything like the dimension that it is in the United States, where it is the tenth most frequent cause of death.

As in the case of suicide, the Chinese I met on this visit were now willing to admit that there might be a few homosexuals in the country. On my first visit I'd been told by Dr. Wu, "We never see any cases of homosexuals anymore because we educate the people from the time they are very young in communist theory." In 1979 when I asked about homosexuality, he remarked that it was "against the social order," but admitted to seeing some cases, "certainly very few."

### The Outlook for the Psychiatric Profession

"During the time of the Gang of Four one dared not talk about it if they were doing research in mental health. Research was considered a capitalist idea," Dr. Wu Chen-i told me in 1979. The period of the Cultural Revolution was indeed a low point for research in all the sciences in China. I heard many stories from the Chinese about scientists and educators who were criticized and persecuted during the Cultural Revolution. There was general agreement that a decade of scientific advance and education had been lost. Now that the ideas of the Gang of Four have been discredited, there is a new emphasis on science, research, and

Mental Health Care in China Today

new technology, including expanded and more thorough education.

Accordingly, departments of psychiatry and medical schools throughout China are resuming research programs. Using surveys that have been conducted over the last fifteen years measuring the frequency of mental illness, psychiatrists have established the number of psychiatric beds, clinics, doctors, and nurses needed in each community. These surveys are variable, however, because some surveys included the mentally retarded and epileptics, while others were limited to psychotics. Now new surveys of mental illness are being conducted which have a more carefully planned research design, so that the results will be more useful. (In one of these community surveys, done in Beijing in 1979, a particularly interesting observation emerged when 540 people over age fifty were interviewed. None of them were found to have involutional psychosis, a mental illness that frequently attacks people between forty-five and sixty in the U.S. with symptoms of depression, suspicion, agitation, and sometimes delusions. Nor did any of them have another mental illness, senile psychosis, a disease of those over sixty-five involving degenerative changes of the brain, memory loss, and confusion. This preliminary finding, although not conclusive, suggests the absence in older Chinese of such problems—the result, probably, of the importance of older people in family and community life, where they have a role to play.)

The first phase of the return to professional publication in psychiatry was the reemergence of the *Chinese Neuropsychiatric Journal* in 1979. This journal carries an update of the last fifteen years of Chinese psychiatry, written by Professor Wu Chen-i, thus ending the drought of information about this subject since 1965. Another improvement is that the length of training for psychiatry has been increased for the doctors who work in mental hospitals; it was only one year in 1975. Also on the horizon is a textbook which will summarize all new developments in the field, scheduled for publication in the near future. This book will be a cooperative effort by five psychiatrists from different cities.

Child psychiatry was discontinued during the Cultural Revolution because of the accusation that it served only the elite (although Dr. T'ao Kuo-t'ai, China's only child psychiatrist, assured me that this had not been the case). A psychiatrist I talked to in 1975 told me that Chinese children had no serious emotional problems and did not need psychiatry, but Dr. T'ao, who is now head of Nanjing Mental Hospital, is busy restoring his child psychiatry department. He told me that he sees cases of children and adolescents with disciplinary problems, autism, and hyperactivity caused by "minimal brain damage."

Mental Health Care in China Today

With the turn toward western scientific ideas and technology that has come with modernization, the Department of Psychiatry at Beijing Medical School is studying the transmission of nerve impulses by chemicals in the brain, called neurotransmitters, in collaboration with the biochemists. At the same time, research in the use of acupuncture and herbal medicine in the treatment of mental illness is also being encouraged. Some fascinating discoveries in this field have already been made, according to Dr. Wu Chen-i. He fortuitously came upon one early discovery concerning the treatment of auditory hallucination during the Cultural Revolution, at a time when he had been shifted from the Third Beijing Teaching Hospital to practicing general medicine in a circuit of seven villages near Beijing. Here, among other treatments, Dr. Wu and the two nurses working with him performed acupuncture. He had had no training in this field before Liberation because there had been a stigma against this ancient folk technique. However, shortly after Liberation he had received six months of training in acupuncture from a venerable doctor of traditional medicine. Up to the time he was transferred to village practice, he had had little personal opportunity to use the method because of his teaching and academic responsibilities. An experience he had during his time in the countryside, when he had relieved a painful cramp in his own leg with acupuncture, increased his interest and confidence in the method. His important acupuncture discovery came about one day in 1967 when he was treating a woman whose complaint was "noise" in her ear. Dr. Wu applied an electrode with mild current at the acupuncture hearing point in her ear. After one treatment the woman told him that she no longer heard "the voices," and Dr. Wu realized that he had just relieved a case of auditory hallucination and had discovered an acupuncture "psychic point." He and other psychiatrists have been using this psychic ear point to treat auditory hallucinations since that time with good results. More research is being done with a new herbal medicine for schizophrenia in Nanjing, while in Beijing the use of herbal medicine for insomnia has been very successful. "We say every doctor has to use two hands; one hand is western medicine and the other is Chinese traditional medicine," Dr. T'ao told me.

## 1981: THE OUTLOOK FOR CHINESE PSYCHOLOGY

Studies in psychology were largely discontinued during the Cultural Revolution and were revived only in 1977. Very few psychologists are working in mental hospitals or clinics as yet. But Professor C. C. Ching, the first psychologist to visit the United States since Liberation, told Paul that he plans programs in which clinical psychologists will work in hospitals along with psychiatrists. He feels that some of China's eleven hundred psychologists, recently restored to professional respectability, can make a valuable contribution to research and to the treatment of mental patients. As for social work, however, we cannot discover any evidence that it exists as a separate profession in China; but plenty of social work is being done in every part of the mental health system.

A new era of give-and-take between China and the United States is just beginning. Chinese psychiatrists, who formerly asked no questions at all about western psychiatry, are now eager to exchange ideas. Instead of interviews, as in the past, we now have conversations with these doctors. Western textbooks are much sought after by the Chinese medical establishment, and many Chinese doctors are visiting the United States.

The United States, on the other hand, has much to gain from studying the unique philosophy and theories of Chinese traditional medicine, which may bring about a new understanding of stress and mental illness and new treatments. We feel it is quite likely that in the 1980s the United States and China will join in research projects on the origins of serious mental illness, including studies of schizophrenia, hallucinations, and depression.

It seems clear to us from discussions with Chinese colleagues that psychologists are now hard at work holding conferences, publishing papers, establishing priorities for future research. Dr. Ching reports that the Chinese Psychological Society now has eight hundred members and twenty-six branches throughout the country, and is divided into seven sections: Developmental and Educational Psychology, Medical Psychology, Physiological Psychology, Psychology of Sports, Experimental and General Psychology, Industrial Psychology, and Psychological Theory. *Acta Psychologica Sinica* resumed publication in August of 1979.[68]

In the area of developmental psychology, research of interest includes a study on how children learn Chinese characters by associating the design of the character with the meaning of the word it represents. A rating scale for diagnosing mentally retarded children has been devised which is said to be very useful, assessing gross and fine motor skills, self-care, language and number skills. Research in other areas is also mentioned by Dr. Ching in his article, in which he eloquently concludes,

*The experience we Chinese psychologists have gained from the thirty years of work since Liberation offers us the following lessons:*
*1. Dialectical materialism is the guiding principle for psychological*

Mental Health Care in China Today

*science, but psychology cannot be replaced by philosophy. Marxism should serve as a guide to our research work, but rather than citing quotations from Marxist writers as evidence, we must adhere to the principle that the only standard for the verification of truth is practice.*

*2. Free and democratic discussion of scientific matters should always be encouraged and must persist, as we learned from the painful lesson of treating different scientific viewpoints as political problems.*

*3. Psychology is international and some theories or schools of psychology abroad may or may not fit into our own culture, but we must acquaint ourselves with them, borrowing anything that is good for and useful to us. The blindly anti-foreign attitude can only result in loss for ourselves. We should promote scientific contact and exchange with colleagues overseas.*[69]

As students of psychology and psychiatry in China, we welcome the opportunity provided in this period to work with our Chinese colleagues.

# Notes

1. Reprinted from *China: Science Walks on Two Legs* by Geri Steiner. Copyright © 1974 by Science for the People, Inc. Reprinted by permission of Avon Books, New York.
2. Ibid. p. 250.
3. Ruth and Victor Sidel, *Serve the People: Observations on Medicine in the People's Republic of China* (New York: Josiah Macy, Jr. Foundation, 1973), p. 166.
4. Wu Chen-i, interview with Paul Lowinger, 1980.
5. Wu Chen-i, "New China's Achievements in Psychiatry," *Collection of Theses on Achievements in the Medical Science in Commemoration of the 10th National Foundation Day of China,* Vol. II (Beijing, 1959). Translated by U.S. Joint Publications Research Service, No. 14,829, p. 601. In the U.S., ECT is often used alone, and psychosurgery is on the rise. See Peter Breggin, "The Return of Lobotomy and Psychosurgery," in *The Congressional Record,* Vol. 118, No. 26 (Feb. 24, 1972).
6. Donald Y. F. Ho, "Prevention and Treatment of Mental Illness in the People's Republic of China," *American Journal of Orthopsychiatry,* Vol. 44, No. 4 (July 1974), p. 628; Ruth and Victor Sidel, "The Human Services in China," *Social Policy,* Vol. 2, No. 6 (1972), p. 28.
7. Yi-chuang Lu, "Social Values and Psychiatric Ideology in Revolutionary China," paper presented at the annual meeting of the American Sociological Association, New York (Aug. 30, 1973), p. 9.
8. Sidel and Sidel, "The Human Services"; Ho, op. cit. p. 629; Phillip Shapiro, "Mental Illness: A Social Problem with a Social Cure," *Getting Together,* Vol. 5, No. 3 (Feb. 1–5, 1974), p. 7.
9. Science for the People, op. cit. p. 260.

Mental Health Care in China Today

10. R. Kupers and T. Kupers, "Mental Health in China: An Evening with Al Wasserman," *Rough Times,* Vol. 3, No. 3, (Dec. 1972), p. 16; Leigh Kagan, "Report from a Visit to the Tientsin Psychiatric Hospital," *Far East Reporter* (Apr. 1973), p. 16; F. Adams, "Mental Care in Peking," *China Now,* Vol. 18 (Jan. 1972), p. 8.
11. Sidel and Sidel, *Serve the People,* p. 170.
12. Marvin F. Miller, *"Psychiatry in the People's Republic of China,* World Studies in Psychiatry, E. R. Squibb & Sons, 1978, p. 16.
13. Kagan, op cit. p. 13; Science for the People, op cit. p. 255.
14. Kagan, op cit. p. 16.
15. Shapiro, loc. cit.
16. Eve Sheringham, "Viosit to a Mental Hospital in China," unpublished manuscript, 1974; Sidel and Sidel, "The Human Services," p. 27; Sidel and Sidel, *Serve the People,* p. 163.
17. For instance, Ilkka Taipale, and Vappu Taipale, "Chinese Psychiatry: A Visit to a Chinese Mental Hospital," *Archives of General Psychiatry,* Vol. 29 (1973), p. 315; David M. Ratnavale, "Psychiatry in Shanghai, China: Observations in 1973," *American Journal of Psychiatry,* Vol. 130 (1973), p. 1083.
18. Maurice J. Sainsbury, "Psychiatry in the People's Republic of China," *The Medical Journal of Australia,* Vol. 1, No. 17 (1974), p. 671.
19. Philip D. Walls, Lichun Han Walls, and Donald G. Langsley, "Psychiatric Training and Practice in the People's Republic of China," *American Journal of Psychiatry,* Vol. 132, No. 2 (Feb. 1975), p. 123.
20. Sainsbury, loc. cit.
21. Shapiro, loc. cit.; Taipale and Taipale, loc. cit.; Sheringham, loc. cit.
22. For instance, Taipale and Taipale, loc. cit.; Shapiro, loc. cit.; "Mental Health in China," *U.S.-China Friendship Newsletter,* San Francisco, Vol. 2, No. 4 (1972), p. 1.
23. Ken Grimes, "Mental Health Care in Shanghai," unpublished manuscript, 1978, p. 7.
24. Shapiro, loc. cit.
25. For instance, Taipale and Taipale, loc. cit.; Walls, Walls, and Langsley, loc. cit.
26. Seymour S. Kety, "Psychiatric Concepts and Treatment in China," *China Quarterly,* Vol. 66 (June 1976), pp. 318–319.
27. "Mental Health in China," op cit. p. 2.
28. Ibid.; Taipale and Taipale, loc. cit.
29. Kagan, op. cit. p. 14.
30. Grimes, op. cit. p. 8.
31. Sidel and Sidel, *Serve the People,* p. 164.
32. Grimes, loc. cit.
33. Sidel and Sidel, *Serve the People,* p. 166.
34. Yi-chuang Lu, "The Collective Approach to Psychiatric Practice in the People's Republic of China," *Social Problems,* Vol. 26 (Oct. 1978), p. 7. Acknowledgment is made to Dr. Yi-chuang Lu of the Department of Psychiatry, University of Chicago and to *Social Problems* for permission to use this quotation.

35. Virginia Goldner, "The Politics of Mental Health in China," *State and Mind* (Spring 1978), p. 13.
36. Science for the People, op. cit. p. 262.
37. Grimes, loc. cit.
38. Ruth Sidel, "Social Services in China," *Social Work* (Nov. 1972), p. 12.
39. Ibid.
40. Mao Tse-tung, "On Contradiction," (Aug. 1937), *Selected Readings from the Works of Mao Tse-tung* (Beijing: Foreign Languages Press, 1967), pp. 70–108.
41. Mao Tse-tung, "Where Do Correct Ideas Come From?" (1957), *Selected Readings . . ., p. 405.*
42. Ibid.
43. Goldner, op. cit. p. 15.
44. Mao Tse-tung, "On the Correct Handling of Contradictions Among the People," (Feb. 27, 1957), *Selected Readings . . .,* pp. 350–387.
45. Grimes, op. cit. p. 9.
46. Sidel and Sidel, *Serve the People,* p. 108.
47. Mao Tse-tung, "On Practice," (July 1937), *Selected Readings . . .,* p. 63.
48. Sidel and Sidel, "The Human Services," p. 27.
49. Sidel and Sidel, *Serve the People,* pp. 163–164.
50. Grimes, op. cit. p. 5.
51. Walls, Walls, and Langsley, op. cit. p. 126.
52. Sidel and Sidel, *Serve the People,* p. 164.
53. Science for the People, op. cit. p. 254.
54. Taipale and Taipale, op. cit. p. 316.
55. Grimes, op. cit. p. 4.
56. Taipale and Taipale, loc. cit.
57. Ibid. p. 315; Sidel and Sidel, *Serve the People,* p. 167; Lu, op. cit. p. 5.
58. Paul Lowinger, "Psychiatric Opinions in Peking," *Psychiatric Opinion,* Vol. 15, No. 5 (May 1978), pp. 36–39.
59. Arthur M. Kleinman, "Social and Cultural Context,". . . *Renewal in Psychiatry,* eds. Theo C. Manschreck and Arthur M. Kleinman, (Washington, D.C.: Hemisphere Publishing Corporation, 1977), p. 107.
60. Wu, "New China's Achievements," p. 596.
61. Lin Yang, "Medical and Health Service," *Beijing Review,* Vol. 23, No. 25, (1980), p. 20.
62. Xia Zhenyi (Hsia Chen-yi), interview on Sept. 2, 1981, with Paul Lowinger.
63. Denis Lazure, "Politics and Mental Health in New China," *American Journal of Orthopsychiatry,* Vol. XXXIV (1964), p. 930.
64. Sheringham, op. cit.
65. Shen Yucun (Shen Yu-tsun), interview on Sept. 2, 1981, with Paul Lowinger.
66. Lowell Dittmer, *Liu Shao-ch'i and the Chinese Cultural Revolution: The Politics of Mass Criticism* (Berkeley & Los Angeles: University of California Press, 1974), p. 338.
67. Martin King Whyte, *Small Groups and Political Rituals in China* (Berkeley & Los Angeles: University of California Press, 1974), pp. 233–234.
68. C. C. Ching, "Psychology in the People's Republic of China," *American Psychologist,* Vol. 35, No. 12 (Dec. 1980), p. 1088.
69. Ibid. p. 1089.

Mental Health Care in China Today

# Appendix 1
# Brief Biographical Sketches of Four Chinese Psychiatrists

### DR. WU CHEN-I

Dr. Wu Chen-i grew up in Hangzhou (Hangchow), and went to a missionary school in Suzhou (Soochow) where he got a bachelor's degree in biology. He was invited by a professor to become a student assistant and get a master's degree "without competition," but chose to go to medical school instead. This choice was encouraged by his father. After finishing at Chilu College, he went to the west of China during the war against Japan and studied psychiatry. He then proceeded up the academic ladder from assistant resident to resident to associate to assistant professor. He then finished his medical training in the United States. Returning to China, he went to Nanjing University, where he started the Nanjing Mental Hospital and the medical school's department of psychiatry shortly after World War II, when this city was China's capital. He was never a Communist, but had many friends who were Communists. He could see the Revolution coming, and apparently welcomed this change, because he saw the pre-Liberation reactionary government as an impediment to progress.

Dr. Wu stayed in Nanjing, to which he had been invited by a Professor Chen, a former classmate from Suzhou. There he was involved in teaching and clinical work and administration. He invited Professor T'ao Kuo-t'ai to join him; Dr. T'ao was a year or so behind Dr. Wu in the residency program, and they had been quite close over the years. Dr. Wu then worked in Western China in neuropsychiatry before Liberation, but has never done private practice. He was invited to Beijing as a professor in the late 1950s. He visited East Germany for two months in 1954, returning home via the Soviet Union, where he visited with two professors in Leningrad and one in Moscow.

During the Cultural Revolution Dr. Wu worked in the clinic and hospital, a change for him, since he had been primarily involved in teaching before that time. At one point during the Cultural Revolution he did general medicine with two nurses in some southern villages near Beijing; it was during this time that he acquainted himself with acupuncture, and discovered a psychic acupuncture point which he has since used many times in treating auditory hallucinations.

In 1980 he started to spend more time working at Beijing's An Ding Hospital, organizing clinical work there. He still retains the title of professor, but Dr. Shen Yu-tsun has become the leader of the Third Teaching Hospital. Dr. Wu now spends much of his time teaching students and young doctors at the National, or First, Medical School.

Dr. Wu's wife is an accountant, now retired, who worked in a bank. They have two sons, who are both aeronautical engineers. One son lives at some distance from Beijing, and rarely gets to visit his parents. The other son is an instructor of aeronautical engineering at Beijing. Both sons are married and have children.

Dr. Wu is also working, along with five other professors, on a psychiatry textbook, which should be finished soon. He still enjoys teaching, but would like to retire and do more traveling. He has a brother in Sweden who is a professor of philosophy in Malmö, a brother who lives on Taiwan, and a sister who is married to a university teacher.

## DR. T'AO KUO-T'AI

Dr. T'ao Kuo-t'ai is the head of the Department of Psychiatry at the Nanjing Neuropsychiatric Institute, and professor of psychiatry at the

Nanjing School of Medicine. Born in Nanjing, Dr. T'ao is China's leading child psychiatrist, and the only child psychiatrist in China who has received any training outside of China. He spent about two years in the United States in 1949 and 1950, studying at the Langley-Porter Clinic, University of California at San Francisco Department of Psychiatry.

Dr. T'ao has written numerous articles on child psychiatry, which was abolished for a time during the Cultural Revolution, and is particularly concerned with the effects on children of the one-child family of the future.

Sixty years of age, Dr. T'ao is married to a doctor; it is his second marriage. He is also a father.

## DR. LIU XIEHE

Dr. Liu Xiehe visited San Francisco and stayed in Paul's home in October, 1980. He had read an article of Paul's about psychiatry in China that had been published in an English journal while he was spending nine months studying in London, and had written to Paul to inquire whether he could look over psychiatric facilities in San Francisco while he was visiting the United States. He was spending one month in America before his return to China after his time in England.

Dr. Liu was born in Hunan Province. His grandfather was a wine merchant and his father was an official in the educational system. One gets the impression that his family must have been well-to-do and scholarly before the Revolution. Dr. Liu's mother died when he was six and his father when he was ten. He and his brother were then brought up by his stepmother. These facts are not filled in by Dr. Liu, either because of reserve or lack of great facility with English, although he speaks and understands English well. Dr. Liu went to Hunan Medical School and graduated second in his class. It was unusual that he elected to go into psychiatry as a specialty (because of his longtime interest in how the mind works), as psychiatry was considered an undesirable specialty— "the end of medicine," Dr. Liu says they called it—by most medical school graduates who were assigned by the government to various jobs. By the time of the Cultural Revolution Dr. Liu was teaching psychiatry at Sichuan Medical College in the city of Chengdu. This medical school was closed during the Cultural Revolution, like all other medical schools in China, for a period of two years. During this time Dr. Liu was dismissed from his professional activities and sent to work in an orchard in the countryside. He obviously feels very bitter about the time wasted in his work, when there was no research and education. His eyes become clouded and withdrawn as he speaks of this time. He definitely feels that no good at all came out of the Cultural Revolution, nothing but setbacks. When the medical school reopened after two years, he was allowed to return. With modernization and the fall of the Gang of Four, his research and teaching at the medical school were allowed to proceed, and he was sent to England to find out more about Western psychiatry. He feels the Chinese are far behind in psychiatric knowledge and is very anxious to learn and use Western ideas. When asked if he felt Freudian ideas were being studied, he said, "No, young psychiatrists in China have never heard of Freud." One felt he meant by the tone of bitterness and frustration that Freudianism was just one of many psychiatric concepts that had been kept from Chinese psychiatrists because of the brevity of their training and the disinterest in Western ideas during the Cultural Revolution.

Dr. Liu is married to a secretary in the department of psychiatry at his school. He hasn't seen her for almost a year, but he has sent some things home. They married eleven years ago, after a short courtship. It was short, he volunteered, because he was older (twenty-eight) when they decided to marry. They have one child, a girl, adopted from someone in his wife's family in Chengdu. She comes from a very large family there. (A common practice in China is to give childless couples an infant from within the family of someone with many children.) Dr. Liu had come to San Francisco after visiting one of her brothers who lives in Houston.

The weekends or days off of the Lius are spent cleaning and shopping and with a lot of friends and family dropping in. "It is not like here. In China, friends and relatives drop in any time they please."

Dr. Liu has written a history of psychiatry in China, which will soon be published in that country. He gives a very scholarly impression, spending his spare moments every evening at his desk writing. While in England he wrote a paper, "Mental Health Work in Sichuan," and also a history of the use of Chinese medicine in psychiatry. Dr. Liu is a thin and intense man with a self-effacing manner. His Western-style suit hangs on his spare body. He smiles often and claims not to study politics when Americans press him about this. He does not drink because "one little bit goes to my head," nor does he smoke. He travels with very little luggage for one away for such a long time. He feels that the greatest needs for improvement in Chinese psychiatry are in child psychiatry, community psychiatry, day care for chronic patients, and psychological tests. There are no trained child psychiatrists among the three hundred psychiatrists in Sichuan. United States community psychiatry interests Dr. Liu, es-

Brief Biographical Sketches of Four Chinese Psychiatrists

pecially in the way it is organized, including special techniques for helping chronic mental patients such as day care and halfway houses, which are uncommon in China. Dr. Liu also feels that the intelligence and personality tests used in the American mental health system could play a useful role in his hospital.

Regarding the Chinese attitude toward the mentally ill, Dr. Liu commented that mentally ill people are somewhat stigmatized in China, but this attitude is decreasing because of the education of the community about mental illness. Urban dwellers and younger people are less apt to look down on the mentally ill than are those in rural areas and older citizens who are sometimes superstitious about mentally ill people, associating them with ghosts. Dr. Liu smiled a bit at this admission of a continuing remnant of the past. Although China is changing very fast, Dr. Liu said that Mao's works and stories of revolutionary conduct, which were much used in psychotherapy before the modernization program, are still an important element of treatment in Sichuan heart-to-heart talks and group discussions to acquaint the patient with their illness. Also, he assured Paul, criticism/self-criticism continues to be used in various ways, as in therapy with patients and in staff meetings to solve problems of productivity and interpersonal relations.

Chengdu, the city to which Dr. Liu was returning, after having sent ahead a color television set to his eager family, is a city of 3.6 million people. The province in which Chengdu is located, Sichuan, has almost 100 million people, about half the population of the United States. In this province there are a mere 300 psychiatrists and 2,500 psychiatric beds. For the same number of people in the United States there are 13,000 psychiatrists and 137,500 psychiatric beds. Are there fewer psychiatrists per person in Sichuan because there are so few mentally ill people there? Or is it because most mentally ill people are cared for within their families? Or could it be because in Sichuan the population is much younger—40 percent under the age of fifteen—than that of the United States, which has an aging population more prone to mental illness? Dr. Liu himself feels that there are not enough psychiatrists and facilities, especially in the rural areas of Sichuan, to treat the number of mentally ill people. He hopes to remedy this by using psychiatrists and nurses in mobile teams.

## DR. SHEN YU-TSUN

Dr. Shen Yu-tsun heads the Beijing Number Three Hospital, one of the major mental institutions in China. She is also associate professor and chair of the department of psychiatry at the medical college.

Brief Biographical Sketches of Four Chinese Psychiatrists

Dr. Shen is originally from Hubei Province, and in addition to her studies in China, she spent four years studying in the Soviet Union. Other more recent travels include a 1979 visit to Denmark, where she studied psychopharmacology, a 1980 visit to the United States with an eight-person delegation from the Chinese Neuropsychiatric Association and a 1981 visit to the United States to plan Chinese-American psychiatric collaboration.

Dr. Shen is especially interested in psychopharmacology and in research on the possible biochemical basis of schizophrenia, and has published a number of articles on these subjects, several of which are available in English. While in the United States, she discussed the possibility of joint biochemical research with a number of American psychiatrists.

Dr. Shen is married to the Minister of Health of the People's Republic of China, a man somewhat older than she, who was on the famous Long March in the early 1930s. They have two daughters who are studying medicine.

# Appendix 2
# Selected Articles From China

1. Ling Ming-yu, "Psychiatry in China Today," *National Reconstruction Journal,* Vol. 6, No. 3 (1946), pp. 20–30. This article provides a historical setting for the period just before Liberation, and an understanding of traditional Chinese values, by a Chinese psychiatrist.
2. "The National Mental Illnesses Prevention Work Plan (1958–1962)," *Compendium of Laws and Regulations in the People's Republic of China,* translated by U.S. Joint Publications Research Service No. 14,335, pp. 562–575. This document is the first national plan put forward by the profession of psychiatry in the People's Republic.
3. Wu Chen-i, "New China's Achievements in Psychiatry," *Collection of Theses on Achievements in the Medical Sciences in Commemoration of the 10th National Foundation Day of China,* Vol. II. Beijing: 1959. Translated by U.S. Joint Publications Research Service No. 14,829, pp. 594–617. This article provides a summary of work done in psychiatry in the first ten years after the founding of the People's Republic, and suggests directions for future work.
4. *Neurology-Psychiatry in the People's Republic of China.* Bethesda, Md.: DHEW (NIH) No. 74-56, 1973 (translated), pp. 71–95. Included here is the psychiatry chapter from this Chinese textbook, originally published in the People's Republic in the 1950s, and revised in 1971. Badly translated, it nonetheless provides the reader with some understanding of the Chinese approach to various of the mental illnesses.

5. Interview with Wu Chen-i: Paul Lowinger, 1979.
6. Wu Chen-i and Zhang Ji-zhi, "The Last Fifteen Years of Progress in Our Country's Treatment of Mental Diseases," *Chinese Neuropsychiatric Journal,* Vol. 12, No. 3 (1979). This recent summary of Chinese work in mental health is not otherwise available in English, having been translated by a friend of ours. Dr. Wu has given his permission for us to use the article.
7. C. C. Ching, "Psychology in the People's Republic of China," *American Psychologist,* Vol. 35, No. 12 (December, 1980), pp. 1084–1089. Although this article, unlike the others included in this Appendix, is readily available in the U.S., we are including it because it gives an excellent account of the current situation in the field of psychology in China.

# PSYCHIATRY IN CHINA TODAY
## by LING MING-YU, M.D.

Modern psychiatry looks to person-in-situation or inter-personal relationships for the understanding and control of the problems presented by mental patients. A psychiatrist no longer considers his patient as a "case" but as an integrate dynamic personality developed from the interaction between himself as an individual and his environment. The individual as he is today has been changed from what he was yesterday, by environmental forces in the process of development; and he is going to be different tomorrow from what he is today. In dealing with mental conditions, therefore, although one cannot minimize the importance of the biological organism of the individual on which personality is developed, it is always interesting and fruitful to view our problems in the social and cultural backgrounds which have produced wide differences in political and economic thinking in different countries, since the influence of these backgrounds shows up in the incidence and manifestations of mental illnesses, and more or less predetermine the general course of their treatment.

China, we must remember, is a very old country, with a continuous history of over five thousand years. She is also a very big country, her geographical boundaries extending from 25.5° N. Latitude to 55.5° N. Lat., and from 75° E. Longitude to 135° E. Long. Her population is something over 450 million souls.

It is beyond the scope of this paper to attempt a full and adequate discussion of all the social and cultural factors which have a bearing upon the psychiatric problems of the Chinese people who, in many ways, differ widely among themselves. Some of these differences are due to the tremendous expanse of the country, with its varying climatic and geographical peculiarities, and the consequent development of different customs and habits in communities remote from each other. Added to these factors is the lack of modern communications between different sections of the country.

In this paper the author will, first of all, describe briefly a few general features of Chinese life which have had great influence upon the formation and development of individual personality. Later on, he will point out the urgent need of the psychiatric help that can be given them, as well as outline a few principles to be followed in approaching the whole problem.

## BACKGROUNDS

### Family Ties

Up to very recent times, the Chinese people lived in very large family groups, members of several generations being housed under the same roof and on common property, with the senior member of the group or his deputy as the head of the family. The authority of the family head had to be respected and his commands followed without question. Should there be any difference of opinion in the family, it was always that of the senior member which prevailed.

Of the five important human relationships continually stressed by Chinese philosophers through the ages, three concerned those between members of the family: the relationships between father and son; between husband and wife; and between brothers. Inside the family there was emphasis on the equal protection and welfare of all its members. Thus a weak person, who might have difficulties in earning a living if he had to depend solely on his own ability, could take comfort from the fact that his brothers and cousins could be counted on for help. Each member of the family would look upon any honors conferred upon the family, or any disgrace that befell it, as something inseparable from himself—in fact as even more important than himself. It is not surprising, therefore, that family interest or family pride, more than any other one thing, became the nucleus around which individual personality developed.

Due to the impact of western civilization, China, in recent decades, has been making a great effort toward modernization. This has involved changes in many aspects of Chinese life. The old family system began to break down about thirty years ago; also, the recent war with Japan has produced such an unprecedented and widespread upheaval in Chinese society, that large families have disappeared from most parts of the country. However, the close emotional ties among family members, developed through many centuries, are still very strong, and will continue to exert great influence upon the psychology and behavior of the Chinese people for years to come.

## Attitude Toward Authority

One's attitude towards authority is an important aspect of one's personality. It often determines the adjustment or maladjustment of an individual to his environment. In the highly elaborate and complex organization of modern society, we are always taking as well as giving orders. Undue indulgence in the exercise of authority, or resentment to it, as well as an ambivalent frame of mind where it is concerned may be considered important causes of personality difficulties. The Chinese, in their family life, are trained to be obedient to their parents, and while in school, they are expected to show the utmost respect for the dignity of their teachers. Both parents and teachers stand, in a sense, on a higher level than young people, and must, therefore, be accorded the utmost courtesy and consideration. This kind of disciplinary training in regard to authority arouses different types of psychological reaction in different individuals. In some it engenders intense feelings of loyalty; in others a respect for authority; in still others a resentment to it or an ambivalent frame of mind regarding it. But whether these attitudes are reflected in an individual's social life to such an extent that they are responsible for some of the difficulties experienced in his adjustment to society, is a question which must be thoroughly investigated.

## Attitude Toward Sex

Since sex life plays such an important role in personality difficulties, it will be discussed quite frankly. In general, in Chinese society, male individuals are allowed much more latitude than members of the opposite sex. Virginity and purity on the part of unmarried girls, and chastity on the part of married women, are considered virtues of the highest order; in fact pre-marital or extra-marital sex relations on the part of women are socially condemned as inexcusable "crimes." Restrictions regarding the sex behavior of men are, however, much less rigorous. A widower or a divorced man may, without question, marry a virgin, while a widow would have great difficulty in finding a second husband who had not been married previously.

Selected Articles from China

The old teaching with regard to the lack of a male descendant being a disgrace to one's ancestors still carries great weight, since the primary function of marriage has been considered the production of offspring. And it has always been the wife who received the blame should there be no male child born to the family. This peculiar marital position of women may easily generate in them sex feelings of inferiority and insecurity which are manifested in various mental symptoms not infrequently seen in our patients. However, with the development of modern education and its emphasis on sex equality, women have begun to enjoy equal rights in this field with men. This should help to smooth out the peculiar psychological differences between them.

Sex taboo used to be a somewhat rigid one in Chinese culture. The separation of the sexes obtained to such an extent that there was even no handshaking allowed between male and female. Talking about sex was regarded as immoral and was strictly prohibited. However, in the old days, the universal custom of early marriage must have helped greatly in eliminating or avoiding a lot of personality difficulties which are, nowadays, found to be due to sex frustration or anxiety about sex problems.

At present free marriage is common in the country. Youngsters are very frequently given the freedom of choosing their own mates. Also, coeducation has been widely introduced. This will not only give the young people an equal opportunity in the field of education; it will also help them to cultivate a healthier attitude towards sex. However, owing to the fact that the modern type of education requires so many years; and owing also to the far-reaching changes which are taking place in China's national economy, each individual will, increasingly in the future, be forced to fight his own way to the establishment of a satisfactory family life, and marriage will thus inevitably be delayed. This is really a very important change in the sex life of the Chinese people, and one which, for better or worse, will have great influence on the personality and behavior of the younger generation.

## Religion

By and large the Chinese people have quite a liberal attitude toward religion. All kinds of religious faiths are found in the country. Each community has a local god who is believed to be in charge of births and deaths and the good fortunes or misfortunes of the local inhabitants. In most communities there are temples to historical heroes and to men of unusual ability and accomplishment. In the minds of worshippers, these heroes and great men might have had a supernatural origin and could in some mysterious ways exert influence on living people. One's ancestors are thought to be closely related to one's own prosperity or misfortunes. Mental patients who have feelings of guilt in one way or another frequently complain of symptoms which are quite often due to the idea that punishment is being inflicted on them by their ancestors. People in the country districts exercise unusual care in choosing what they consider favorable geographical locations for their ancestors' remains. This is believed to have so much to do with the prosperity of offspring, that changes in the outward appearance of a grave or even a change of its location have sometimes been employed as a means of treating mental conditions.

Religions which originated outside of China have been introduced into the country at different periods of time. Buddhism, Mohammedanism and Christianity are now well established throughout the country. Among the Christians there are Catholics as well as Protestants of all denominations. Each religion has its special appeal and has attracted different types of individuals. In general, it is the aged and tired people, or those who have had repeated frustrations and misfortunes in life who seek refuge and consolation in Buddhism. Mohammedanism has for a long time had great influence in the northwestern part of China. The Christian missionaries, along with their religious teaching, brought a knowledge of medicine, of other sciences, of modern education, and a modern way of living, all of which the Chinese people found interesting. The number of Christians increased rapidly and Christianity is now widely accepted by the Chinese people.

Except in the matter of their relations to their ancestors—an attitude which has been evolved through thousands of years—the Chinese as a people are less fanatical in their religious beliefs than any other people in the world. They readily absorb the ethical values of any religious teaching, but they do not adhere to any one religion to such an extent that they would fight against each other over it. Every religious faith can find a place in China and followers of different religious faiths manage to live harmoniously with each other. The role played by religion in the development of individual personality among the Chinese people is quite different from the one it plays in most western countries.

The old philosophical teaching about life placed great emphasis on the value of spiritual satisfaction in preference to physical comfort; on compliance rather than belligerency; on leisureliness rather than haste; on reserve rather than frankness. Such teaching invariably leads to the development of a personality which can bear misfortunes philosophically. Now, it is generally recognized that the average Chinese, through all the vicissitudes of life, can take so much more than his western counterpart, that certain frustrations which would drive a man crazy in the West, are stoically accepted by him. Another important viewpoint about human conduct which is stressed in Chinese philosophy is that of "balanced behavior along the middle-of-the-road." Too much, according to the ancient sages, is to be avoided just as much as too little.

Things of an extreme nature, or events that are extraordinarily exciting are not commonly experienced in the daily life of the average Chinese. This would seem to be one of the important reasons for the relatively low incidence of mental illness generally found by psychiatric workers in China.

## Alcohol and Drugs

Alcohol in relation to personality changes is probably not so serious a problem in China as it is in the United States or in other western countries, although it has been widely used in the former country for thousands of years. Chinese drink alcohol mostly at social gatherings along with the consumption of a lot of food, and thus its absorption is much delayed and the likelihood of intoxication reduced. Individuals with psychological difficulties or dissatisfactions who seek refuge or temporary comfort in alcohol, as so many seem to do in the western world, might in many instances find satisfaction in going to a Buddhist Temple. Although individuals affected by alcohol are occasionally seen in China yet not many cases of personality changes have so far been attributable to alcoholism.

On the other hand, the problem of drug addiction demands our immediate attention. In areas occupied by Japanese troops, due to the malicious and purposeful spread of narcotic drugs like opium, heroin, morphine, etc., by the enemy, addicts of all ages have been reported. After addiction to any drug is once formed, the craving for it, as is well known, is so strong that an individual will often run all sorts of risks to procure it; and in overcoming the drug habit, the individual himself is often so unreliable, that external help is absolutely needed.

## Infectious Diseases

Syphilis as an important cause of personality disorder has been universally recognized. In China it also deserves special attention. According to the reports of some city hospitals in which routine serological tests are supplied to every new patient admitted, its incidence is put at 6 to 8 percent. This figure is comparable to that resulting from most western studies. Among rural populations, it is thought to be lower. In those areas where there have been active military operations, the disease has undoubtedly become widespread because of lack of medical control of the soldiers.

Many other infectious diseases like malaria, typhus, typhoid, etc., have been prevalent in different regions of the country due to lack of adequate sanitation; and these diseases have contributed in no small measure to undermining the general health and disturbing the balance of personality.

The recent long protracted war with Japan has produced unprecedented changes in the social life of the Chinese people. Millions have been killed or wounded, hundreds of thousands of homes have been broken up, and a vast amount of property has been destroyed. There has also been mass migration of people from the eastern to the western part of the country in the face of almost unbelievable difficulties. In many communities scattered throughout China the normal social structure has been uprooted to such an extent that not a single native soul was left. City inhabitants had to stand the terror of aerial bombing for years. Millions of soldiers had to fight under most unfavorable conditions. The amount of emotional shock sustained by the whole nation therefore is almost beyond imagination.

At a time of emergency when the collective existence of a nation is threatened, each individual, under the illusion of national vanity and the influence of his own internal secretions, is likely to make every possible effort to stand all kinds of hardships and suffering in the hope that victory will solve every personal problem. When the war is over and repatriation and rehabilitation begin, he will see his own problem at a conscious or subconscious level. Then every recent wound or old scar he received will probably, in one way or another, stir up many emotions which will affect his personality, thus making trouble for himself and others. So it is to be expected that more varied psychiatric problems will arise in China after the war than at the time it actually was going on.

### Industrialization

The chief aim of post-war reconstruction in China will be industrialization, which undoubtedly will bring about a great change in Chinese social life. In a big organization like a modern factory there is a mechanization of human relationships. The intimate interpersonal relations enjoyed on small farms or in handcraft establishments will no longer be possible. Individual ability or aptitude will count so much in fitting an individual into a certain niche in an industrial organization that members of a family will have to be separated from each other and lead their own individual lives. There will be more mingling of the sexes. In this new and more complex society, a proper attitude toward authority is very important in one's adjustment to his work. One's philosophy of life will undergo important changes when one faces a differently organized objective world. When people are crowded together, social evils and social diseases are given a greater chance to spread, if no adequate preventive measures are taken. In a word, the industrialization of China will require so much readjustment in the lives of the Chinese people that the psychiatric profession will be called on for much intelligent planning for the prevention and cure of such personality difficulties as are sure to arise.

## PRESENT PROBLEMS AND PRINCIPLES OF APPROACH___

With the above cultural and historical backgrounds it is evident that the development of psychiatry in China will be by no means a simple matter. A consideration of the vast numbers of people who have recently suffered serious physical injury and enormous emotional shock from long years of war, and in addition have to face a new period of industrialization, will immediately reveal the greatness and complexity of the problem. It is not only too big a situation for the very small number of available Chinese psychiatrists to handle, but is also complicated enough to challenge the talents of the psychiatric profession of the entire world.

Unfortunately the history of psychiatry in China is a very short one. It was only in the thirties of the present century that China began to build mental hospitals or to remold the old asylums into hospital forms at Peiping, Shanghai, Canton, etc. The Chinese medical profession was then awakened to the importance of psychiatric help to its clients, and young physicians underwent special training in this field. Among the pioneer workers who sowed the seeds of the science of psychiatry in China, the author is particularly grateful to an American psychiatrist, Dr. Richard S. Lyman, whose unusual enthusiasm for this work and whose talent for inspiring his colleagues and students would have speeded up the development of psychiatry in China, had not the war broken out in 1937. Then all the rudimentary physical set-ups for mental patients, which China had had only for a short time along the sea coast, were either destroyed by or lost to the enemy. During the eight years of war, there was only routine undergraduate teaching of psychiatry, carried on by a few young psychiatrists in a few refugee medical schools, but there was practically no hospital service, and no postgraduate training or research to speak of. At the present time the lack of trained personnel is one of the most serious problems demanding our immediate attention.

The training of psychiatric personnel has become such a pressing and important matter that immediate measures must be taken to meet the situation. But it has to be deliberately considered and carefully planned. Due to limitation of space, the writer will not go beyond the statement of a few essential ideas. In order to facilitate training, a few training units will have to be set up. These can be profitably incorporated into the C-UNRRA's program for medical relief and rehabilitation in China. In each of the three national training centers suggested in that program, a psychiatric unit with a definite hospital service is to be organized. To start with, more emphasis shall be laid on the quality of work. As time goes on, the training program should be gradually expanded and only then can we talk about quantity on a sound basis. Owing to the lack of Chinese psychiatrists available for the work, the help of American specialists is urgently needed. However, differences in language and cultural backgrounds between the two friendly nations makes it imperative that not more than technical help should be expected from our American friends. Administrative responsibilities must lie with Chinese psychiatrists.

A well formulated general course of psychiatry is to be given in the training center and every trainee should be required to take it, as it is now generally recognized that every medical practitioner should have psychiatric orientation if he wants to do his job well. Additional courses are to be provided for those who intend to work in the special field of psychiatry. The minimum course for training specialists should be three years. In order to encourage young physicians coming into this important field and to prepare training officers for the future, adequate foreign fellowships should be provided. Certainly this will not be lost sight of by such important organizations as The Rockefeller Foundation and UNRRA, whose wise policy and deep interest in China have been generally recognized.

The teaching of psychiatry in medical schools now existing in China has to be strengthened. The main difficulty of efficient teaching has been due to a lack of clinical facilities. C-UNRRA has planned to provide 52,500 additional hospital beds for general relief and rehabilitation in China. It is suggested that some of the additional hospitals should be specially equipped for psychiatry and affiliated with medical schools of good standard. These will serve as the nucleus of a permanent training program. In medical schools, psychiatric teaching should stick to the broad general principle that psychiatry is not to be regarded as a specialty monopolized by a few people called psychiatrists, but as a general knowledge of personality, of which every member of the medical profession has to have some idea. Instead of elaborately describing to the students a few clinical entities, as most psychiatry textbooks do, much more attention should be given to the importance of social and cultural influences on personality development and functioning; to the principles of general psychopathology; to psychosomatic relations; and to the early recognition of personality deviations and prompt management of them.

## Research

Research is to be incorporated into the training program. It should be a part of training. But on account of the limitation of personnel and facilities, it seems more profitable to concentrate research attention and effort only on a few important problems. What type or types of personality difficulties are peculiar to Chinese culture? What are the factors or situations in Chinese culture that would determine a healthy or unhealthy attitude toward modern life? How would the changes in the economic life the Chinese people are going to face affect their attitude? What are the new personality problems to be expected? What kind of mental hygiene program would be the most useful and practical? What are the most economical and efficient ways to take care of the sick? To give answers to these questions on a scientific basis requires a great deal of research indeed. It seems, however, to be the only rational approach to the whole problem. Otherwise, the development of psychiatry in China would not be sound.

Probably no country in the world could ever provide adequate hospital facilities for all the mental patients it might have. Because of the nature of the present situation in China, the problem of the care of the sick has to be attacked from different angles. Except those who have definite homicidal or suicidal tendencies and for whom institutional facilities must be provided, all other patients will have to be attended to in dispensaries or cared for in families. A well organized and properly equipped dispensary really can do a lot of diagnostic as well as therapeutic work. As described in the first part of this paper, the Chinese have an unusually close family relationship and it is not only necessary but also easy to emphasize the importance of family care for mental patients. As a matter of fact, practically all such patients up to the present time have remained in their own homes. But it is important for the medical profession to spread the knowledge of modern psychiatry to the general public, and to get in close touch, through social workers, with the family members, so that a more intelligent handling of patients will be made possible.

There are two groups of patients that have greatly burdened American mental institutions during recent years. One consists of elderly people undergoing senile changes; the other consisting of the feeble-minded. But in Chinese culture the aged are always to be respected; no family would let an aged father or grandfather be cared for by others no matter how poor his mental condition. As to feeble-mindedness, the problem is also comparatively simple. It is only idiots and imbeciles who have to stay at home and who require close attention; all higher grades can be easily placed on small farms and taught to do some simple farm work.

The incidence of epilepsy in Chinese communities is fairly high. The modern treatment of epilepsy consists in control of the attacks with drugs and the segregation in institutions of those who need close supervision because of uncontrollable and frequent seizures. Under the present circumstances in China, while drugs can be easily dispensed in dispensary service, family care again has to be resorted to in place of segregation in institutions.

## CONCLUSION

In dealing with mental conditions, it is the integrate dynamic personality of the patient that occupies the attention and interest of modern psychiatrists. Social and cultural backgrounds are strong determinants of individual personalities. The author has made a special effort to describe the factors in Chinese culture and social conditions that have made important contributions to the formation and development of individual personalities.

Psychiatry in China has only a short history. The recent war with Japan undoubtedly has created numerous psychiatric problems that demand immediate attention. The prospective changes in the economic life of the Chinese people following post-war reconstruction will make the situation more complicated. It is high time to develop psychiatry in China. The most urgent demand at present is that of training personnel which will require the joint effort of China and the United States. For the time being we have to rely chiefly on dispensary service and family care for the management of mentally sick people. It seems that these would be more workable in China than in any other country because of the unique Chinese family relationship.

Selected Articles from China

# THE NATIONAL MENTAL ILLNESSES PREVENTION WORK PLAN (1958–1962)

## A. THE BASIC CONDITIONS OF MENTAL ILLNESS PREVENTION WORK

Mental illness is one in which the higher nervous activities of the human body are chaotic, and there is a mental block. It brings not only pains and distresses to the patients, but also brings certain perils to industrial and agricultural production as well as to social security.

Before liberation, the reactionary ruling class was unconcerned with the prevention of mental illnesses. There were then only a few mental hospitals in China in such places as Canton, Peiping, Shanghai, Nanking and Ch'eng-tu, with about 1,000 beds in all, and the number of mental disease specialists did not exceed 50 or 60. Most of these mental hospitals were poor in equipment and management, and they had no positive cure and no humane treatment for the patients. A great many mental patients became vagabonds, with nobody to care for them, and their perils constituted a serious social problem.

Since liberation, under the correct leadership of the party and the people's government, close collaboration has been effected among the pertinent departments, and great strides have been made in the prevention and cure of mental diseases. Old hospitals have been revamped and expanded, and new hospitals and clinics for the mentally ill have been established. According to incomplete statistics, there are now in China 46 mental hospitals and clinics, with 11,000 beds in 21 provinces and municipalities, and the number of professional personnel for mental illnesses has been increased to 5,000 or more, among which some 400 are doctors (including some 30 doctors of Chinese medicine). Ending 1957, some 73,000 mentally ill persons were treated, and among them, some 27,000 recovered. Considerable work has also been done in learning from the Soviet Union, in unfolding the treatment of mental patients in the various mental hospitals, and a protective clinical system has been promoted, thus giving more rational treatment to the patients. In Peiping, Shanghai, Tientsin, Nanking and Soochow, restrictions on patients have been basically removed, and this reform not only relieved the distresses of the patients, but it also has a great political significance. In Shanghai, Nanking and Changsha, investigations were made on the rate of incidence of the mental illnesses, thus furnishing useful data to prevention and clinical work. In order to enable medical students to be more steeped in the knowledges of mental illness, courses on mental diseases have been inaugurated in various medical colleges. As a result of the above works, basic changes have occurred in the prevention of mental illnesses since liberation. This has not only safeguarded the health of the broad laboring people, but also produced positive catalyst functions in the socialist economic reconstruction.

Although the achievement in our mental disease prevention work is tremendous, nevertheless, there are still certain problems in this work.

1. The health administrative departments have not done sufficiently to implement the policy of efficient and economical development of enterprises in their mental illness prevention work. They failed to rely on the masses and cooperate closely with the pertinent departments, and lacked the spirit of adapting to local conditions and utilizing simple equipment. In the process of developing their mechanisms, they still have the deviations of seeking what is new, what is big, and what is "regular." They emphasize clinical organs, but neglect the organs for hospitalization and convalescence. They also lack adequate arrangements for patients. In the area of clinical treatment, they stress the medical treatment, but neglect methods of labor cure and spiritual cure; they emphasize treatment in hospitals, but neglect clinical consultations; they prefer Western medical treatment, but neglect Chinese medical treatment. They also lack comprehension in the importance of prevention, early treatment, and early diagnosis, and as a result, many patients have failed to get timely and rational treatment.

2. The management system in some of the mental hospitals is still far from being rational. When systems are enacted, they usually think more about the convenience of working personnel than about the patients, and they have not paid sufficient attention to protective clinical system. Some of the working personnel lack the ideology of serving the patients wholeheartedly, and their professionalism for mental illness prevention work is not firm enough. There are still some working personnel who dislike the patients, discriminate against them, and despise them. They would think that since the patients are spiritually odd, there is no need to consider their views and suggestions even though they are sound. Consequently, irrationalities still prevail in the treatment and living of mental patients.

3. In the mental illness prevention work, there exist still conditions in which the number of patients is too large and the strength for their cure too limited, thus resulting in disparity between demand and supply. About 2/1000ths of the people in China are mentally ill, according to estimates. This means that there are some 1,000,000 mentally ill persons,

though there are only 11,000 sick beds, and the number of people who go to the clinics for treatment is relatively small. Many of the mentally ill persons, because of the unavailability of timely and proper treatment and hospitalization, have affected productive reconstruction and disturbed social order. There are still some of the masses that lack correct understanding about mental patients, and take wrong attitudes toward them, while there are also patients who cannot get proper care at home.

## B. THE BASIC PRINCIPLES FOR MENTAL ILLNESS PREVENTION WORK

In the work for prevention of mental diseases, it is necessary to implement the general line of efficient and economical development of socialism and the policy of frugal and industrious development of hospitals with the attitude of rendering wholehearted service for the people. We should unfold prevention work by coordinating ourselves with the masses, by assuming local control, and by key-point accommodation. Preventive institutions should be set up systematically. There should be coordination between urban medical care and area medical care, between rural villages and the various clinical units and health stations. The specialists should leave their laboratories and hospitals to guide this work. Next, we must have industrious and economical collaboration (including three-man groups, inter-area and inter-unit collaboration) and serve as catalysts for our enterprises. Finally, we must discard superstitions, have self-confidence, establish ourselves academically, follow the mass line, and solidify and help mutually.

In methodology, there should be centralized leadership from the party and government organs of the various provinces and municipalities, and centralized planning should be made in business arrangements. We advocate the following: 1) three kinds of organizational patterns: medical base, preventive unit, and sanitarium; 2) two kinds of dispersion: those who live in their homes and those who are dispersed in rural villages for convalescence or other places with labor prerequisites; and 3) four kinds of cure: cure by Chinese and Western medicines and physical therapy, proper labor therapy, therapy through organized sports and cultural amusements, and systematic educational therapy. It is necessary to seriously summarize and propagate the clinical experiences of Chinese medicine. The frontal lobotomy or other clinical methods that can injure the lives and health of the patients should not be used. We must implement the system of protective treatment and resolutely oppose the binding or imprisoning of patients.

## C. FIVE-YEAR PLANNING FOR MENTAL ILLNESS PREVENTION WORK

1. In provinces, municipalities and autonomous regions where no mental illness prevention center or mental hospitals have been set up, they should be established within one or two years; where there are such establishments now, more such centers and hospitals should be set up according to conditions of population distribution and the size of the area in order to accommodate patients, and to guide the mental illness prevention work in the various nearby *hsien* (municipalities). In provinces and autonomous regions where the foundations for prevention work are better, a mental illness prevention center or mental hospital should be developed to assume charge for guiding prevention work and training professional personnel. Mental disease sanitariums and mental disease convalescent villages should be set up in the various provinces, municipalities, and autonomous regions. These organs should have a suitable farmland to be used for labor therapy. On one hand, there must be sustained planning for the establishment of sanitariums and convalescent villages, and on the other hand, the method of gradual expansion should be resorted to. Labor therapy should be used in these sanitariums and convalescent villages, coupled with certain cultural and amusement activities, and simple cure. In the process of labor therapy, various types of agricultural, forestry, husbandry and handicraft production should be adopted, based on the conditions of the patients, in order to effect labor cure and save state expenses. Additionally, handicraft and agricultural labor may be arranged in some *hsien* and municipalities for light cases of mental illness. Concentrated control on a small scale may also be experimented on mental patients in agricultural cooperatives who cannot work and cannot be controlled. There are still in various mental illness prevention centers and mental hospitals long-time inmates afflicted with chronic mental illness, thus preventing the full use of their potentialities. In order to fully develop the potentials and to enlarge the number of beds for treatment, it is necessary for these hospitals to remove these chronic patients to sanitariums or convalescent villages for the mentally ill for prolonged care. The expansion of mental care and clinical organs should be based on the principle of retrenchment and local adaptability.

Selected Articles from China

Some of the old houses suitable for such use and some ordinary buildings that are newly built may be provided for mental patients.

In order to strengthen the leadership in preventive work and bring about its smooth progress, three-man small groups comprising representatives of the civil affairs, public security, and health departments should be set up to jointly undertake the work.

2. The work of treating visiting patients should be greatly expanded. Mental illness prevention centers should enlarge their scope of their visiting clinics, while the general hospitals in various localities should also open clinics for mental patients and designate a certain number of beds to accommodate them. The mental illness prevention centers should also undertake the tasks of prevention, propaganda, investigation, and research in conjunction with "medical service by zoning."

3. It is necessary to energetically foster the professional personnel for prevention and treatment of mental illnesses, and enhance the professional knowledges of administrative cadres working in organs that treat and accept mental patients. In order to speedily meet the demands for the prevention and care of mental illness, medium-grade personnel should be fostered massively. For the purposes of mutual support, mutual study, exchange of experiences, and joint enhancement in order to solve the problem of cadre training, we have decided to divide the entire country into five collaborative areas, in which Peiping, Shanghai, Nanking, Ch'eng-tu and Ch'ang-sha shall serve as centers. (The Peiping An-ting Hospital and the mental illness teaching and research division of Peiping Hospital should serve as the collaborative centers for the Northeast, Inner Mongolia, Hopeh, and Ninghsia; the Nanking Nervous and Mental Illnesses Center should serve as collaborative center for Kiangsu, Anhwei, Shensi, and Shansi; the mental illness teaching and research division of Szechwan Medical College should serve as collaborative center for Sinkiang, Tsinghai, Tibet, Szechwan and Kansu; the mental illness teaching and research division of Hunan Medical College should serve as collaborative center for Hunan, Kwangei, Kweichow and Yunnan; the Shanghai Municipal Mental Hospital and the Shanghai First Medical College's mental illness teaching and research division should serve as collaborative centers for Kiangsi, Chekiang, Fukien and Hupeh; and the Canton Municipal Mental Hospital should serve as the collaborative center for Kwangtung.) Diverse measures should be taken to foster cadres and strengthen technological guidance.

4. In unfolding the work of mental illness prevention, Chinese and Western medical treatments should be undertaken simultaneously, and Western-oriented doctors should learn from Chinese doctors. It is nec-

essary to canvass and collate the experiences of mental disease therapy in the medical heritage of the fatherland, summarize their therapeutic laws, and fully apply the efficacious experiences of Chinese medicines in curing mental illnesses.

5. Scientific research on mental diseases should be unfolded in order to improve the quality of treatment. Besides the study of schizophrenia, nervous weakness, epilepsy, and various other items of work in mental illness prevention centers in accordance with Central government stipulations, we must also study the causes and prevention of mental diseases in factories and mines, enterprises, organs, and schools, and experiences and theories of Chinese medicine. Additionally, we must study children's mental illnesses and cooperate with political and legal departments to study mental illnesses in forensic medicine. In these studies, we should adopt the communist working style of imagination, outspokenness and daring. We should believe the masses, believe ourselves, but must not be superstitious about foreign countries. We must fully rely on the broad technical cadres, strengthen the collaboration among specialists, apply data extensively, and absorb the experiences of Chinese medicine and doctors in treating mental illnesses as well as the advanced experiences of various countries in the world, especially those of the Soviet Union, so that significant results will be achieved in two or three years.

6. Workers engaged in prevention of mental illness should strengthen their study of Marxism-Leninism as well as Comrade Mao Tse-tung's writings by unfolding criticisms on the bourgeois idealist viewpoints in the theory of insanity and by hoisting the standard proletarian dialectical theory of insanity and mental illnesses of the Chinese people.

The task of unfolding the work of mental illness prevention is an arduous one. To consummate this task, we must strengthen the political and ideological leadership of the party and overcome conservatism and superstitions. It is necessary to implement the policy of industrious and economical development of enterprises and coordination between Chinese medicine and Western medicine, and among the rank and file of workers engaged in prevention of mental diseases, establish the ideology and working style of love for patients, enthusiasm for profession, arduous struggle, and dedication for the service of the people. If we will, under the leadership of the party and government, closely cooperate with the various pertinent departments, fully develop the positiveness and creativeness of the masses, and resolutely implement the general line of efficient and economical development of socialism, we are confident that during the second five-year planning period, there will be great achievements in the work of mental illness prevention in China.

Selected Articles from China

# NEW CHINA'S ACHIEVEMENTS IN PSYCHIATRY
## by WU CHEN-I

Since Liberation, following the construction of socialism, our country has made rapid strides in the field of psychiatry. These last few years have seen many newly built hospitals, as well as increased facilities in the old ones. A large staff has been trained, and definite progress is being made in the area of preventive care. We should especially point out that while the light of socialism shines, the mental patient is, for the first time, freed from all forms of bondage. He is now being treated as humanely as everybody else and lives a normal life.

With respect to healing, a medical system has been established and perfected during recent years. The system took over and developed much of the precious medical heritage of our fatherland. We have improved many of the healing techniques as well as having created some new ones. These measures and efforts have brought about obvious results in the quality and effectiveness of our system.

The first Conference of Psychiatry was held in Nanjing in June 1958. The Conference clearly formulated the goals and regulations in prevention and healing, as well as giving the workers of that field all over the country a chance to exchange experiences. A new wave of the Great Leap Forward began after the Conference.

The major achievements in the field of psychiatry are briefly as follows:

## 1. HISTORY OF DEVELOPMENT

Before Liberation, our reactionary government did not pay the slightest attention to psychiatry. As a result, it was the weakest field in our country's medical sciences. In old China, only in the big cities and the medical universities were there psychiatric wards, which were poorly staffed and had a capacity of just a few beds. Their equipment was scanty, and it was not cleaned and maintained properly.

The patients ate bad food, wore rags as clothing, and were regularly mistreated. Sometimes they were bound up, scolded, or even beaten. They received none of the care and medical attention they needed. The idealism of the capitalist class ruled during that day and age. It obstructed the development of psychiatry.

The establishment of the People's Republic of China stimulated the growth of psychiatry, and within a short time it has completely changed its original appearance.

In order to be able to admit and to heal the mentally ill, the government developed psychiatry as a special field with its own organization. It made plans to have the old facilities enlarged, and 62 new hospitals were built all over the 21 provinces and autonomous regions, with a total number of beds 14 times greater than before Liberation. In 1950 the number of beds in the psychiatric wards and hospitals was 1.1 percent of the total capacity, and in 1957 it was 3.6 percent. There are now quite a few psychiatric sanitariums in various areas for the chronically ill.

The hospital staff increased as more hospitals and more beds became available. The number of doctors in 1958 was 16 times that in 1949. The increase in the number of nurses was more than twentyfold.

We adopted a double-track method of training a specialized staff. On top of the regular high and medium medical colleges, we also regularly have training programs, and advanced training classes. Just in the two cities of Shanghai and Nanjing, during the years between 1953 and 1958, there were 375 high and medium level specialists graduated. The National Conference of Psychiatry formulated a system by which each of the five areas was made responsible for training a certain number of specialists for certain definite provinces, autonomous regions and municipalities.

Through the attention and concern of the Party and the government, the hospitals were quickly and amply equipped. Generally speaking, every psychiatric hospital has its own healing equipment and laboratory. Aside from the original insulin, electric shock, and heat treatments, we are now gradually introducing hypnotherapy, all types of drugs (including herbal medicine), acupuncture, electric needles, stimulation of the nerves, psychotherapy, and the method of combining several of these treatments. Recently, artificial hibernation is also being tried. We can now, in this country, produce all the medicine needed by the above treatments as well as X-ray equipment, electric shock instruments, and others. We no longer need to import any of them.

Because of the aforementioned factors, the healing results of recent years have been improving and encouraging. From sources gathered in Shanghai and Canton (Guangzhou), the recovery rate was shown to be 40 percent to 50 percent in 1950 and 80 percent in 1958. The death rate has also been lowered considerably.

The prevention and healing of children's mental diseases are currently being developed in this country. An outpatient clinic for mentally ill children was established in Nanjing soon after Liberation and later in a few other areas. In 1956, the Nanjing Mental Hospital added its children's ward to admit children for observation and therapy, and at the same time began its home visit program. Through the combination of outpatient care, the clinic, and the home visit program, experience is being gathered, and it is becoming invaluable material for future study.

Regarding the criminally insane, the Party and the government have always been concerned with this problem. Much progress has been made in this field during the last 10 years and more. When local legal courts suspect any criminal to be insane, they always ask specialists to observe and diagnose, and the specialists' opinion is decisive in such cases. The specialists in the mental hospitals take this responsibility very seriously. Moreover, the law schools of many universities have established classes to study laws regarding the mentally ill. Many specialized books in that field were translated from Russian so as to enrich the specialized knowledge of legal workers in this field.

The treatment of the mentally ill has undergone basic changes since Liberation. In the past, mental patients were looked upon almost as criminals. They were often kept behind locked doors, and they were often physically restrained to keep them from hurting others or themselves. Only after Liberation were these harmful treatments changed, especially during the Great Leap Forward of socialist construction in 1958. Medical workers popularly raised their ideas and awakening. They realized that it is their responsibility to serve the patients well. Therefore, there was a suggestion in many mental hospitals to let the mental patients enjoy the real humane treatment of socialism, and that they should live the life of normal people. In order to make this new reform possible, the medical workers studied effective measures of controlling overexcitement. They established new methods of protection, improved and strengthened their contact with the patients, and began to give careful and individualized therapy.

On the other hand, being encouraged by the Great Leap Forward, our mental hospital workers further developed physical therapy. The mental patients were assisted by the medical workers to organize themselves for collective cultural and physical activities such as chorus, dance, and evening parties, which greatly enriched the life of the patients. They were also organized to learn about political science and current affairs. They made reports, held meetings, and discussed various subjects. All these activities were used to keep the mentally ill from being isolated from society. Our medical workers also changed the individualized, nonproductive labor the mental patients had been made to do in the past, to productive group labor. This measure caused the patients to feel that although they were inside of a hospital, they were every bit linked with the whole socialist construction, and were thus greatly encouraged. They recovered faster and better.

With regard to the philosophy of mental disease, in the past, all forms of idealism ruled this field. Mental disease was considered either as a symptom of a certain partial or total physical illness, or as the combination or accumulation of various types of abnormal behaviors. Many symptoms of mental disease were explained with the theories of psychoanalysis. This is why there had been little development in mental health work.

After Liberation, our mental health workers began to learn materialism and the philosophy of Marxism-Leninism. They gained understanding of the contest between materialism and idealism, as well as what idealism really is. Then, they learned the new medical philosophy of the Soviet Union, which has Pavlov's biology as its foundation. In 1953, a conference on the theory of Pavlov was held in Beijing, which further promoted a wave of study. Because of using this theory as a weapon, the mental health workers of our country can diagnose, cure, and prevent mental illness, as well as progress swiftly in all aspects of scientific study.

## 2. ACHIEVEMENTS IN HEALING AND SCIENTIFIC RESEARCH

Much work has been done and definite success obtained in healing and in scientific research on mental illness. The following is a brief account of the achievements in the various fields:

### A. Achievements Concerning the Major Mental Diseases

*(1) Schizophrenia.* This is currently one of the most serious mental diseases. According to the statistics of a few areas, as well as the estimates made by Hsia Chen-yi, T'ao Kuo-t'ai, and Wang Chih-yuan from analyzing 3,875 hospitalized mental patients, 35 to 40 percent of all the mentally ill are schizophrenics, and they make up 50 percent of all the hospitalized mental patients. Regarding the age of the patients when they first contract the disease, it was found to be mostly between 21 and 30 (50 percent on the average).

Considering the types of this disease, according to the study of Hsia, T'ao, and Wang, on the average 2.8 percent are the simple type of schizophrenics, 16.5 are the sexual maniacs, 11.4 percent are the excited type of patients, 48 percent are the paranoiacs, and 21.3 percent are other types. Healing results were found to be best in the excited type, second best in the paranoiacs, and worst in the simple schizophrenics. One third of all the patients have the acute form of the disease. With regard to duration and recovery, 82 percent of those who had contracted it for six months or less were improved or completely recovered. When the duration was between one and two years, the rate was only half. When the duration was more than five years, the rate was only 26 percent (T'ao Kuo-t'ai). This information shows that the sooner the disease is discovered and treated, the better chance the patient has for recovery.

With respect to therapy, aside from the original shock treatment, now we have more than ten different methods, as well as the combined use of all of them. They are hydergine, roots of rauwolfia serpentina, hypnotherapy, artificially-induced hibernation, and Chinese herbal medicine and acupuncture.

In this country, specialists are divided in their opinions about electric shock treatment. They are generally quite cautious in its use. In recent years, hydergine has shown obvious effectiveness, and the use of shock treatment has been greatly reduced. It seldom is used alone, and if it is used at all, it is in combination with other methods.

We can now produce hydergine ourselves. It is popularly used all over the country, especially in outpatient clinics and in the farm villages. The method is simple, and effectiveness is high. It has become the major therapy for schizophrenia. There are still quite a few problems about the dosage, how long it should be given, and how dependable is the recovery. Ch'en Ch'ang-hui pointed out in his study of 154 cases that if we can watch very closely the patient's reaction to the medicine, we can quickly increase the dosage, so that the effective amount can be reached quickly, and the duration of treatment shortened. In this manner, it is easy to decide the least dosage for effectiveness (average 100 to 400 milligrams) so that we may prevent overdosage. To make the effectiveness stable, he thinks that within a definite period after recovery the largest possible dosage should be given by mouth, and then a smaller dosage should be continued for a few days.

With regard to the causes of schizophrenia, some research has been done in our country in recent years. According to T'an Chien-chiu, there are many obvious factors which help to bring about the disease. Among them, the most apparent ones are nervous reactions, and physical illness. This type of patient has a better recovery rate. The patients' histories show that 22 percent of them have relatives with the same illness. This shows some hereditary tendency in this disease.

Selected Articles from China

The type of central nervous system has a definite relationship with this disease. According to statistics, the patients tend to have the weak type of central nervous system; about 70 percent to 80 percent of them do. Relatively few patients have strong central nervous systems, and their chances of recovery are much better.

Chi Ming and others made acetaldehyde tests on 172 patients, and the results were compared with the tests made on 158 mental patients with a different disease and 58 normal people. They think the schizophrenics may possibly have physical difficulty in digesting amino acids. Ch'en Ch'ang-hui, in his bedside study of patients suitable for hydergine and artificial hibernation, discovered that the patients on the average had 2.24 mg./ml. of amino nitrogen in the blood. This is about double that of a normal person. After treatment, the amino nitrogen rate was duly reduced, and the patient felt better at the same time. These biochemical studies show that this disease is related to difficulties in absorbing protein.

The study of electrobiology is gradually being developed in this country. T'ien Shou-chang and others made a study of 34 mental patients (16 of them were schizophrenics) to check the changes in their electroencephalograms. They think most patients showed an apparent sign of change, or very small change. However, these changes had no obvious relationship with the change in symptoms.

On the contrary, Hou I, in his analysis of the electroencephalograms of 40 patients suffering from paranoia, reached a different conclusion. He thinks the changes are relatively obvious and definite. Before taking the medicine, 32 of them had alpha wave as the major one, and four of them had beta wave as the major one. Generally, the waves are rather straight, especially around the forehead. The majority of them showed asymmetry on the right and left sides. The silent period is longer, the value of alpha was gradually reduced, and reaction to outside stimuli was poor. We may explain these phenomena to mean that at that time regarding the surface of the cerebrum the suppressing process was dominant. After treatment, the major wave rate did not show much change; however, the wave length was apparently higher, symmetry improved, regularity improved, and the alpha value increased, and there was an improvement in reaction to outside stimuli. All these changes were parallel to symptoms of recovery. Generally, the patient showed signs of recovery before the electroencephalograms became normal.

*(2) Psychasthenia.* Since Liberation, through studying the theory of Pavlov, we have gradually changed our past errors regarding psychasthenia and established a new and correct concept. This is why we have made such progress in treating the disease as well as in scientific research.

In treatment, we have adopted many established forms as well as creating a few new ones, among which there are Chinese herbal medicine, hypnotherapy, physical therapy, and psychotherapy, and the combination of these.

Treatment with drugs is still preferred by most doctors. Aside from bromine and its combinations, we make use of many different western and Chinese drugs, and sometimes use them in combination. Chinese herbal medicines have shown considerable success, and currently we are seeking further development in their use. There are some reports on the experience with amino acids, insulin and low blood sugar. Leng Yen was the first to apply this method to the treatment of psychasthenia. Inspired by the novocaine method in the Soviet Union, she began her experiment, and recorded that among the 88 patients, 88.4 percent were better or completely recovered.

Acupuncture to stimulate the nerves and electric stimulus have both shown effectiveness. Of course, more study is needed to make these treatments produce a complete cure.

Other physical therapeutic treatments such as electric heat, hydrotherapy, vinegar, or sparks are all being applied, and found to be effective if combined with other methods.

On the basis of learning and being very acquainted with Pavlov's biological theory, we have further developed psychotherapy for psychasthenia. Regarding group psychotherapy, the Graduate School of Psychiatry in the Beijing College of Medicine, in cooperation with the Institute of Psychology of the Academia Sinica, tried an experiment in 1953 with a group of 29 patients at a certain hospital. All 29 showed definite improvement. Group psychotherapy was combined with a small amount of drugs to treat 500 patients in the Nanjing Mental Health Institute. The result was very good.

In 1958 Li Ch'ung-p'ei and Li Hsin-t'ien created a rapid combination therapy for the treatment of psychasthenia. It is currently being practiced in many areas, and appears to be very effective. This undoubtedly opens up a new road for the treatment of psychasthenia.

It has been noticed that physical labor is very meaningful in the cure of psychasthenia. A group of 35 patients were sent to a farm village to participate in production as part of the treatment. The psychiatric division of the First Hospital in Shanghai made a study of them. Patients of similar age, trade and symptoms are compared with one another. Among them, 57 percent showed improvement, the others thought physical labor definitely helped relieve them of certain symptoms.

Four hundred patients of a certain school in Beijing were sent to work at Shihsanling. And 51 percent of them showed obvious improvement. These experiments show that physical labor has positive effects on this disease, and is worth looking into.

In 1958, the Nanjing Mental Health Institute investigated more than 4,000 people in schools and hospitals in search for the causes of psychasthenia. The Graduate Research Center of the Beijing College of Medicine in cooperation with the Institute of Psychology of the Academia Sinica made a similar study among 25,741 people of various professions. These studies provided useful material for future study, as well as offering suggestions for preventive measures.

In the laboratory, Chang Pao-tsun, Wang Yin-hsiang, and Ch'en Chung-keng made speech and conditional reflex tests on 57 patients. They discovered that most patients have weak suppressing processes, and this condition was in proportion to their symptoms. Ch'en Chung-keng used a cardiograph to record the line graph movements of the electric reflex of the skin. He thought these tests were truly meaningful to compare a normal person and a patient to show the difference in their psychological function. Liu Tso-ting and the graduate research section of the Department of Psychiatry in the Beijing College of Medicine made some electroencephalogram tests. Their results show that the study of the functional change of the surface of the cerebrum of a psychasthenic is definitely relevant.

*(3) The Manic-Depressive.* The frequency of this disease in China is second only to schizophrenia. According to the analysis made by Hsu Tao-yuan on 135 patients and Yu Chin-han on 100 patients, most of those suffering from this disease are from 16 to 25 years of age. The next largest group of patients are from 26 to 30. There is no apparent difference between the sexes. Before Liberation, according to the statistics obtained from the hospitals in Canton (Guangzhou), Suzhou, Beijing and Dalian, the patients with this disease made up 17.6 percent of the mental patients there. After Liberation, the ratio is 14.2 percent in Sian, 7.2 percent in Nanjing, 11.62 percent in Beijing, and 8.2 percent in Heilongjiang. The proportion seems to be far smaller everyplace else.

With respect to treatment, the above two authors thought electric shock seemed to be more effective than the rest. Insulin is satisfactory in the extremely violent cases. In this respect, our opinion is different from that of the Anglo-American scholars. According to the analysis made by Lo Ho-tsun of the Beijing College of Medicine, the effectiveness was about 95 percent; of these, 77.5 percent had lessened symptoms. After being released from the hospital, their follow-up visits also showed relatively stable recovery. The results in the Nanjing Mental Health Institute and the Heilongjiang Mental Hospital are comparable. Although insulin does not act as rapidly as some other drugs in controlling excitation, yet its effect is more lasting, according to these reports. Therefore, it remains a dependable treatment.

Hypnotherapy is definitely meaningful in treating manic-depressives. According to the tests made by Chai and Ch'en on 54 patients, of which 22 were manic-depressives, the effectiveness was 88 percent.

To use the method of artificial hibernation by reducing the body temperature externally offered a new, easy, quick and cheap method. It is now in the process of being developed.

*(4) Paralytic Mental Stupor {Tertiary Syphilis}.* Before Liberation, 10 percent of hospitalized mental patients were of this type. (Shenyang, 11.9 percent; Guangzhou, 10 percent). These last ten years have seen an apparent reduction of cases. According to statistics, the rate is now 2.5 percent in Nanjing, 2 percent in Heilongjiang, and 1.23 percent in the Beijing Medical College Hospital. This fact fully demonstrates the superiority of socialism. Under the rule of our socialist system, syphilis is almost non-existent. The very few people who do contract this disease are immediately and thoroughly cured. Aside from a few older patients who had suffered from this disease since before the revolution, recently, no case has been reported in which the incubation period has been less than ten years.

## B. Concerning Some Especially Effective Treatments

*(1) Artificial Hibernation.* Shen Yu-ts'un and others first applied artificial hibernation on mental patients. Since 1958, they have observed the patients systematically, made electroencephalograms, and carefully compared them. They have also conducted many other laboratory tests. The author summarized the effective results of 79 mental patients. She pointed out that the total effectiveness was 72.5 percent. There were 57 schizophrenics, and the effective rate for them was 72.4 percent. This method, she said, was especially effective for those affected with the type with delusions (90.1 percent).

This method offered a new, easily available, quick, good, and cheap treatment. In many areas throughout the country, tests are currently being made on this. However, the durability of its effect, its way of improvement, and its function remain to be studied.

Selected Articles from China

*(2) A Rapid Combination Treatment for Psychasthenia.* In the past, all the treatments for psychasthenia required a long period of time, and their effectiveness was generally poor. They cannot meet the urgency of today. In 1958, the year of the Great Leap Forward, Li Ch'ung-pei, Li Hsin-t'ien and others created a rapid combination method, which has been tested for more than a year in various hospitals. According to the observations made by K'uang P'ei-ken, and at the Chinese College of Medicine, as well as at the Shandong College of Medicine, it was 80 percent effective among the 1,042 cases observed. This method only requires three to four weeks, and its effectiveness is quite durable. Among 163 follow-up cases, 79.3 percent were still improving or remained the same three months after their release from the hospital. Half a year afterwards, 76.8 percent still remained well. On the basis of the 401 cases reported by K'uang, this method was effective even with the older patients, who had been ill for a long time, and no other treatment had worked. For instance, among the 401 patients, 80.5 percent had contracted psychasthenia for five to fourteen years, and in 114 cases, the follow-up (after four months) showed 77 percent effectiveness.

This method is not only effective as a medical treatment, it also improves the positive function of the patient's subjectivity. It helps him to accept the power of the group to fight the disease together. This method has certainly greatly strengthened group psychotherapy. It can also be easily combined with other methods of treatment, and make them more functional.

*(3) Electric Stimulus.* In 1955, Wang Ching-hsiang, based upon the pathological theory of hysteria suggested by Pavlov, used an electric-stimulus treatment. He designed an $L_2$ type electric-stimulus instrument. This method is different from Berkowitz, Delmas-Marsalet, Hirschfeld, and Alexander's nonconvulsive type. Wang's method is not only quickly effective, but also is not painful or frightening. He treated 220 cases of hysteria, and obtained an effective rate of 83.6 percent. Compared with other suggestion types of treatment, his method is almost twice as effective. This method is also effective in cases of psychasthenia, hemicrania, insomnia, depression, and seasonal depression. More study and improvement are needed in this method.

*(4) Hypnotherapy.* Various forms of hypnotherapy have been in use all over this country since 1951. According to published and soon-to-be-published reports, among the 2,794 cases of various types of mental diseases, very good results have been obtained. Chou Yen-k'ai, Wu Chen-

ting, Chung Yu-pin, Liu Chang-yung, and Chai Shu-tao summarized the results of 270 cases of drug-induced hypnotherapy. They thought it is generally effective (80 percent); however, it also has shortcomings. Some authors suggested that if drugs were used to prolong normal sleep, or induced sleep by conditioned response so as to make the sleep deeper and longer, we may prevent the toxic effects of the drugs, as well as improve the effectiveness of the therapy.

Chai Shu-tao and Ch'en Hsueh-shih summarized the results of the conditional response type of hypnotherapy, and found it to be effective in 80.8 percent of cases pertaining to nervous diseases, and in 61.5 percent of cases pertaining to split personality. Electric hypnotherapy has also been popular in recent years. According to the report by Chai and Ch'en, it is more effective for psychasthenia and hysteria, and poorer with diseases of split personality (average, 55.3 percent). These two treatments are quite safe. They do not cause pain, and are definitely effective. However, further study should be made in order to make them more effective.

(5) *Insulin Treatment.* Insulin treatment started rather early in China, but it was not used on any great scale until after Liberation. By now, not only have we accumulated a great deal of experience in its application, we have also done considerable scientific research on the subject.

Hsieh Chen-i and T'ao Kuo-t'ai made an experiment by using insulin alone on some patients, and using it in combination with other treatments on others. Among the 3,689 cases of schizophrenics reported, the difference in effectiveness was not very great, 75.7 percent on the average, and only fourteen deaths occurred among them (0.49 percent).

Regarding those mental patients who were also suffering from tuberculosis, the selection of treatment was very important. Li Hsin-t'ien and Fu Ya-ku tried insulin, electric shock and the combination of the two. According to their experience and analysis, if the tuberculosis is reasonably controlled by suitable drugs, electric shock treatments are not necessarily harmful.

As for the amount of insulin used, the Shanghai Municipal Mental Hospital suggested an accelerated method, and a half dosage method, while the Beijing College of Medicine suggested a gradually increased or reduced dosage. The latter method may save 45 percent on insulin compared with Sakel's original method.

Wang Ching-hsiang used Pavlov's theory to explain the symptoms of the patients under insulin treatment. He made new suggestions of dividing the treatment procedure into four stages, according to the signs of activity, food and defensive reflexes.

## 3. CHINA'S CONTRIBUTION TO MENTAL HEALTH

Since Liberation, under the correct guidance of the Party, those who work for mental health have gradually corrected their past mistaken opinions about Chinese medical science. They have begun to learn from Chinese doctors. A great deal of work has been accomplished, to make this first stage a success. Chi Ming, Hsu Yu-hsin, Li Yuan-chi, and Ts'ai Hsui-chun took the first steps to compile, analyze, and recommend some of the theory and experiences concerning mental diseases among the Chinese scholars of medicine. Hsueh Ch'ung-ch'eng discussed the theory of Chinese medical doctors of classifying people according to their temperament. They pointed out that in the last two thousand years, the medical scholars of China have contributed some excellent opinions, and accumulated a rich store of experience concerning the causes of mental illness, knowledge of its physical systems, and description of the symptoms, and measures for cure and prevention. There is a wealth of material in this field waiting for us to explore further.

The Beijing Municipal College of Chinese Medicine used the dialectical method to study the special characteristics of psychasthenia, and suggested six different types of mixed herb medicine as treatments. These were tried in 115 cases, and good results were obtained. Among the six, Yan-kan-ning-shen mixture, and the combination of Yang-kan and Kuei-p'i are better than the rest.

Li Chi-kuang, Wang Hsin-hua, and Wang Shen-chih tried several different kinds of mixtures to treat 640 cases of psychasthenia, and found them obviously effective in eliminating or lessening some major symptoms. The Beijing Municipal An-ding Hospital staff used Fu-fang (seeds of Rhaphanus) and Ch'ien-niu-tzu (Pharbitis nil) mixture or erh-shih combined with hydergine. Ts'ai Hui-ch'un used Ch'ien-chiu Wen-tan T'ang and its variations while P'ei Shen used some liquid form of iron. In areas such as Siping, Chia-wei-lan-wang-hsin-t'ang and others were used too. All these are being tried to treat serious mental disorders, and they are showing good results.

Acupuncture is used quite popularly, and has solved many difficult problems. It is especially effective for psychasthenia and hysteria. A report summarizing the experience of the Chen-chiu Hospital, the Shandong College of Medicine, the Chen-to Hospital, the Chang-chia-k'ou

Hospital, the Mental Hospitals in Kirin and Heilungjiang as well as Kuo Fang-hsueh and Huang Yun-chih in treating 2,133 cases of hysteria, showed that acupuncture had quick and obvious results in controlling the attacks. Generally speaking, the following positions are used: Na-kuan-jen-chung, ho-ku, yung-ch'ien, tsu-san-li, and ch-e, etc.

The nerve stimulation method of Sun Hui-ch'ing is also being used for treating psychasthenia. A report of 331 cases showed that it was apparently effective.

The aforementioned methods are simple, using simple and economical instruments, and have no side effects. They are not painful to the patient. They are entirely compatible with the principle of achieving more "quicker, better, and cheaper results." However, it is up to all of us to study them and improve them.

## 4. FIRST ACHIEVEMENTS IN PREVENTIVE MEASURES

Since Liberation, preventive work has been greatly emphasized so as to comply with the principle of being provident with lives which conforms with a directive of the Party. Mental health is listed as one of the three largest subjects for scientific research. We should particularly mention the June, 1958 National Mental Health Conference, which set forth the principles and plans for the future. This Conference may be said to be a milestone in China's mental health program.

A good mental disease survey is a prerequisite for a good preventive program. Since Liberation, directed by the Party and the government, some areas have long completed their survey and have gained understanding of the program. After the Conference, many cities earnestly carried out large scale surveys. At present in the cities of Shanghai, Nanjing, Beijing, Hunan, Siping, and Chengdu alone, a survey of 18 million people has been completed. In some areas (such as Nanjing, Siping, Hunan and Beijing) the work was done in the farm villages also.

Each area used different methods for the surveys, but they are generally about the same. The doctors specialized in mental diseases, the nurses and mental health social workers organized themselves into small groups. They checked with the local police offices, the resident councils, and block committees to gain some knowledge of the condition of mental diseases in each area. Then they made door-to-door visits, and collected information concerning each patient (including potential patients). They gave these patients mental and physical check-ups, made diagnoses, and kept the files.

Selected Articles from China

For the purpose of making the survey a success, the groups organized the masses, families of the patients, and the Red Cross Committee of the block. Meetings were held, and informative literature was distributed. They began a program of mental health education, and helped the residents to correct their past misgivings about mental diseases, so that all of them may not only take good care of the afflicted, but also report new cases quickly.

This survey helped to make known the extent of mental disease in China, and the distributions of the various types, so that we may be better prepared to carry out our preventive program. It also provided much valuable material for scientific research.

Preventive clinics are now being established. In Beijing, mental health organizations have been formed as part of the birth control agencies in thirteen districts. Some of these organizations have grown to be small-scale hospitals admitting patients. In Shanghai, there are mental health outpatient clinics in fourteen districts and four *hsiens*. In Nanjing, district hospitals have added mental health clinics and have equipped more than 200 sickbeds in various homes. We are very earnestly carrying out this program, and hope that a mental health network will be established all over the country.

## 5. FUTURE MISSIONS AND DIRECTIONS

The field of mental disease has been developed in China on a very weak foundation of the past, and has made tremendous achievements in the last ten years in healing, prevention, and scientific research. However, we still have many problems and shortcomings to be solved and improved. Our future job is not an easy one.

A. The preventive program is especially important in mental disease. We must carry out the resolutions of the First Conference to strengthen investigation and research work so as to formulate a better program of prevention.

B. The quality of our care and treatment is steadily improving. We should continue this good work to study and further improve. We must raise the rate of complete recovery, and reduce recurrence, so that the patients may soon resume their productive labor.

C. In order to quickly develop preventive and healing programs, we should train a large staff. We should emphasize both native and foreign methods to cultivate a new force for mental health work.

D. Our scientific research work in mental health began not long ago. The foundation is still weak at this stage. In the future, we should continue our study in the fields of biology, pathology, physiology, and anatomy, as well as the incorporation of many other sciences.

E. In order to fulfill all of our responsibilities, we must diligently learn the philosophy of Marxism-Leninism and Mao Tse-tung thought. We must arm ourselves with dialectical materialism. We should learn the advanced experience of the socialist countries, among which the first is the Soviet Union. We should also learn and study our own medical legacy, and absorb from all these sources treasures of experience and theory to enrich our own specialized knowledge, so as to do our work well.

# PART TWO: NEUROLOGY-PSYCHIATRY IN THE PEOPLE'S REPUBLIC OF CHINA: DISEASES IN PSYCHIATRY_____

## CHAPTER 1. HOW TO RECOGNIZE MENTAL ILLNESS_____

### What Is a Mental Disease?_____

A mental disease is pronounced expression of abnormality in mental activities due to a confusion in cerebral function, such as quarrelsome excitement, irregular crying and laughing, hurting people and destroying materials, talking nonsense, being suspicious, being depressed, reacting slowly, and idiocy. Commonly, people call these actions "an attack of nerves" or "nervous disease." In reality, nervous diseases are damages to the nervous system (such as inflammation, vessel disease, tumors, injury, and degeneration) which cause disease symptoms of numbness, pains, paralysis, convulsion, and coma. Thus, mental diseases and nervous diseases are diseases of two different categories.

### What Are Expressions of Mental Diseases?_____

Symptomatic expression of a mental disease is often the simultaneous existence of several symptoms forming a symptomatic group which attracts the attention of others. The following is a brief introduction of several common symptomatic groups:

*1. Quarrelsome Excitement:* This is the most pronounced symptomatic group of mental diseases; it may occur to all types of mental diseases. The expression of the excitement is as follows: increased activity, emotional excitement, restless activity, quarrelsome day and night, increased speech, yelling and screaming loudly, hitting people and screaming at people with other excited behaviors, and even producing destructive results.

2. *Depressed and Dull:* When the depressive symptom occurs, the patient's expression is melancholy and depressed. The eyebrows are tightened and the facial expression is sad. He sighs and draws his breath. His emotion is low and he is not interested in his surrounding environment. His thinking process is dull and he speaks very little. His language is simple and his voice is low. His actions are slow and he eats little. When the condition is severe, there are often thoughts of self-accusation and self-incrimination, pessimistic viewpoints, and suicidal behavior.

3. *Hallucinations and Delusions:* Hallucination means when there are no voices in the environment but the patient hears voices (auditory hallucination), when there is nothing in the environment but the patient sees things (visual hallucination), smells odors (olfactory hallucination), tastes special tastes (imaginary taste), and feels electrical shock on the body (imaginary touch). Auditory and visual hallucinations are the most common. The attention of the patient may be completely distracted by the hallucination. He concentrates his attention to listen or to converse or debate with the imaginary voices, or directly obeys the order of his imagination and acts abnormally, such as refusing food and hurting people. Delusion is a sick way of thinking about something the patient believes to be true but there is no factual basis. The most common ways of thinking are persecution, exaggeration, and self-accusation, with imaginary persecution as the most common. For example, the patient may suspect a member of his family is trying to hurt him and produces all types of ridiculous evidence. Delusion often co-exists with hallucination and the two strengthen one another.

4. *State of Stupor:* Stupor means the patient is completely quiet. He does not speak and he has no reaction to outside stimulation. When it is severe, he may have defensive behavior. For example, if he is asked to open his mouth, he not only does not open his mouth but closes it even tighter. He may refuse to eat and the saliva may accumulate in his mouth and refuse to either spit it out or swallow it. He may even refuse to go to the bathroom. Under the state of stupor, the patient does not react to any external stimulation but he is, in fact, conscious and is often capable of observing the surrounding activities; therefore, conversation around these patients should be very careful.

5. *Confused State:* When such diseases as poison and infection affect the cerebral activities, the patient may be confused to the extent that he

cannot correctly recognize people, places, and time. He may express fear as well as a great deal of hallucinations, mistakes, and excitement.

Mistakes are different from hallucinations. Mistakes mean that there are actually things in the environment that cause the patient to have a twisted reflection. For example, he may see patterns on the wall but mistake them for falling insects. He may actually see shadows of a tree outside the window but believe that someone is there waving hands at him.

6. *State of Idiocy:* This means the patient's memory is degenerated. He speaks of something and then forgets; he performs tasks disorderly; and makes all kinds of mistakes in simple calculation. His ability to distinguish events and things is obviously reduced and his emotional fluctuation is great. His anger and happiness are not reasonable and his behavior infantile, and he cannot even take care of himself in daily living.

## What Are Different Kinds of Mental Diseases?

The common mental diseases are the following: schizophrenia, manic depression, menopausal depression, cardiac reactive disease, hysteria, compulsion, mental retardation, mental abnormality caused by brain diseases (hardening of brain blood vessels, brain atrophy, acute and chronic inflammatory diseases), one of which is senile idiocy. Epilepsy may also have mental symptoms.

Infection, poison, and metabolic confusion may cause many kinds of mental symptoms. The patient may appear confused or idiotic. In order to control this type of mental symptom, emphasis should be placed on treating the infection, poison, and metabolic confusion.

## How to Diagnose Mental Diseases

Aside from ordinary physical examination and necessary chemical examination, it is extremely important to gather complete materials relating to the history of the disease and to perform a careful mental examination.

1. *Collecting History of the Disease:* Because the mental patient is confused and often does not recognize his own sickness, family members, neighbors, friends, colleagues, and the organizational unit of the patient must provide the history of the disease. The data relating to the disease must not be collected in the presence of the patient. Emphasis must be placed on the developmental process of the illness, the family's condition, a brief personal biography, and the political attitude of the patient. Certain doubtful key problems (such as the pathogenic factors and delusions) should be investigated repeatedly and substantiated. A detailed record must be kept.

Selected Articles from China

*2. Mental Examination:* Mental examination is a method used to observe the behavior of the patient and through contact and conversation to understand the mental state of thoughts, emotions, and memories of the patient.

In the practice of mental examination, it is necessary to observe carefully the actions and expressions of the patient. Pay attention to whether the patient answers questions relevantly, whether the patient has hallucinations and delusions, and whether there is a degeneration of intelligence such as memory. It is also important to understand the patient's attitude toward his own illness. The investigation must be thorough and the understanding must be profound, and through understanding one aspect of the disease the other aspects may be inferred. Through the appearance, the reality may be understood. As much as possible, the major characteristics of the patient's mental activity should be grasped. Regarding both patients who are excited and quarrelsome, or quiet and speechless, there is no way to perform mental examination, but the patient may be carefully observed during different times and under different conditions to produce a detailed record.

After the history of the mental patient, the various mental symptoms, and the results of examination are gathered together, viewpoints of class and class struggle should be adopted and the dialectic viewpoint of "dividing one into two" should be used to proceed with comprehensive analysis, scientifically to eliminate the false from the true and to obtain the actual condition which should correspond with the objective reality to derive a diagnostic conclusion.

Most mental patients are not willing subjectively to be treated. Those patients whose disease progresses slowly and who live a lazy life become separated from their environment farther and farther. These are the so-called "civilized insane." They are often not easily discovered to be sick by their family and the people close to them for early treatment. It is therefore extremely important for the great masses to be aware of the general and specific manifestations of mental diseases so that the patients may be discovered early and treated in time. The mass prevention work for mental illness is extremely important for patients to regain their health at an early date.

### Class Analysis and Scientific Analysis of Mental Patients Are Necessary

The mental activities of people all have a class characteristic. As mental disease is a disease, while the contents of mental symptoms are closely related to the actual class struggle, the symptoms often reflect the ideas, culture, tradition, habits, of different societies and the feelings of different classes. This is why class and scientific analysis of mental patients is necessary.

### Feeling of Concern and Care for the Mentally Ill Brothers and Sisters of the Same Class

Mentally ill patients should not be looked down upon and laughed at. They cannot be tied up and punished at will. The attitude which regards the so-called "flower madness" to be easily cured by marriage is an incorrect viewpoint. Facts prove that this measure brings very bad results to the family and the future generation. When a member of the family has mental disease, the family should accompany the patient to the physician for treatment as soon as possible.

Mental diseases are curable. The past attitude which regarded mental disease as "incurable" was a pessimistic and do-nothing viewpoint. It must be thoroughly criticized.

### CHAPTER 2. SCHIZOPHRENIA

The origin of this disease is most closely related to the original thoughts and conscience of the patient. It is closely related to the characteristic of activity of the function of the nervous system and various induced mental factors. After the onset of the disease, some patients continuously appear to be mentally abnormal while others regularly have repeated acute attacks. For some patients with slow development of the disease, people often do not understand and consider it as a matter of personality or a common thought problem. Most of the patients do not have an understanding of their own illness and are not willing to seek treatment on their own; therefore the treatment is delayed. If the disease is discovered early and treated early, it is easier to regain health. Recognition of symptoms of this disease is therefore extremely important and careful investigative study and thorough observation are necessary. Due to the fact that people's mental activities all have a class characteristic, people of different classes have different feelings. When people's mental activities are being observed, the medical workers must use the class viewpoint to treat everything and analyze everything.

### Symptoms

Symptoms of this disease are numerous. Different patients have different manifestations and in a single patient the manifestations may vary during different times. The medical workers should have frequent contacts and conversations with the patient in order to grasp the primary symptoms of the disease.

*1. Broken thoughts:* This is one of the typical symptoms of this disease. Broken thoughts mean that the patient does not have a centralized consideration of problems. Between the first thought and the second thought there is no connection whatsoever. As a result the patient's conversation does not form a continuity. It is confused and there is no beginning and ending. There is no order. Sometimes the conversation stops suddenly and sometimes when one problem is being discussed, the patient suddenly speaks some sentences which are completely unrelated to the problem. Sometimes the patients talk a great deal but the language is so disorderly, without a centralized theme, that others cannot understand what the problem is that the patient is trying to explain. Some patients may have an acute attack during which they scream without end and talk to themselves all the time. Sometimes the conversation does not form sentences. There are also patients who do not make a sound and will not answer any inquiries. The phenomena of these broken thoughts may also be observed in the writings and letters of the patient. These letters and articles are disorderly and others cannot understand them.

*2. Disharmonious Feelings:* It is possible that early in the illness the patient begins to change his feelings about others. He stays away from those who have been close to him and becomes cool or even antagonistic. He becomes very unconcerned and uninterested in all things and events around him. He has no concern toward happiness or sadness. He sits at home all day and thinks confused thoughts. Some patients may appear to be very lazy. He does not comb his hair, shave, and his clothing is very dirty. The patient's feelings are often not harmonious with the content of his conversation. For example, he may talk about his thinking that others are trying to kill him but his facial expression appears to be very glad. A little unimportant matter may cause him to be very angry.

*3. Delusions and Hallucinations:* These are common symptoms of this disease. Among hallucinations, imaginary hearing is relatively more frequent. For example, the patient may hear someone talk to him or he may hear others discussing him, or hear someone ordering him to do something. The behavior of the patient is often affected by the hallucination or he may even obey the order of the hallucination to do some dangerous things. There may also be imaginary vision. For example, he may see the shadow of a person who is not present. Some patients seem to smell some very bad odors or feel there are insects crawling on their bodies or electrical current running through them. The contents of delusions are numerous and very strange. Some patients insist that someone has placed poison in their food. They may think others use coughing, spitting, and scratching their heads as some sort of "special signals." There is also another type of patient with "flower madness." This type of patient thinks that he is loved by a particular person and will not stop bothering that person. There are also patients who feel that their own thoughts, behavior, and body are controlled by electrical waves, supersonic waves, and machines.

The above medical symptoms are relatively common ones for this disease. Clinically, a patient often has one type of primary symptom but it is also possible to have concurrent symptoms in one patient. For example, a patient with a primary manifestation of broken thoughts may also have symptoms of extreme excitement, crazy laugh, and making strange faces. There are also patients using actions as the most pronounced manifestation. He may stand on the side in a frozen posture with no speech or motion. There may also be a behavior of resistance. He may not be willing to eat and then he may suddenly become very excited and have attacks of destroying things and hurting people. Following the excitement, he may again return to his frozen, motionless state. The thoughts and feelings of this type of patient also have the general characteristics of this disease. If this disease is not treated, during the later stage the feelings of the person may become even colder. He may have no concern whatsoever about the things around him. He may often laugh or cry or talk to himself and cannot take care of his own living. His eating and everyday living must be taken care of by others, but these patients may still have hope of recovery after treatment.

## Treatment

*1. New Acupuncture Treatment:* Acupuncture treatment of mental diseases is a new creation. Practice has proven that it has obvious effects on mental diseases while it is easily performed with little pain or damage. It meets the demands of the masses of workers, farmers, and soldiers.

a. Deep acupuncture method in points of *ta-tsui* and *t'ao-tao:* Major points: *ta-tsui, t'ao-tao,* and *sheng-chu,* once a day, once a point, use alternatively. When the condition of the disease is improving, select one point every other day or twice a week, one point at a time. Accessory points: *ya-men, jen-chung, ho-ku* penetrating to *lao-kung, nei-kuan, tsu-san-li, ch'u-ch'ih* penetrating to *shao-hai, san-ying-chiao,* and *t'ai-ch'ung.* When the symptoms have disappeared, select two or three accessory points every day for acupuncture in order to stabilize the effect. The duration of stabilization treatment is 2–3 weeks.

*Important items:* When applying deep stimulation in points of *ta-tsui, t'ao-tao,* and *sheng-chu,* the patient should sit straight, with arms, head and face leaning on the back of the chair, and with the head bent as low as possible. The local skin should be regularly disinfected with iodine and alcohol. The technician should use alcohol to rub his hands and use 75 percent alcohol to disinfect the No. 24 needle before proceeding with the puncture at the upper edge of the vertebra below the selected point. The needle should slant slightly upwards to puncture to a depth of about 2.5 *ts'un* and the needle should be withdrawn when the patient has the feeling of the acupuncture (an electrical impulse all over the body and a sudden jump). If there is no reaction to the needle, push the needle until there is a feeling of the needle being in an empty space before slowly pushing the needle forward for 3–5 mm, then withdraw the needle. The needle must not be retained, must not be pushed and pulled, must not be squeezed, and the needle should be advanced slowly and withdrawn quickly to prevent damage to the central nervous system. If the work is performed carefully and grasped properly, there are almost no side effects. Some patients may demonstrate weakness over the body and a loss of appetite. Some may suffer headaches, dizziness, nausea, and vomiting. If this occurs, the treatment may be temporarily suspended for a few days and these side effects will spontaneously disappear after a week. If the spinal cord is damaged, there may be weakness and paralysis of the lower limbs and this condition will normally recover in 1–2 days. Severe damages may create such serious side effects as paralysis of lower limbs, anuria, and subarachnoid hemorrhage. For this reason, ideological work must be done well before acupuncture to obtain the cooperation of the patient. Carefully stabilize the body of the patient; the technician should have the spirit of being extremely responsible and work with superb concentration. The needle must advance steadily and it must not be poking around or changing directions even if there appears to be obstruction. In case of obstruction, the needle should be withdrawn to the position just under the skin for re-entry. Following the puncture, the patient should be closely observed in order to discover changes in the condition in time.

b. Method of simultaneous stimulation of many points: First group of points: *Ting-sheng* (located one-third below the nose in the groove of the upper lip; the needle should be advanced in a 15 degree angle toward the center of the nose to a depth of 1.5–2 *ts'un*); *hou-pien* (located 1.5 *ts'un* above the joint between the index finger and the palm; *ho-ku* is located 0.5 *ts'un* below; the needle should be directed toward *ho-ch'i* for a depth of 2–2.5 *ts'un*); *t'ai-ch'ung*.

Second group of points: *t'ou-nien* (located one *ts'un* toward the rear of the temporal; at the inner side of the temporal artery, along the edge of the bone, the needle should be directed parallel to the upper rim of the ear, for a depth of 1.5–2 *ts'un*, *chien-shih*, and *san-ying-chiao*.

The third group of points: *jen-chung, nei-kuan, tsu-san-li*.

*Method of treatment:* For excited and quarrelsome patients, as well as for the condition of stupor, the three groups of points should be used alternately. Select large No. 26 or No. 24 needles. Several technicians should perform the acupuncture simultaneously. Using the large-scale strong stimulation twisting needle technique, the person who is responsible for the head and facial points should be in command. The patient should be induced to go to sleep. When the patient's muscles are relaxed and the pulse is slowed down, the acupuncture action should be weakened. After the patient falls asleep, the needles should be slowly withdrawn. Each acupuncture action should last about half an hour. The needles of the lower limbs should be withdrawn first, then those of the upper limbs, finally those of the face. If the patient becomes agitated once again, the needles may be advanced again; if necessary the point may be changed to *yung-ch'ien*. In this manner, the acupuncture treatment is applied once a day. If the patient is severely agitated, a large number of technicians may be gathered for continuous acupuncture technique; that is, to apply acupuncture treatment twice, three times, four times, even five times within a single day. When the new acupuncture treatment technique is applied, the technicians should analyze concretely each individual patient, and different treatment methods should be adopted for different patients or for different stages of the disease. Generally speaking, the technique should be more powerful and the duration of stimulation longer during the first stage of the treatment. When the symptoms are somewhat controlled, the technique should be lessened and the duration of stimulation should be shortened. During the recovery stages of the patient, weak stimulation should be applied and as soon as the patient feels the needle, it should be withdrawn. Normally a period of treatment is two weeks. When the condition of the disease is stabilized, the technique of quick single needle acupuncture should be adopted and the following points should be selected: *ya-men, feng-chih, an-nien, t'ou-nien, ting-shen, ch'u-ch'ih, chien-shih, nei-kuan, t'ung-li, shen-men, tsu-san-li, san-ying-chiao, chao-hai,* and *t'ai-ch'ung*. Select several points in each treatment to stabilize the effect of the treatment. The period of stabilization should last 2–3 weeks.

_Selected Articles from China

c. If there is the symptom of auditory hallucination, points of *t'ing-kung, t'ing-hui,* and *i-feng* may be added; if there is visual hallucination, *ch'an-chu, yu-yao, yang-pai, szu-pai, ch'eng-hsi,* and *chin-ming* may be added.

d. For cases of high degree of excitation, electrical needles may be added for control. The points to be selected may be divided into two groups. First group: *ting-shen* and *pai-wei.* Second group: *t'ou-nien* (both sides). The needle should be applied 2–4 times every day, one group each time. After the needle is in place, add electrical pulsations of six volts. Use relatively high frequency to conduct the electricity intermittently. The patients will have localized muscular spasm and the feeling of numbness will be strong. During treatment the patients should be closely observed, and according to the condition of the patient, the amount of electricity and the duration of the conduction should be adjusted. Generally speaking, the symptoms may be controlled within 2–3 days and thereafter the number of electrical needle treatments may be reduced or the method may be changed to the new acupuncture or ear acupuncture treatment to stabilize the effects.

*2. New Method of Treatment Combining Acupuncture and Chlorpromazine:* In case the symptoms of agitation are severe or the new acupuncture technique does not control the patient fast enough, while applying the new acupuncture technique, chlorpromazine treatment or injection of chlorpromazine in the points may be a technique to be used with the new acupuncture technique. For injection, 25–50 mg of chlorpromazine may be used in the points every day. Alternately select points of *hsin-yu, ke-yu, chien-shih, tsu-san-li,* and *san-ying-chiao,* once a day, 1–2 points each time.

*3. Ear Acupuncture Method:* Select points of *shen-men,* hypodermic, internal secretion, heart, sympathetic nerve, stomach, forehead, and occipital, one treatment each day; one side each treatment, using 1–3 points. The points to be selected for both sides may be identical, but may also be different. Normally the penetration method is used in 2–3 points, and the points are changed every day. It is also possible to search for sensitive points among the above for acupuncture and after the needle is in place electricity may be applied (use electrical needle machine, or electrical pulses). The electrical conduction should be applied until there is muscular spasm on the face of the patient. Generally the effects are better if the patient feels a burning and numb sensation in the ear, head, and on the face. One treatment is effective for 18 days. When the patient is better, the application of electricity may be continued, with reduced quantity.

The ear acupuncture method may be used in all the aforementioned

types of schizophrenia, but only when the symptom of agitation is not very severe. This method is also often used to stabilize the effects and to prevent recurrence.

4. *Herb Medicine: Wu-mu-t'ang:* use one *chin* each of the branches of the following trees: willow, mulberry, elm, and peach. Cook the branches with water and use the water to bathe the patient. The temperature of the water should be as hot as the patient can tolerate. Bathe once a day, 1/2 to 1 hour per time. After the bath, use cloths to wrap the patient without drying him. At this time, the patient will be suffering from high fever but the fever will soon drop spontaneously. After several baths, the state of agitation may be controlled. Patients with cardiac diseases and patients of weak constitution shouldn't take these baths. After the soaking bath the patient should also be protected from heat stroke.

*Huang-yuan-hua* (also called *ho-su-yao-hua*): A certain People's Liberation Army hospital adopted the method of using *huang-yuan-hua* for treatment and found it to be effective. Use the buds and leaves of this plant, dry them, and grind them into powder. Give the patient 2–4 g orally each day. The patient may take this dosage all at once or divide it into several doses. The treatment should be continued for 3–7 days. If the effect is not obvious, the patient should rest several days before starting another treatment. This medicine has been tested to be effective for excited patients. Some patients may develop stomachache and diarrhea after taking this medicine, and weak patients may develop shock.

There are many forms of experience in using herb medicine to treat schizophrenia in many parts of China. These experiences should be summarized in the future for improvement.

5. *Tranquilizing Drugs.*

Chlorpromazine: It has a very powerful tranquilizing action and is often used for patients of agitation, or delusions and hallucinations. Apply by mouth 25–50 mg of chlorpromazine, three times daily. According to the condition of the symptoms, the dosage may be increased to 300–500 mg per day. After a treatment of 4–8 weeks, if the condition is better, the dosage may be reduced to below 300 mg per day for maintenance. When the patient is violently agitated, 50 mg of chlorpromazine may be injected in the muscle with 0.3 mg of scopola; or 50 mg of chlorpromazine may be added to 20 mg of cotarnin for muscular injection, 1–2 times a day. During the drug treatment, the blood pressure must be watched closely. The patient should not get up out of bed too fast in order to prevent shock. When there are drug reactions, such as increased muscular tension, slanted neck, upturned eyes, shaking hands, 0.2 mg of scopola may be given orally, three times a day; or 2 mg of artane, three times a day. In an emergency, apply hypodermically 0.3 mg of scopolamine. If jaundice, rash, or reduction of granular cells occur, the drug application must be stopped and positive treatment of the condition should start immediately. This drug treatment should be adopted with extreme care for those patients with serious diseases of the heart, the liver, and the kidney, and those patients with too low a white cell count.

Perphenazine Chlorpiperazine: It is rather effective for controlling patients with delusion, hallucination, and stupor. Use 2–4 mg, three times a day; it may be increased to 20–40 mg per day. If the condition is better after 4–6 weeks, the dosage should be reduced to below 20 mg for maintenance. It may also be used with chlorpromazine. Important items for using this drug are the same as chlorpromazine.

*T'ai-erh-teng:* It has the effect of tranquilizing and anti-depression. Use 25–50 mg, three times daily. According to the condition of the patient, the dosage may be increased to 300–500 mg per day. If the condition is improved after 4–8 weeks, the daily dosage may be reduced to below 300 mg for maintenance. The important items for applying this drug are the same as chlorpromazine.

Trifluoperazine: It is to be used for patients with delusions and hallucinations and for chronic patients. Use 5 mg, twice per day, and after 3–5 days, the dosage should be increased another 5 mg every day until the condition of the symptoms are improved. At this time, the daily dosage should be about between 20–40 mg. After 2–6 weeks, the dosage may be reduced to below 20 mg per day for maintenance. This medicine often causes restlessness, slanted neck, and turned-up eyes. When these side effects occur, scopolamine may be used to relieve them.

*Li-hsueh-p'ing* [Reserpine]: It is applied to patients with agitation or stupor. Use 0.25 mg, three times daily. The dosage may be increased to 2–6 mg per day. If it is necessary, one mg of reserpine may also be used for muscular injection. Reserpine is often used in combination with chlorpromazine. When the patient is on reserpine, electrical acupuncture should not be applied at the same time; and attention must be given to the possibility of the occurrence of depression and suicide. Patients with stomach and duodenal ulcers should not be given this medicine.

6. *Preventing Recurrence and Others:* For patients who have been cured of schizophrenia, it is necessary to help them to learn Chairman Mao's works with specific problems in mind in order to correctly resolve the various factors that have caused the disease in the first place. Use heroic figures as examples to help the patient to improve his awakening

in class struggle and line struggle. After he is recovered, new acupuncture and ear acupuncture techniques may be applied to stabilize the cure. Drug maintenance may also be adopted. For some patients, before a recurrence, there may be symptoms of insomnia, restlessness, etc. If acupuncture treatment or tranquilizer application are given at this time, recurrence may be avoided.

For those who are suffering from schizophrenia and have not been cured, marriage and reproduction are not favorable for the health of the patient or for the education of the children.

## CHAPTER 3. MANIC DEPRESSION

Manic depression is primarily a disease of emotional confusion. It is manifested in the two primary expressions of manic state and depression state; these two expressions may occur alternately with the same patient and one of the states may occur as the dominant state. The intermission between recurrences is often very regular.

### Symptoms
The major expressions of manic depression are excessively violent emotional reactions. If the patient is not excessively excited then he is excessively depressed. The special characteristics are the fact that the emotion, the language, and the action are in neutral harmony. The manic state is manifested as an extreme emotional excitement. The patient is happy and self-satisfied all day, but when he is slightly dissatisfied he may scream and yell very loudly and jump up and down like thunder. His mental activity is very fast and he is very sharp in observing his surroundings and events. He talks consistently and can carry on a discourse on any subject. He changes his subject on any pretense and when his lips are cracked and his mouth is dry he still will not stop talking, and he can write many letters and articles. He has an abundance of energy and has numerous activities. His hands and feet move all the time and never stop. He is busy all day long and while each action has a specific purpose, he is often affected by outside influences and changes constantly. He often starts something and does not finish. He usually is a troublemaker and affects all his neighbors. He even has destructive behavior. When the condition is serious, due to excessive excitement, he is too busy to eat and becomes physically exhausted. The patient may become obviously thinner within a short period of time.

Selected Articles from China

2) The depressive state is manifested as the complete opposite of the manic state. The patient tightens his brow and has a sad face all day long. He bends his head low and sighs all the time. And he is obviously in a bad mood. His thinking is dull and he speaks very little. He has difficulty writing and speaking, and he has an answer only when the question is repeated. He sits in a corner or lies in bed all day long. His actions are simple and slow while his daily living must be urged by others. When the situation is severe, he begins to blame himself and thinks of himself as having no energy whatsoever, and cannot work and learn like others. He becomes a "waste"; therefore, he feels guilt-ridden and increasingly pessimistic. He may commit suicide when others are not watching.

## Treatment

Based upon the different manifestations during different periods of the disease of manic depression, different treatment methods should be adopted.

1. *Manic state:* The new acupuncture, electrical acupuncture, *wu-mu t'ang,* and chlorpromazine may be adopted. See the section on schizophrenia for details.

2. *Depressive state:*

a. The medical worker should have a high degree of sense of responsibility. He should closely observe the condition of the patient in order to understand the thoughts of the patient. He should carefully prevent the patient from committing suicide.

b. New acupuncture treatment: The multiple points simultaneous stimulation method and the electrical needle method may be adopted. See the section on schizophrenia.

c. Drug treatment: *T'ai-erh-teng:* apply the drug orally as in the section on schizophrenia. When the depressive state is serious, 30 mg of *t'ai-erh-teng* with 0.3 mg of scopolamine for muscular injection, 2–3 times daily.

Imipramine: apply by mouth, in the beginning, 25 mg, 2–3 times a day. The dosage is gradually increased to 150–200 mg per day. When the effect begins to be noticeable, the dosage is reduced to 50–100 mg per day for maintenance. During the drug application, there may be side effects of thirstiness, fast heartbeat, blurred vision, constipation, skin rash, insomnia, and shock. Patients with diseases of the liver and kidney, hypertension, and heart disease, especially diseases of the coronary artery, should not be treated with this drug.

Selected Articles from China

# CHAPTER 4. MENOPAUSAL DEPRESSION

Aside from symptoms of ordinary depression, patients with this disease also have anxiety, tension, and suspicion. These symptoms often occur during menopause, 55–60 years of age for males and 45–55 years of age for females. The disease occurs more frequently in females than in males.

The patients appear to be depressed and worried. There are tensions and fear. He cannot sit or stand still and cries a great deal. He loses his appetite and cannot sleep. He is thin and looks old. At the same time, he often accuses himself of wrongdoing and brings up minor events of the past. He thinks of himself being wrong here and bad there, and accuses himself of having committed serious mistakes and having done irreversible bad things. He also believes he is becoming a burden on his children. Some patients come to believe all the organs of their bodies have become rotten and their lives are in danger. He worries a great deal and often hurts himself. It is common to observe these patients pull their hair out and scratch their skin. They may bang their head on the wall and sometimes purposely twist facts in their quarrels with others. They are very suspicious and often believe other people are out to hurt them. A few of these patients may suddenly commit suicide. The treatment for this disease is the same as for the depressive state of manic depression.

# CHAPTER 5. SENILE IDIOCY

Senile idiocy is an expression of brain atrophy, with the primary symptom of idiocy. The disease occurs during old age, after 65 years of age for males and after 55 years of age for females. This disease occurs to males more than to females.

The symptom of idiocy is often more severe every day. The manifestation is that the patient sleeps during the day and is awake at night. There is an obvious change of personality. He becomes quarrelsome and often screams for nothing. There are also suspicions and hallucinations. His memory degenerates rapidly and he cannot remember what he said a moment ago. He often cannot remember where he put his clothing, shoes, and hat. When he leaves his house for a few steps he will not remember how to return. He speaks of something repeatedly or he may make up totally false stories. For example, after he gets up from the bed he says he has already had his lunch. Then he says he has gone out and walked around for a while. He cannot understand other people's language and often cannot remember the names of the members of his family. He cannot do simple arithmetic and whatever he does he makes all kinds of mistakes. His ability of recognition is obviously degenerated and his behavior is infantile. In some cases, the patient keeps waste paper and rags as precious things and stores them very carefully. When the disease is severe, the patient may not be able to get up from the bed and cannot go to the bathroom on his own.

Special attention must be given to take care of these patients to prevent infection and fracture due to falls. They cannot be allowed to wander out-of-doors because they may not be able to find ways to return. Patients who smoke cigarettes should be especially taken care of to prevent them from starting a fire by forgetting where they may have put down lighted cigarettes. For the patients who have been in bed for a prolonged period of time, careful nursing is necessary to prevent bed-sores. Extreme care should also be given to cases of incontinence. Chinese traditional preparation of aconite, cinnamon, and *rehmannia* or the six-ingredient *rehmannia* preparation may be applied orally to those patients whose condition is discovered early. For those patients who are extremely quarrelsome, with behavior confusion, chlorpromazine or *t'ai-erh-teng* may be given orally, but the dosage should not be excessive.

## CHAPTER 6. EMOTIONAL REACTION SYMPTOMS (REACTIONAL MENTAL DISEASE)

In the process of accelerated contradiction between man and his environment, man's emotional reaction may become excessive, exceeding ordinary limits and producing a mental disease, with common mental symptoms. As a result, the patient can no longer maintain his work and daily living, and he requires the care of others. These mental symptoms often last a long time and cannot improve within a short period. When these patients require medical treatment, we call this condition "emotional reaction disease."

### Symptoms
The onset of the disease may be fast or slow. Clinically, most patients have satisfactory contact and conversation with others. Their language is clear and logical and they have good judgment. The content of their conversation mostly reflects various contradictions between the patient and his environment. The content of the mental symptoms is closely

related to the mental factors which induced the disease. Just as in hysteria, this disease has its pathogenesis in the mental aspects of living. Hysteria, however, is generally manifested in repeated attacks, and "emotional reactional disease" is relatively sustained and continuous. In some patients, the feelings are low, and they are burdened by worries. Their brows are tightened and their expression is sad. They complain and sigh. They do not think about eating and drinking, and are depressed and pessimistic. They blame and accuse themselves and there are suicidal tendencies. The patients talk very little or they do not answer questions. It is also possible that they are very slow in answering the questions of others. Patients may speak of the mistakes they have made in the past and may also talk about the unfortunate deaths of their relatives. They may also talk about past failures in work or study. Some patients may also appear to be emotionally excited and quarrel a great deal. They may cry, sing, or laugh uncontrollably. Some patients may also have hallucinations, auditory in most cases. Some patients may also talk about rich physical experiences of hallucination, but the contents of the hallucination normally reflect the patient's wishes, fantasies, and demands. The attitude of the patient toward such hallucinations varies. The behavior of some patients may be affected by the hallucination to a certain extent, but a few patients may also have certain delusions similar to schizophrenia. For example, they may suspect that someone is trying to harm them and may also consider the actions of others to be related to themselves. The content of the delusions is often related to the mental factors of the patient. Due to the violent contradiction and sudden onset of the disease, the patient may also appear to be confused and agitated. They may go out wandering all day long in a daze, or they may be in a state of passive stupor. These types of patients are relatively rare.

## Treatment

1. This disease may be prevented. The key is in the correct attitude toward various problems in daily living. The comrades, members of his family, and members of his organization should cooperate to demonstrate a high degree of concern and care for the sick class brothers and sisters, to help the patients to resolve these contradictions reasonably in order to prevent the occurrence of this disease. Or if the disease has begun, they should help the patient to recover his health.

2. The complicated contradiction which is the origin of this disease and the cause of its development should be concretely analyzed from the viewpoint of class struggle. The method of resolving contradiction also varies with the nature of the contradiction. The different conditions

should be distinguished and different methods should be adopted to handle them. For the class brothers and sisters with this disease, the medical workers should perform good political ideology work and sincerely help these patients to handle their problems.

3. Aside from ideological education, proper medical treatment is also necessary for patients of this disease. For acupuncture, select points of *ta-tsui, nei-kuan,* and *tsu-san-li.* Or they may be given appropriate tranquillizers. For example, if there are symptoms of depression, 25 mg of *t'ai-erh-teng,* 2–3 times daily, may be applied. In severe depression, the dosage may be gradually increased according to the state of the disease. When the condition is improved, the dosage should be reduced. For cases of agitation, hallucination, and delusion, additional chlorpromazine or perphenazine chlorpiperazine, or a 2 ml of chlorpromazine may be added to 0.3 mg of scopolamine for muscular injection.

## CHAPTER 7. HYSTERIA

Hysteria is a common disease, more in females than in males. In most of the cases, there is a factor of emotional disturbance before the onset of the disease. The disease is usually manifested in periodical attacks.

## Symptoms

*1. Mental symptoms:* During the attack, the common symptoms are crying, laughing, screaming, stamping of the feet, beating the chest, tearing apart clothing, talking nonsense, singing songs, waving hands, dancing, and making all sorts of faces. The patient uses exaggerated actions and expressions. He may sing folk songs and local tunes to express the unhappiness he feels within himself. In a crowd he may become violent, or when he is extremely excited, he may suddenly fall down. He may not answer when called, and his body may be very stiff while his limbs may be shaking. He may be out of breath or may breathe in but not out. His face may be red and may appear to be in an epileptic attack. Normally, an hysterical attack can last from 10 minutes to several hours. Some patients may appear to be in a severe stupor, and may not remember their own name and age. He may even say, for example, two plus three equals four or six. It appears as if he is making the mistake intentionally, but he may recover and become normal within a short period of time.

*2. Physical Symptoms:* The patient may suddenly become deaf, blind, voiceless, or paralyzed in the limbs, or he may lose sensations in the skin, but after careful physical examination, the symptoms appear not to correspond with human anatomical and physiological principles. For example, a paralyzed patient may not have changes in tendon reflex and there may not be any pathological reflex. The deaf patient may be able to be awakened from sleep by noise. The person who loses his voice may be able to cough with a sound. The person who loses his skin sensation may have feelings on the opposite side of the body.

These symptoms are mostly related to the patient's actual living condition and his imagination. Under the influence of other people's words and actions, the contents of the symptoms may change.

Before the onset of the disease, some patients are highly emotional and imaginative. They are often boastful and are very capable of expressing themselves. They are emotionally extremely excitable. They cry and laugh easily and they are not broadminded. And they have a tendency to be dramatic and eager to attract attention. Patients who have the above special characteristics have a greater likelihood of recurrent attacks.

### Treatment

1. New acupuncture treatment: Select points of *jen-chung, nei-kuan, ho-ku, chiu-wei, san-ying-chiao, shao-shang,* and *yung-ch'uan;* apply strong stimulation.

2. Two *liang* of *huai-wheat,* 10 jujubes, and 5 *ch'-ien* of *glycyrrhiza;* cook ingredients in water and drink the liquid.

3. Tranquillizers: 10 mg of urethane, three times daily; 10 ml of tribromal compound, three times daily. For those with obvious agitation, apply 25 mg of chlorpromazine, 2–3 times daily; or 25 mg of *t'ai-erh-teng,* 2–3 times daily. The dosage may be increased if the disease is severe; or 2 ml of compound chlorpromazine may be used with 0.1 ml of phenobarbital for muscular injection.

## CHAPTER 8. DISEASE OF COMPULSION

Compulsion is a disease with the primary symptom of compulsion. The so-called compulsion symptom means that the patient understands clearly that his way of thinking, his behavior, and his emotional reaction toward certain things and events are unnecessary and meaningless, but he repeatedly thinks and does these things because he cannot control himself. The patient feels extremely miserable and this feeling is often accompanied by depression and anxiety. There are all kinds of compulsion symptoms: such as his hands may not be dirty at all but he washes them repeatedly; he may be afraid of other people bumping into him and consistently avoids others; or he may change his clothes continuously. He may be afraid that his doors are not closed when he leaves the house, therefore he examines them repeatedly and cannot leave his house at all. Or when he walks in the street he feels he must touch every tree on the road. Or he cannot stop repeatedly thinking "why one plus two must equal three," or such meaningless problems. Besides, he may be afraid of contracting cancer; he may be afraid to enter a high building; he may be afraid to walk across a large market square; he may be afraid of glass; or he may be afraid of knives, scissors, and other sharp instruments.

The patient should understand that it is not a horrible thing to have this disease and if he has patience and confidence he can overcome the disease. Suitable participation in physical labor is beneficial.

New Acupuncture Method: Select points of *ya-men, hou-ch'i, chien-shih, chao-hai, tsu-san-li,* and *san-ying-chiao;* the treatment period should be longer in order to be effective. Certain drugs may also be used with the acupuncture treatment, such as 1–2 tablets of 10 mg of urethane, three times daily; or a small amount of trifluoperazine, or perphenazine chlorpiperazine.


## CHAPTER 9. MENTAL RETARDATION

Incomplete development of intelligence is commonly called stupidity. In most cases the origin is congenital (such as birth injuries, postnatal suffocation, and high fever and injury during infancy). These incidents may have affected the development of the brain.

The major characteristic of this disease is a very slow development of mental abilities. The intelligence of these patients is very different from other children of the same age; and the condition of the disease varies a great deal, therefore the symptoms are also greatly different. These patients appear to have no understanding of their surroundings and events. They lack power of judgment and the ability to think independently. Sometimes because of their lack of intelligence, class enemies can talk them into being utilized to do bad things. When the disease is severe, their ability to remember, understand, and reason is inferior, and they do only very simple work with other people's help. They may often suddenly become very quarrelsome and show a great deal of anger and may even be violent. When the condition is severe, even basic daily living such as going to the bathroom or eating cannot be taken care of by themselves. They do not understand how to avoid danger. They even cannot speak, or can only make meaningless sounds or speak only a few words.

## Treatment

New Acupuncture Method: Select from two groups of points: first group— *ta-tsui, an-mien,* and *tsu-san-li;* second group—*ya-men, an-mien,* and *nei-kuan.* Apply acupuncture once a day in alternated groups of points, with strong stimulation. One treatment period should last 10 days, and the patient should rest 3–5 days between treatment periods. Generally, improvement may be observed after one treatment period, but long-term maintenance is necessary.

Bloodletting Treatment Method: The major points to be selected are *chung-ch'ung* and *t'ien-ch'u;* the accessory points are *yung-ch'uan* and *lao-kuan.* The method is to use a prism-shaped needle to puncture the skin of the points to a depth of one *fen,* to let out 4–5 drops of blood, one bloodletting a day, alternating the major and the accessory points.

During treatment, the patient should be properly cared for and given patient training and education. According to different conditions, patients should be assigned simple labor. During childhood, some drugs may also be given to improve intelligence. For example, the patient may be given orally 0.3–0.6 g of glutamic acid, three times daily; or 0.25-0.5 g of gamma-tyrosinic acid, three times daily. If the patient is overly excited and quarrelsome, a proper amount of chlorpromazine or *t'ai-erh-teng* may also be applied.

## CHAPTER 10. CARE OF MENTAL PATIENTS AND ITEMS TO BE EMPHASIZED

*1. Proper Attitude Toward Patients:* First of all, the patients must be respected and cared for. Ways must be found to understand the patients' needs and as much as possible the patients should be reasonably helped. Care and concern can win their confidence and obtain their cooperation so that the disease can be conquered.

Mentally ill people may sometimes make unreasonable and impossible demands. Medical workers should be patient and explain to the patients very carefully. If the explanation is ineffective, methods may be found to transfer the attention of the patients when the opportunity arises. For example, during a discussion, the medical worker may change the subject or may request the patient to do something in order to cause the patient to concentrate his attention on something else so that he may give up his unreasonable demands.

When family members are looking after the patient, they should be patient and understanding. They should not scold, threaten, or treat the patient with cruelty. Family members should not give in to the patients without regarding principles.

*2. Productive Labor and Collective Activity:* Organizing the patients for suitable labor and collective activity is also a method for promoting recovery of health. Suitable labor for the patients includes ordinary housework, such as making the beds, washing the dishes, washing and mending clothing. Patients may also participate in productive labor. Combined with the patriotic public health movement, the patients may be organized for cleaning work indoors or out and for maintaining their personal cleanliness. The specialties of the patient before he became sick may be taken into consideration in organizing productive labor.

Patients may also participate in such collective activities as broadcasted physical exercise and recreational groups, singing revolutionary songs and watching movies.

In productive labor, attention must be given to the commonly used knives, scissors, and agricultural tools. After the patient has finished using these implements, they must be taken away from the patient. They should not be given to the patients for safekeeping so that unexpected accidents may be prevented.

*3. Preventing Accidents:* Suicide is a common dangerous behavior of mental patients and it must be strictly prevented. Attention must be given to ideology and to the sense of responsibility. The patients' actual thought processes must be carefully understood so as to adopt effective measures in time. Serious pessimistic ideas, sudden "improvement" of the condition of the disease with no improvement in appetite and body weight, are signs to be alarmed about. Special attention must be given to these patients toward the evenings and before daybreak. The residence areas of the patients must be kept simple and all tools that can be used for suicide, such as knives, scissors, ropes, and drugs should be taken from the patients. Drugs should be kept by family members to be given according to the directions to prevent the patient from taking the whole contents at once to create an accident.

Injuring others and violent behavior are also common among mental patients. These patients should be prevented from obtaining dangerous instruments. Their behavior must be controlled. If a dangerous situation occurs, the medical workers should remain as calm as possible and must not react with haste. They should ask others to help to make the patient put down the dangerous weapon voluntarily. If the patient will not co-operate, then the weapon must be taken from him when the opportunity allows. A blanket or a quilt may be used to grab the patient suddenly from behind in order to prevent the patient from hurting himself or others.

Escape is also common among mental patients. The thinking process of the patient should be regularly understood. If the patient is suspected of attempting to escape, measures may be adopted to prevent it. If the patient is discovered to be out of his residence and not returning as expected, he should be traced from all possible clues. If necessary, the public safety organizations should be informed so that they may help look for the patient.

4. *Food, Nutrition, and Sleep:*

a. Refuse food and overeat: Some patients may refuse food or may not be able to feed themselves. The reason for refusing food should be found, and if necessary the patient should be fed. Some other patients may be extremely contrary. The more you give them food the more they refuse. In such a case, food may be left by his side and the patient may start feeding himself when there is no one looking. In some cases, the patient may suspect poison in the food and is thus unwilling to eat. Others may eat the same food first in order to eliminate the patient's suspicion. There are also patients who are unwilling to eat under any circumstance; these patients may be fed liquid food through the nose.

There is another tendency of not knowing how much to eat. Food intake for these patients should be properly controlled. The quantity may be limited in order to prevent overeating. At the same time, this kind of patient should be prevented from eating unclean food and causing inflammation of the intestines and the stomach.

b. Insomnia is a common symptom of mental patients. The disease may become worse due to insufficient sleep. During the depression state, insomnia is very common; during the excited state, the patient may stay awake all night. Thus, measures should be adopted to improve the pa-tient's sleep and this is also an important link in the treatment of mental disease.

5. *Preventing Recurrence:* The patient should be encouraged with positive factors so as to improve his confidence in struggling against the disease to eliminate his mental burden. This is favorable to the recovery and stabilization of health. Secondly, during the treatment period and during the recovery period, proper dosage of drugs and acupuncture should be regularly applied so that the recovery condition may be sta-bilized. It is best to continue the treatment for a certain period of time.

Selected Articles from China

After the period, according to health conditions, the drug application and acupuncture may be applied intermittently. During the period the mental patient is under tranquillizing medication, if fever, sore throat, yellow-colored eyes, skin rash, and bleeding spots are discovered, the drug should be stopped immediately. The patient should be sent to nearby clinics for examination and treatment in order to prevent severe reaction to the medication.

When the patient is recovered, the unit in which he works, his family members, and his colleagues should have a proper attitude toward this type of disease. They must not look down upon the patient, neither should they ignore him. They must not give in to him or brush him off. They should encourage him. The attitude should be sincere and compassionate to cause the patient to feel the friendship and collective warmth of comradeship so as to create, for the patient, the condition of reentering the movement to grasp revolution to promote production. If the conditions permit, simple and light labor may be arranged to provide the patient a trial period so that he may gradually recover to his original level of work. As far as the patient is concerned, he should establish the spirit of revolutionary optimism. He should develop an open mind and an alert spirit. He should not be overly sensitive. Whenever necessary, he should talk with his leaders, colleagues, and family members to obtain help.

## INTERVIEW WITH WU CHEN-I
by PAUL LOWINGER, 1979

*L:* I am very interested in knowing how health and medicine have changed since the fall of the Gang of Four.

*W:* During the time of the Gang of Four, really they were extremely left. They were so extremely left that if you were doing some research work, it was not considered proper, you dared not even talk about it, it was a capitalist idea.

*L:* Did that interrupt any of the work you or your department had been engaged in earlier?

*W:* No, but you could not do research, especially laboratory research. You must do practical work. That is not good public policy.

*L:* In the long run, it is better to have some time committed for research for the entire nation and the needs of the people.

*W:* Yes.

*L:* Did you see any effects on patient care during the time of the Gang of Four? Was there less training, perhaps?

*W:* You mean training of doctors?

*L:* Yes.

*W:* We have always trained the doctors in different ways; it is mostly on a practical basis. We still carried this on. We did more practical work and less theoretical study. Medical school was cut down to three years so we had fewer hours for lectures in psychiatry. We still had some doctors who came to our department and we gave them training. Now we offer practical experience and there is more time put into theoretical studies.

*L:* What has happened in psychiatry since the fall of the Gang of Four? I guess you date that from 1976.

*W:* We can discuss different opinions in regard to theory. Now, in China, we can learn more about American psychiatry. You can express your ideas with more freedom. We have more free discussion.

*L:* Do you feel that you will be able to get more laboratory facilities for research?

*W:* Yes, we have the plans now. We will study neurotransmitters, using a laboratory in the biochemistry department of Beijing University.

*L:* Do you work with the biochemistry department?

*W:* Yes, we have our own doctor studying serotonin and 5-hydroxytryptamine.

*L:* What about training, has that changed since 1976?

*W:* Yes, it's quite changed, from three to five years for medical school.

*L:* Are medical students admitted by examination, including those who have been barefoot doctors?

*W:* Every student has to take the examination. If you pass the exam then you can enter college. In medical school and some other schools, you have to pass with a much higher grade. Before that we didn't have any examinations, even in middle school. Now, if you do not pass the examinations you cannot go to college. This is very big change.

The problem before the nation now is modernization in four areas: industrial, cultural, scientific, and national defense. So people are working very hard and students are studying very hard. Things operate more regularly. Before you couldn't plan in advance.

*L:* Do you think the day-to-day operation of your clinical service has changed since the fall of the Gang of Four? Is the experience of the patient who comes to your hospital any different now?

*W:* No, not too much.

*L:* I saw your psychiatric department in 1975 as a busy, active, thoughtful kind of approach. Do you think the selection of treatments for patients has changed? Are you using more treatments now? Are you doing anything differently when you decide on a treatment plan for a patient?

*W:* There is not much difference. Even during the time of the Gang of Four, we used similar treatments. But now we pay more attention to Chinese traditional medicine. Our government wants us to have our own medicine, Chinese medicine. We accept a lot of wisdom from this, but we also continue to learn from Western medicine. We also learn from research projects in the medical school and we pay more attention to basic science. In medicine, not only have we learned from Western medicine but, at the same time, we pay more attention to Chinese traditional medicine. Chinese traditional medicine has lasted for several thousand years, so there are many good things. For example, we are doing a lot of research work on acupuncture.

*L:* Is that going on in Beijing?

*W:* There will be a meeting on acupuncture in Beijing, and Professor Loh of the University of California at San Francisco will attend this conference.

*L:* He is one of those who discovered the endorphins.

*W:* We are doing work at Beijing Medical College on endorphins and their role in acupuncture.

*L:* Do most of your patients get Western medication, traditional medicine, and acupuncture—all three treatments?

*W:* We are still working on that issue.

*L:* Do most patients find something in each area from which they can benefit?

*W:* We have lots of side effects from the neuroleptic drugs; we also find more dyskinesias. Besides, some patients need much higher doses of neuroleptics. So we are studying how to give the patient traditional medicine.

*L:* Does that reduce the dose of neuroleptic which is needed?

*W:* Yes, we are working on that. We use a herbal medicine with a neuroleptic.

*L:* I think you mentioned two of the herbal medicines when I was with you in 1975.

*W:* We are working on this with the department of pharmacology.

*L:* Are your doses of neuroleptics low by San Francisco standards?

*W:* Yes.

*L:* Do you notice any difference when you treat patients from the west? I assume you occasionally have patients from North America or

Europe who get ill and enter your hospital. Do you think there is any difference between a patient from Europe and a Chinese patient if they are treated in your hospital in Beijing?

*W:* We have some patients from other countries. We treat them the same way. Usually we use smaller doses of neuroleptics. Personally I have found that larger doses don't work better but they cause more side effects. We are working with acupuncture too, especially the ear points. We have herbal medicine for neurosis and insomnia, and this medicine has no side effects.

*L:* Do you use electroshock?

*W:* That is a problem we are now discussing in China. In some places they don't, but in some places in China they do. Most anti-depressant drugs usually take two weeks or even more to act. In those cases where there is very severe depression, there is more chance for suicide. The memory loss with electroshock is temporary. Shock must be given in the proper way, using the proper machine. Now, several hospitals in China use electroshock. For depression, they will give two, three or more treatments. Then they can start on the medicine and the safety of the patient is assured by the shock, which is a life-saving measure. We don't have succinylcholine so we use a barbiturate like sodium amytal.

*L:* Do you have much of a problem with suicide?

*W:* Not much. We have had some in cases of depression and schizophrenia. It seems that you have more in the United States.

*L:* Yes, but it's also common, isn't it, in Hong Kong?

*W:* We had a discussion yesterday in the Richmond MaxiCenter about Oriental patients, because most people who come from Hong Kong and Taiwan have environmental stress factors.

*L:* Hong Kong life is quite stressful. They have quite a bit of drug abuse, narcotics, and suicide.

*W:* Here in the United States, the American Chinese are impressed with the old Chinese culture, but they are also impressed by the American culture. It is different for them.

*L:* Have your heart-to-heart talks continued as both group and individual work?

*W:* Yes, my opinion is that we should do psychotherapy with individuals and groups. They should be integrated so there will be more benefits. We ask the family to help and they respond. We get good cooperation from the families.

*L:* Do the patients themselves form a group and talk together?

*W:* Yes, group therapy has different forms. One is when the patients get together and exchange experiences. This is very good because we have found that the patient would rather receive the information from other patients than the doctor. The doctors are educated to treat the patient as their brother. Otherwise you can not have heart-to-heart discussions. The patient won't believe you. They'll think that you don't really want to help them. This is very important. We are working on a reference book on psychiatry.

L: You are doing this with the institute in Beijing?

W: Beijing and also Nanjing.

L: What kind of reference book is it?

W: It's a textbook of psychiatry.

L: So you have been working on this quite a bit of the time—mostly you and Professor T'ao?

W: Also Professor Shen and several doctors from the Beijing Psychiatric Hospital. Also a doctor from Xian and a doctor from Gansu. We come together to write the book.

L: It takes a lot of effort. You couldn't have done that during the Gang of Four period.

W: That's right, this book is for the young psychiatrists.

L: Are you going to increase training in psychiatry? Do you think there will be more trainees?

W: Yes, more young doctors, so I am very interested to learn from your country about the postgraduate training of psychiatrists.

L: Did you find out everything you need to know? Of course, you will find out more in Chicago when you see the training institutions there.

W: We have some lectures from Los Angeles, and also from Langley Porter, and I find this very interesting. In our country we have a different system and different conditions, so we cannot copy. We have to take from your experience and work out what would be the best training for our young doctors.

L: How frequent is psychoneurosis in Beijing?

W: We have quite a number of psychoneuroses. We have three main kinds of neurosis: neurasthenia, hysteria, and compulsive neurosis. There are also anxiety neuroses. We have a lot of neurotic patients, but most have somatic manifestations.

L: Do they go to the barefoot doctor or the family physician?

W: They are seen in the medical clinic. In the psychiatric clinic we have more psychotic than psychoneurotic patients.

L: Do you think most psychoneurotic patients are treated in the medical department of the general hospital?

*W:* There are quite a number of neurotic patients treated there, including those with gastrointestinal and cardiovascular symptoms.

*L:* Do you consult on those patients?

*W:* Yes, they are referred to our outpatient department. We have more neurasthenia; we don't have too much compulsive neurosis. We have quite a number of hysterics, especially in the emergency room. Next time you come to China, if there are some hysterical cases we shall be happy to demonstrate them for you. I found that acupuncture is good for hysterical cases. Three acupuncture points are used. We combine it with suggestion and sometimes no suggestion.

*L:* Do you have many people with sexual problems?

*W:* No.

*L:* Why do you think that is?

*W:* I don't know. Maybe a cultural thing. Premarital sexual relationships cause shame.

*L:* Do people worry much about masturbation?

*W:* Yes, some youngsters. Some schools have sex education. Mostly they don't. If I get any youngsters with problems about masturbation they have some wrong education.

*L:* Do you see people who worry about sexual problems a lot? Do they come to the psychiatrists sometimes because of worry?

*W:* Yes, some people worry about premature ejaculation. They come to talk about that.

*L:* What about homosexuality?

*W:* Yes, we have some cases, but certainly very few.

*L:* Is it more common in women than men or about equal?

*W:* I have seen some statistics that show it is more common in men. It is against the social order.

*L:* What about family difficulties between husbands and wives? Are those handled mostly in the community?

*W:* Yes, in the family and in the community, using the organizations where they live and work. There are responsible persons there to come together with them and discuss problems with them and to try to harmonize them and give them education. Most problems can be solved that way.

*L:* Do you make any distinction between therapy and education? I notice you use both. Do you think they are the same? Does a couple having marital difficulties undergo education or therapy?

*W:* We have no such special therapy.

*L:* Is the criticism/self-criticism still widespread?

*W:* Yes, we think it is a very good way to solve problems. Some are willing to accept this, but some don't. You have to take time to educate them. During the time of the Gang of Four there were very few effective criticisms.

L: The unity:criticism-self-criticism:unity has been going on since 1949. Have you seen any change in that since the fall of the Gang of Four?

W: Before the Gang of Four we had better criticism-self-criticism but during the time of the Gang of Four it was not so good. Now we are educated to be criticized not only by others, but by ourselves.

L: Do you practice criticism/self-criticism in the hospital too?

W: Yes.

L: Do you still have a Revolutionary Committee? When I was at your hospital in 1975 there was a Revolutionary Committee, and a woman from the Committee attended our meeting.

W: Now we have restored the system of a superintendent and an assistant superintendent.

L: So you don't need a Revolutionary Committee. You have returned to a more hierarchical system. If you personally go to a criticism/self-criticism group, who goes to your group?

W: Sometimes the doctors meet with the nurses and sometimes they meet separately. It depends on the topic being discussed.

L: Do you think criticism/self-criticism is a prevention for psychoneurosis or personality disorder?

W: Not only prevention, but also curative. You see, we have to educate the patient to recognize or realize their situation and how to improve it, to face reality.

L: Do you see people at times who have become emotionally upset because they have been in criticism groups?

W: Yes, we recognize that there must be time to permit them to think it over. We discuss it with them individually. Certainly it is much better to discuss with them individually at first, to listen. We also try to explain. But there is also help from the group.

L: Do you find that people who are engaged in criticism/self-criticism where they live or work sometimes get upset, or is there enough support so they don't get upset about what is said?

W: In a community or in a factory, usually there are people who are responsible and they will talk to the people who get excited.

L: Do you participate in the examination of people accused of crime? Do you examine them to see if they are competent?

W: We have forensic psychiatry. Patients are referred from the court or the police. We are asked whether the act is due to disease or is an

ordinary criminal act. Usually we give our conclusion and suggestion to the court.

L: Do they generally agree with you?

W: Yes, we get good cooperation, but sometimes they don't agree. If
they don't agree, they can send the patient to another hospital and
get two opinions. Sometimes doctors from two psychiatric hospitals
come together to make a report.

L: What about the process of commitment?

W: If the patient is committed as psychotic and has no responsibility, he
is sent to the hospital for treatment. It is different from the United
States. You have a lot of laws in the United States to protect the
patient, but sometimes too much is decided by the judge. In China,
the patient stays in the hospital until the doctors decide he should
be discharged, just as the doctors decide that he should be admitted.
You have a different social system, so your commitment system is
different. Personally, I think that when the patient lacks insight
about his illness, it is better to have the psychiatrist decide. We
find that the first admission is extremely important, and it is important to help the patient be entirely cured. Otherwise, he has
more chance to become chronic.

L: What is your approach to the patient with delusions?

W: In order to understand delusions, you must know the law of their
development. A lot of patients have delusional ideas. I always teach
my patients about their delusions. If you trace the history, first you
have suspicion, later it may develop into delusion of persecution.
We discuss how to make a plan. The patient himself can handle
that, can handle the law, whenever he gets some suspicion if he is
aware that something is wrong; otherwise, if he doesn't talk to
somebody else about his suspicion, nobody will ever know. If he
understands it, he will be able to handle it and he will say "there
must be something wrong with me." He will go to the psychiatrist
voluntarily. Then he can cure the disease. As you know, Chairman
Mao taught us that it is possible for a spark to start a big fire. But
we can handle it very easily. When the smoke is just smoke you
may step on it. But if you start the fire, it's very hard and you have
to go to the hospital. If the patient understands his suspicion, he
will take the medicine voluntarily, and go to the doctor. He says
he has suspicion, and then the doctor can give him the treatment.
It will be very easy to treat him; otherwise it would be very difficult.
This is what I do in my work.

L: That's very helpful to understand.

*W:* The first part is to give the knowledge to the patient so he understands it, and then the second is to help the patient to handle it correctly. Then comes revolutionary optimism. This is the way I handle it.

*L:* When Dr. Phil Shapiro was at your hospital in 1972, he was told about a case in which a man in his thirties, a teacher of physics in medical school, was admitted to the hospital when he was plagued by the conviction that he was being spied on. He had been in the hospital for two months. He said he was much better and looking forward to returning to his job and he had a letter from his fellow teachers then, saying that they hoped to have him back. When he was asked what helped him he mentioned the essays of Mao Tse-tung, "Where Do Correct Ideas Come From?" He went on to tell the group in 1972 that some time after he arrived at the hospital he saw a man whom he recognized as an electronics technician from the medical school and at once he concluded that they were spying on him. Then he thought maybe it was subjectivity and he thought of Mao Tse-tung's essay. What has happened to him?

*W:* He is working very well now.

*L:* Has he come back to the hospital?

*W:* No.

*L:* Does he come for treatment?

*W:* Yes, no matter if he is completely cured, he must come back for treatment once every month or two.

*L:* Does he take medicine?

*W:* At times he takes medicine.

*L:* Which medicine?

*W:* Trilafon (perphenazine), 4 mg a day. He doesn't have any side effects. He sleeps well.

*L:* Is he married?

*W:* Yes, he gets along well with his wife and with his co-workers. He has some other problems, including suspicion, but he can handle it. He may have trouble for a few days when he is at home. I still see him. We don't know the etiology of schizophrenia, so prevention is very important. We try to prevent a disease from beginning. It is difficult to treat later. This is one reason why we have a team for outpatients.

*L:* Does this man get acupuncture or traditional medicine?

*W:* No. I think that psychotherapy is very important not only for the psychoneurotic, but for the schizophrenic. It seems to me that Mao Tse-tung Thought comes from reality, from real practice, so it teaches patients how to face reality. Revolutionary optimism encourages patients in facing reality. It encourages them after they have lost self-esteem. If you don't believe that you will be able to make change, it's not easy to overcome the many difficulties you must face. Patients need to be armed by revolutionary optimism. Sometimes we speak of a loss of revolutionary faith.

L: I am interested in your results. I think you said you are able to keep about eight out of ten from coming back to the hospital.

W: Yes, patients are given medicine and then we have a follow-up team and tell them to come back in a certain number of days. We telephone or we go pay a home visit if they don't come.

L: Who is on the team, the nurse and doctor?

W: Usually the nurse can make the home visit.

L: One person, then what happens?

W: Mostly we can arrange it by a telephone call to the family members or to those people who are responsible. Then they bring the patient in.

L: What about the patients who cannot return to their families or work? How can you help them?

W: If they are still not completely rehabilitated, and still some symptoms such as hallucinations are present, then they still get the medicine. It is very good that when the patient is in the hospital he still gets full pay, and he won't lose his job, even if he does not have a full recovery. He can still keep the job. He may get seventy percent to eighty percent of his salary and this will last for many years.

L: Do you find that some people need day care like at the Richmond MaxiCenter?

W: Yes, day care is especially well developed in Shanghai. Before the Cultural Revolution we had community health stations in Beijing that were preventive and curative, but during the Cultural Revolution they were closed. Only a few are left.

L: Why did they close during the Cultural Revolution?

W: Because of the view of psychiatry as related to thought or idealism instead of Marxist materialism.

L: Do you think that during the Cultural Revolution there was less support for psychiatry than for the rest of medicine because of the relationship of psychiatry to idealistic philosophy?

W: Yes, but not just psychiatry. In some places it was argued that, somehow, psychiatry was idealistic. However, ninety percent of the time this was not an issue. In American psychiatry you don't have very equal treatment with the rest of medicine, do you?

L: No.

*W:* The same is true in China, although we are trying to educate our people.

*L:* What proportion of patients coming to a medical department in Beijing have emotional illnesses? I asked the doctor at Dazhai (Tachai) about the percentage of the patients who come to him who have mental or emotional problems causing their physical complaints and he said one or two out of the sixty patients he sees a day. I wonder what you think about that. Do you think it is more than that?

*W:* It is higher. His proportion is low.

*L:* In Western Europe and the United States, one third, if not one half or more, of the people who come into the office for help have mental or emotional problems. Perhaps the percentage is quite low in China because many of the emotional complaints are taken care of in the criticism/self-criticism groups?

*W:* Yes, also in the family and community.

*L:* What about personality disorder?

*W:* We have different ideas about this problem. We haven't reached a conclusion. We think that there are personality disorders like juvenile delinquency. But we don't have too much personality disorder in China. Reeducation is very important here. Most of these cases are prevented.

*L:* Does it sometimes begin in the adolescent years?

*W:* Yes, the Communist Party is important here in educating the youth and now school entry requires examinations.

*L:* You feel that preventing personality disorders takes a lot of education, so you have physical and general education and recreational and political education?

*W:* Especially political education. Youth now has a lot of work and a better social purpose.

*L:* Do you think there was some increase in juvenile delinquency during the Cultural Revolution?

*W:* I don't think that because I have no way of checking on it.

*L:* Do you feel that the Cultural Revolution was mostly positive, or partly?

*W:* That is something very difficult to say. I'm not a political person. But some good things happened during the Cultural Revolution.

*L:* What has been your own special interest in psychiatry?

*W:* Teaching.

*L:* So your main personal interest has been in teaching.

*W:* Yes.

*L:* This is your duty.

Selected Articles from China

*W:* Yes, we also have to do research.

*L:* Research is another commitment, and clinical work? So you combine them?

*W:* Yes.

*L:* As the professor you are responsible.

*W:* I'm chairman.

*L:* When I was in Beijing it seemed that there was a kind of Marxist–Mao Tse-tung Thought about mental problems. I wonder if some development in this has taken place. That is, the use of dialectical materialism in psychiatry.

*W:* This is still our political basis. This is what we teach. The patients we deal with are the reality.

*L:* Has a new theory of mental illness emerged?

*W:* We are working more on new treatment for psychiatric cases. We study how to make an integration of our own traditional medicine with Western medicine.

*L:* Yes, that is very important, and that comes from Mao Tse-tung Thought too. Have you seen anything here in the United States that would be transferable, that you could adapt and that is new to you?

*W:* The time here is very short, less than a week. It is all very interesting.

*L:* But what is important that you found here?

*W:* Community work is important.

# THE LAST FIFTEEN YEARS OF PROGRESS IN OUR COUNTRY'S TREATMENT OF MENTAL DISEASES
## by WU CHEN-I and ZHANG JI-ZHI

Since the Liberation of our country the work on mental illness is under the leadership of the Communist Party. This work, directed by the Ministry of Health, has achieved great success as reported in this journal in 1959 and 1964. During the last 10 years, Lin Piao and the Gang of Four stopped progress toward establishing preventive organizations, the increasing of mental hospital beds, training of mental health personnel, the application of new treatments and methods, the development of outpatient care and the combination of Western and Chinese Traditional Medicine. The Gang of Four disturbed our progress but there has been some degree of development and improvement since the fall of the Gang of Four in 1977. The work in mental health has been improving rapidly as the result of the reorganization during the last 3 years.

Here we can recall from our personal experience some aspects of our history in order to learn for the future. First, the work on the prevention and treatment of mental illness has made definite progress during the last 10 years and it is a cornerstone of our policy. The broad mass of mental health workers from the hospital go to the countryside, the factories and the basic commune units, making surveys and developing programs of mass treatment and prevention of mental illness.

1. The organization of prevention and treatment is formed by local organizations of health officers, civil administrative officers and public security departments. In Shanghai, under the leadership of the City Committee, members of the major organizations including health, civil administrators, security officers, the industrial control department and officers of the housing department, altogether five departments, integrate planning and the division of labor and responsibility. In this way the work has progressed more smoothly. In Northeast China, the work is under the leadership of the provincial and city administrative organization who form an office for prevention and treatment of mental illness. In the Northeast they integrate planning of the preventive and diagnostic services for mental illness using the provincial mental hospital in the city as the center of a preventive network for the whole province and its cities. Preventive services are generally on three levels, the city, the catchment area and the street. In the factory we can take the example of Daqing (Taching), the large oil field in the Northeast. They established a hospital for the area and a three-level prevention network. In the rural country, the three levels come from the district, the commune and brigade. Where the preventive network has not been established in an area, some communities create their own units to do mental health surveys and education and train the medical personnel. They also bring medical service and medicine to the door of the patient. Simultaneously with establishing preventive and treatment organizations, certain cities, to suit conditions in their area, created mass preventive stations outside the hospital on the street level and established worker health and nursing units. For example, in the Shenyang District, the Huang Gu area and the South District of Shanghai, daytime preventive and treatment units were established, with the following services: medical treatment, work and recreation therapy, and environmental therapy. In these units, the patient receives the treatment and the units also consolidate therapeutic effort, promote recovery and rehabilitation, and prevent recurrence. Some of these units even make money through the patients' work and reduce

the financial responsibility of the patients, which is warmly welcomed by the great mass of people.

2. The survey of mental illness. During the last 15 years, many areas of the country have continuously operated large-scale mental survey work. According to the incomplete statistics in Beijing, Shanghai, Nanjing, Sichuan (Szechuan), Honan and Xinjiang (Sinkiang) Province and the autonomous regions, 30 million people have been surveyed. The method of survey and the criteria of mental illness were not the same everywhere, so there are variations in the information. The prevalence of mental illness is about 5 to 7 per 1,000 people. Of this number, two to four per 1,000 have schizophrenia, which occupies first place among mental illnesses. This illness seriously endangers the health of the people, affecting work production and also the security of society. We pay great attention to these two figures when establishing plans for preventive and diagnostic services. We will use these two figures in planning research projects.

3. The mass prevention and treatment of mental illness by the people themselves. The unique characteristics of the work of prevention and treatment of mental illness in our country emphasizes the combination of survey, prevention and treatment. Each local region operates a mass prevention and mass treatment program according to its conditions and circumstances and has obtained a certain amount of experience. For example, in Shanghai, some cotton-weaving factories established a mental health care unit and a sheltered workshop for patients and services for their families. This kind of project is relatively effective in controlling the patient's symptoms and greatly reduces the recurrence rate. The mass prevention and treatment work in Tianjin (Tientsin), continuing over 10 years, has built up a fully developed preventive and treatment network. This permits the great majority of mental patients to have outpatient treatment in the local community and reduces the waiting list for beds at the hospital. This outpatient treatment has also significantly decreased the recurrence of schizophrenia. All over the country, a great many cities and districts provide beds for the treatment of patients at home. For example, in Liaoning Province, mental hospitals have provided over 3,000 home beds for treatment, and this is a unique characteristic of our mass prevention and mass treatment work. In the rural areas, the patients are scattered, so the mass prevention and mass treatment work is operated from the commune health care center bringing medicine to the door of the patient. In areas where mass prevention and mass treatment is in operation, timely treatment is generally possible.

4. Research on the epidemiology of mental illness. Survey work is

combined with epidemiology research in the preliminary analysis. Comparisons in the prevalence of mental illness and the changes in distributions have been made by the Shanghai Institute for the Prevention and Treatment of Mental Diseases, the Department of Psychiatry of Sichuan Medical College and also the Number Three Hospital of Daqing. The Fushan district of Guangdong analyzed a survey of the prevalence of mental illness and the family history of mental illness. The accumulation of this kind of research data has established the epidemiology of mental illness and has laid a very good foundation for further research into factors influencing the etiology of mental illness.

    5. The combination of traditional Chinese and western medicine. Over the last ten years, with the increase in western-trained medical personnel, many units have done a great deal of clinical research and experimental work. Now, a combination of traditional Chinese and Western medicine is used to treat schizophrenia and other common mental diseases. This development can be classified into two areas. The first is traditional diagnosis and the second is differentiation of the illness by western methods. These classifications for clinical research are used in Beijing, Shanghai, Tianjin, and Harbin. The point is that the diagnosis of illness by western medicine can be combined with the differentiation of types according to traditional Chinese medicine. The Shanghai Mental and Preventive and Treatment Institute suggests employing the differentiation of types using the visceral organs for classification. Tianjin Mental Hospital, while studying 77 cases of schizophrenia following the traditional Chinese medicine differential diagnosis of schizophrenia, chiefly involves three visceral organs—heart, liver, and spleen—and on the whole they found that an excess entity predominates. The Harbin Medical College Department of Mental Illness, using forty cases of schizophrenia, following a diagnosis of traditional Chinese medicine differentiated ten types. They consider the principle of vitalizing the blood and dissolving ecchymoses can be used for all these types. However, one should depend on the occurrence of symptoms when selecting herbs for clearing heat and vitalizing blood. In Beijing An Ding Hospital, 320 cases of schizophrenia were analyzed and they found the excess category composed about 70 percent and a deficiency entity composed 30 percent. During the differentiation of the types using traditional Chinese medicine, it is not important whether the category is in an excess or deficient state. Of 123 cases, 38.4 percent involved the symptom of phlegm. Therefore, it is necessary to consider the problem of phlegm during further research work. The Third Affiliated Hospital of the Beijing Medical College analyzed 88 cases of schizophrenia, using the traditional

Chinese medicine method. It was found that the majority involved congestion of the liver and an excess of phlegm. Other hospitals have gone into more research and have other points of view. This research concerning the combination of traditional Chinese medicine and western medicine is just beginning.

6. Principal treatments and selection of traditional Chinese medicine prescriptions. There are many principles in treating mental illness. We will now discuss the most common methods:

A. The method and principle of cleansing phlegm, opening up the orifice, the so-called masking of phlegm. The phlegm fire disturbing the heart is a traditional view of the etiology and the pathology of mental illness by traditional medicine. At this time, many medical units are using this principle for the treatment of schizophrenia. For example, in a Tianjin Hospital, they use an herbal decoction which warms the gall bladder meridian. Its use has been combined with a small amount of Valium in treating 50 cases of schizophrenia with very good results. The Shanghai Institute for the Prevention and Treatment of Mental Diseases uses the same method in treating toxic psychosis and with satisfactory results.

B. The second principle is vitalizing blood and dissolving ecchymoses. Since Wong Qing-ren suggested this method in the Qing Dynasty, the first principle of treatment by cleansing phlegm and opening up the lumen has been used with favorable results in the dilution type of schizophrenia. The vitalizing of blood and dissolving of ecchymoses method originated in the Qing Dynasty by traditional Chinese physicians who thought that the *chi* in the blood had congealed and stagnated and that this was related to mental illness, so a decoction called "awakening the manic dream" was prescribed. Since then the indications for its use have been enlarged. For example, in Henan Province Mental Hospital, using "eliminating ecchymosis decoction" from the blood chamber in treating forty-three cases of schizophrenia produced favorable results. At the same time, an EKG was done and measurements of cerebral blood flow were made. In Shanghai Mental Preventive and Treatment Institute, they are using another decoction by the name of Attaining Ying Decoction for the treatment of sixty cases of schizophrenia. They have observed the blood flow pattern before and after treatment. They found the whole blood viscosity is greatly increased after the treatment. They also have used this method for periodic mental illness, with very good results.

C. The third principle of treatment by traditional Chinese medicine is the "clear heat and purging method." This method is mainly used for a manic excess entity. In these cases, they use three herbs—one is Flos Genkwa, the second is Euphorbia pekinensis Rupr, and the third is

Semen pharbitidis. All these herbs have very strong side effects during the purge, but they can usually control acute symptoms of mania. They should not be used for a long term because they might cause dehydration. It is contraindicated in old and weak constitutions, in pregnant women, and in children.

7. The clinical experiment with a single type of Chinese herb. There are several kinds of single herb in clinical use. We will select just one for example. For 7 or 8 years in Chengdu City they have used an herb called *Ma Sang* for schizophrenia. The literal Chinese name is horse mulberry, or *coria sinica*. This is a kind of parasitic plant. A great deal of research has been done on its pharmacological properties, and it has been found that combining it with other herbs is better than taking it alone. Patients with manifestations of convulsions seem to have better results. Side effects of this type of treatment using *Ma Sang* and Valium include vomiting and convulsions which may cause some injuries, so nursing is very important.

Another herb that is used in schizophrenia is Datura, a kind of belladonna. It has a tranquilizing effect, especially on the restless, excited type of patient. Where the patient has built up a tolerance to Western drugs used in treatment, Datura is helpful. After taking Datura the patient goes to sleep quickly and the duration of sleep is relatively long. According to Jiangsu Province Mental Preventive and Treatment Unit, Datura was used with a small dose of chloropromazine, 200 milligrams a day, to treat 352 cases of schizophrenia, with a marked improvement in 116 cases (33 percent). It was used with all types of schizophrenia. The most serious adverse effect was lowering of body temperature, lowering of blood pressure, and irregular heartbeat in a few cases. The patient should be observed closely.

8. Clinical research on schizophrenia. The cause of schizophrenia is uncertain, and at this stage, the treatment is mostly symptomatic. Besides using Chinese traditional medicine together with western medicine, we are trying some new Western antipsychotic drugs such as pimozide, fluphenazine, and fluphenazine decanoate, the long-acting form of the drug. With the use of antipsychotic drugs, the recurrence problem becomes more obvious. We are doing clinical research on lowering the recurrence rate. In Tianjin Mental Preventive and Treatment Institute they have a follow-up of treated patients. They have preventive classes along with drug and psychiatric treatment in the hospital, in combination with social therapy. Within three years, they have lowered the recurrence rate to 31 percent and the readmission rate is 8 percent. Professor Xia Zhenyi (Hsia Chen-yi) has observed 100 cases of schizophrenia from the

clinical point of view, including subtypes and treatment with a long follow-up. He found that the pattern of symptoms is variable and unstable during the course of the illness. Apathy and degeneration of the mental state becomes more significant in the long term. The subtypes are unstable. In the end, most subtypes become a mixed and undifferentiated type. The result of treatment determines the course and the number of recurrences. The variation of symptoms also influences the therapeutic effect. Consideration is given to the standard diagnosis and the problem of misdiagnosis of schizophrenia. If there are no Schneiderian first-degree symptoms of schizophrenia, we should consider a psychosis caused by a lesion of the brain. For example, Liu Xiehe and others have observed the relation of schizophrenia to organic lesions of the brain. They pointed out the occurrence of schizophrenic-like symptoms related to a local lesion, especially in the temporal lobe. Schizophrenia may be related to dopamine or the function of the neurons or the imbalance of neurotransmitters. Research on schizophrenia is very weak because of the Gang of Four. At that time all research projects were stopped, and now some hospitals are beginning with research on biochemistry and metabolism. For example, Chang Wen-ho observed that schizophrenia in an acute excitatory state has an excess of serotonin, and with the relief of the symptoms the serotonin returned to a normal level. This shows that attacks of acute schizophrenia are related to abnormal serotonin levels. They pointed out that serotonin metabolism may have insufficient turnover or breakdown, and when the breakdown is reduced, the enzyme monoamine exidase is low. After giving specific drugs and evaluating all the schizophrenic patients, it is the apathetic patients who show a change in a monoamine-like CNS transmitter. Also there is research being done on the heredity of glucose and adrenal cortical metabolism.

9. Mental retardation problem. Mental underdevelopment is another very important subject. According to a report, 60 percent of mental retardation is caused by noxious factors of the external environment and 40 percent is related to heredity. In one area, a school for the retarded emphasizes that they need more research, investigation, and control, which should be done with gynecology, obstetrics, pediatrics, genetics, and psychology education.

10. Other fields: An emotional type of psychosis is often seen in China. Professor Xia Zhenyi has investigated its relation to hereditary factors by studying the patient's family. He found that its occurrence is higher than usual in the first-degree relatives of patients who also have a higher rate of schizophrenia. This indicated that these two types of illness, emotional psychosis and schizophrenia, are related in some way

through heredity. In this familial type of mental illness women are affected more than men, although this is not statistically significant. In this type of mental illness, there is no clear inheritance of the emotional psychosis.

Some problems are noticed when using antipsychotic medicines for a long time, including effects on the cardiovascular system, the liver, the skin and eyes, tardive dyskinesia, and a "malignant syndrome." This calls for more research on toxic effects.

11. The direction for the future. The first is the combination of Chinese and western medicine. We have to build up or establish organizations of Chinese and western medicine, using the older, experienced doctors, including those trained in western medicine. We must train an enlarged research group, and they should integrate western and traditional scientific research so the results can be repeated by other scientists. Now, in China, they have single treatments like Chinese herbs, and the results between studies sometimes differ so much that new studies cannot give us a confirmation. The next priority for future reserach is the classification of mental illness. We use ICD-8 and DSM III, and every five to ten years there is a revision. In China since 1958 we have had a draft of diagnostic nomenclature, but after 20 years it is not established, so we have to work on that. This classification is not yet used throughout the country. In 1978, at the Second National Mental Health meeting, we presented a new draft of this classification, and it needs more revision. The third priority is clinical work. Certain clinical systems are very weak, like pediatric psychiatry and geriatric psychiatry. They are mostly lacking. The legal determination of mental illness, forensic psychiatry, needs more effort. Another area needing more emphasis is the psychosomatic or functional nervous disease. It is often seen and the incidence is very high, especially in young people, affecting study and work. The fourth priority is research on theory. We need to establish biochemistry, neurology, genetics, neurophysiology, neuroendocrinology, immunology and pharmacology—we need to catch up in these mental health research areas. The fifth priority is the study of psychopathology. This discipline hasn't been established in China yet, and we will develop it. We can study psychopathology by using psychology, neurobiology and neurochemistry. We are sure the theory of dialectical materialism will help psychologists and psychiatrists in their study of psychopathology. . . . These studies will open up a new understanding of mental phenomena. The value of psychology also lies in the study and development of interviewing.

In order to achieve these goals, we must develop organizations and

administrative structures. We should not isolate ourselves. We must coordinate information exchange within the country and also internationally. This way we can be sure our modernization will be achieved according to schedule.

# PSYCHOLOGY IN THE PEOPLE'S REPUBLIC OF CHINA
by C. C. CHING

*ABSTRACT: The author describes the five periods of the development of psychology in China: (a) the beginnings of Chinese psychology (1910– 1948), (b) psychology in the early days of the People's Republic of China (1949–1957), (c) the period of growth and development (1958–1965), (d) the attack on psychology by the Gang of Four (1966–1975), and (e) the revival of psychology since 1976. This overview emphasizes the development of psychology after the founding of the People's Republic of China in 1949. The disruption of psychology between 1966 and 1975, as well as the progress made in the reconstruction of psychology since 1976, is also stressed.*

The following is an overview of the development of psychology in China from its very beginning as a science to the present time and of how we Chinese psychologists have devoted ourselves to the building of a scientific discipline.

## BEGINNINGS OF CHINESE PSYCHOLOGY (1910–1948)

Ancient Chinese philosophical writings contained a wealth of psychological thoughts. Problems such as the goodness and evil of human nature and the essence of the human spirit were discussed in relation to ethical, political, and educational theories. But the advent of psychology as a modern, independent discipline came about only in the present century. In 1907 the philosopher Wang Kuo-wei translated Höffding's (1893) *Outlines of Psychology,* which was one of the earliest books of psychology in Chinese. The first psychology course was given at Peking University in 1917, and in 1920 the Nanking Higher Normal School established the first department of psychology. In the early 1920s, an Institute of Psychology was established in the then Academia Sinica. The first psychological journal, *Psychology,* was published in 1922, and in 1936 the *Chinese Psychological Journal* came out. The year 1937 saw the founding of the Chinese Psychological Society. After the outbreak of the Sino-

Japanese War in 1937, the Psychological Society and the journals were forced to stop their activities, and only a few universities in remote parts of China were able to continue with teaching and research.

Early Chinese psychology was introduced mainly from the West. In the 1920s and 1930s students were sent abroad, chiefly to the United States, with some going to Europe. Among these early students were Tang Yueh, Luh Chi-wei, Z. Y. Kuo, Tsai Chao, Pan Shuh, Chen Li, Sun Kuo-hua, Siegen K. Chow, Huang I, Hu Chi-nan, and J. C. Tsao. These scholars came back and contributed to the development of Chinese psychology. A few of them later turned to physiology and became prominent physiologists. Among the problems studied at that time were the recognition of Chinese characters, child psychology, psychological testing (revision of the Binet-Simon scale), and animal psychology. Learning and memory were studied primarily in the context of education. The main influences on Chinese psychology were functionalism and behaviorism, although psychoanalysis and Gestalt psychology were also introduced to China. The Institute of Psychology, established in the thirties, did research on neuroanatomy and brain functions. Before the founding of the People's Republic of China, however, conditions were not good for the development of science in general, and psychology was not well regarded by the old Chinese society. At this early stage, psychology was virtually at a standstill.

## PSYCHOLOGY IN THE EARLY DAYS OF THE PEOPLE'S REPUBLIC OF CHINA (1949–1957)

After the founding of the People's Republic of China in 1949, the Chinese government strongly supported the development of psychology. Chinese psychologists believed that Western psychology did not fit well into Chinese culture and that it was necessary to construct a new psychology that would be relevant to China's social system and cultural milieu. The following sections describe the important occurrences in Chinese psychology at this time.

### Psychology Based on Dialectical Materialism
Chinese psychological workers have proceeded along a path aimed at building a dialectical materialistic psychology. They have endeavored to develop a Marxist materialistic interpretation of psychological phenomena and to set up objective principles in methodology. Psychology was to be reformed under the guiding principles of Marxism and Leninism

Selected Articles from China

and on the basis of Pavlov's theory. Regarding epistemology and the mind-body problem, Chinese psychologists hold a materialistic monism: A psychological phenomenon is a product or function of a kind of highly organized matter—the brain. Further, mind is a reflection of objective reality in the outer world. These principles are drawn from Lenin's (1947/ 1973) theory of reflection, expounded in his work *Materialism and Empirio-criticism,* and Mao Tse-tung's (1965a, 1965b) *On Contradiction* and *On Practice.* This viewpoint is the one that most Chinese psychologists embrace today.

## Learning of Soviet Psychology

Soon after Liberation, Chinese psychologists acknowledged that Soviet psychology was more advanced and that we should learn from the Soviet Union. Soviet textbooks and Soviet psychological literature were thus introduced to China in the early 1950s. These works were translated into Chinese and were used as teaching materials in universities and colleges. The three most influential textbooks were Kornilov's (1948) *Advanced Psychology,* Teplov's (1951) *Psychology,* and Smirnov's (1962) *Psychology.* Soviet psychologists came to China and lectured at Peking Normal University, and Chinese psychologists traveled from many cities to attend their lectures. These Soviet psychologists had a strong philosophical orientation. An event that had a great effect on Chinese psychology occurred at the joint meeting of the Soviet Academy of Sciences and the Soviet Academy of Medical Sciences held in Moscow in 1950. A resolution was passed to make Pavlov's theory of conditioned reflexes the scientific foundation of biology and medicine, as well as psychology. As a result, Pavlov's (1928) *Lectures on Conditioned Reflexes* was translated into Chinese. Laboratories for studying classical conditioning were established in universities, and at the Institute of Psychology, salivation experiments on dogs were replicated. Chinese psychologists also studied the theory of the two signal systems put forward by Pavlov in his later years. This theory holds that the unconditioned and conditioned sensory reflex belongs to the first signal system, while language, a higher conditioned reflex of a conditioned sensory reflex that has a generalization function, belongs to the second signal system. This theory explained higher human mental functioning and served as the physiological basis for language and thinking.

In the 1950s in the Soviet Union, Western psychology was regarded as idealistic and bourgeois; psychological testing and social psychology were viewed as reactionary. Some Chinese psychologists at the time shared these views, and no work was done either in testing or in social psychology.

## Critical Reviews of Western Psychology

Articles and monographs written during this period evaluated Western psychological schools and theories including structuralism, functionalism, behaviorism, Gestalt psychology, Freudian psychoanalysis, and Thorndikean educational principles. The pragmatism of James and Dewey, which had a strong influence on Chinese educational thought before Liberation, received special scrutiny. These critical reviews were the first step toward reform of psychology under Marxist principles.

## Debate on the Object, Methodology, and Scientific Nature of Psychology

In the course of studying Pavlov's theory and making critical reviews of Western psychology, differences of opinion arose among Chinese psychologists. These differences were reflected in a debate on the relation between psychological activity and higher nervous activity (Pavlov's term) and on the justification of studying underlying processes of behavior in psychology. Psychologists at one extreme held that psychological activity is nothing but higher nervous activity and that there is nothing else but that. Those at another extreme held that psychological activity is a higher phenomenon which cannot be explained by nervous activity alone. The former group denied altogether that psychology was an independent discipline and reduced it to studies of higher nervous activity. The latter group de-emphasized the role of Pavlov's theory in the reformation of psychology and separated mental phenomena from their material substrate, leading to a psychophysical parallelism, a form of dualistic philosophy. After long discussion, the majority of psychologists came to the conclusion that psychological activity is a result of higher nervous activity that evolved over a long period of phylogenesis; this activity is peculiar to humankind and is far more sophisticated than and qualitatively different from that of animals. While agreeing that it is the task of psychologists to study the material substrate (i.e., the human brain) of psychological phenomena, these psychologists emphasized that psychological phenomena are a reflection of objective reality, which is also a determining factor of the mind.

It should be noted that this discussion on the scientific nature of psychology is of value in setting a methodological frame of reference for our future research: that science should prosper through free exchange of ideas. However, this emphasis on the study of physiological mechanisms of the mind led to a movement in 1958 criticizing the consideration of psychology as a natural science. Critics charged that psychology neglected the "class nature" of people by one-sidedly emphasizing the mind as a function of the brain, a view that was said to violate Marx's principle that a person is a social being involved in class struggle. This trend was called the "biologizing" of mental phenomena. The criticism eventually subsided, and corrections were made afterward.

## Founding of the Institute of Psychology of the Chinese Academy of Sciences after Liberation

Although the Institute of Psychology had been in the planning stages since 1950, it was not formally founded until 1956. It is now the largest research institute of psychology in China. It is involved in basic as well as applied research, whereas all other psychological research units are set up as teaching and research groups under the departments of education or philosophy in universities and colleges. In 1955, after Liberation, the Chinese Psychological Society was reinaugurated, and in 1956 the journal *Acta Psychologica Sinica* began publication.

## PERIOD OF GROWTH AND DEVELOPMENT (1958–1965)

After a decade of struggle to find a unique way for the development of psychology in New China, Chinese psychologists realized that apart from methodological discussions and intake and rejection of Western psychology, it was necessary to initiate work in the laboratory and to conduct field studies related to the practical needs of socialist construction. Working under the principle "theory united with practice," Chinese psychologists started work on research projects in numerous fields. In the period between the Second National Congress of Psychology in 1960 and 1965, some 500 papers were published in various journals in China. Over 30 percent of the papers were on child psychology and educational psychology, and most of these concerned the developmental stages of basic psychological processes and the teaching of school subjects, especially teaching young children to learn Chinese characters. Programmed instruction was also tried out in China and showed some success. Another 30 percent of the papers were on physiological psychology and sensory and perceptual processes. The rest dealt with industrial, clinical, and other applied topics. Ergonomic studies of control design and displays were done to meet the demands of industrialization. Psychotherapy was applied to treatment of chronic diseases such as hypertension, peptic ulcer, and neurasthenia.

It should be noted that research work in this period was no longer confined to the Soviet tradition and developed in a more independent atmosphere, freely borrowing useful ideas from both East and West. Some of the studies of this period, the selection of problems, and the approaches to problems were truly international and of rather high standards. Thus, on the eve of the Cultural Revolution in 1966, after fifteen years of toil, psychology at last had a strong foothold in the ranks of science. During the early 1960s, psychology flourished and was well supported, and it developed more strongly than at any other time in Chinese history. The membership of the Chinese Psychological Society reached an all-time high of 1,087 in 1965.

## THE ATTACK ON PSYCHOLOGY BY THE GANG OF FOUR (1966–1975)

In 1966 a plot by Lin Piao and the Gang of Four to seize power in China was under way. With it, our scientific work, particularly that of psychological investigation, suffered severely. In October 1965, a member of the Gang, Yao Wen-yuan, using the pen name Ge Ming-jen ("revolutionary man"), wrote an article in the *Kwang Ming Daily* (Ge, 1965) entitled "Is This the Scientific Method and Correct Direction in Psychological Research?"; he attacked a paper by Chen Li and Wang An-sheng (1965c) entitled "Color and Form Preferences." Chen was then the vice-president of Hangchow University and a well-known psychologist. This paper was the third of a series (see Chen & Wang, 1965a, 1965b) on the development of color and form abstraction in children and dealt with preferences of children of different ages for the four primary colors and different forms. Yao argued that there is no abstract color and form devoid of concrete objects and that preferences are always related to political attitude, ideological inclination, and the class to which the observer belongs. Yao continued his argument in the following manner: The experimental psychologists who perform experiments by abstraction and manipulation of a few variables are approaching problems that do not exist in reality; such psychological studies are scientifically absurd. Thus the legitimacy of experimental psychology as a scientific discipline was questioned. Yao argued that though science studies common laws of nature, there are no common psychological laws for the whole human race; rather, people from different social classes have different laws for their mental activities, and psychological problems should be approached exclusively by the method of social class analysis. He therefore accused experimental psychology of being disguised as a scientific discipline but of actually trying to do away with the Marxist principle of the class nature of society, thus becoming a politically harmful pseudoscience.

When Yao wrote his paper, he was a relatively unknown writer from Shanghai and had not attracted much attention. But during the Cultural Revolution he joined three other ambitious personages who worked their way into top positions in the Central Committee of the Chinese Communist Party and the government. Yao obtained one of the nation's highest posts, the one responsible for propaganda, culture, and science. With this power in his hands he waged a campaign against psychology, using such terms as *pseudoscience* and *bourgeois psychology*. Free scientific discussion was suppressed, and Yao's ultraleftist view was taken as the standard for evaluating a psychologist's political attitude whether he or she be revolutionary or nonrevolutionary. The Gang of Four upheld a philosophy of voluntarism, stressing the omni-importance of the will by which marvels and feats could be accomplished; scientific principles of intellectual and cognitive development were discarded. In this way psychology was attacked politically, and in the years between 1966 and 1973, psychology in China was completely liquidated. Senior psychologists who disagreed with Yao were called bourgeois, reactionary, academic authorities and were subjected to persecution. Younger staff workers had to turn to other tasks or work as farmhands or factory workers. The Institute of Psychology was closed from 1969 to 1972, and teaching and research practically ceased for almost ten years (1966–1976).

The power exercised by the Gang of Four had such a devastating effect on our nation that economic, cultural, and educational institutions were in a state of chaos. The country was on the brink of destruction. In science and technology a decade without recruitment resulted in a lost generation.

## THE REVIVAL OF PSYCHOLOGY SINCE 1976

In October 1976 the Chinese Communist Party, headed by Chairman Hua Kuo-feng, smashed the Gang of Four, restoring democracy and law. Science was again brought to the forefront. Early in 1977, the National Assembly for the Advancement of Science and Technology convened and laid out a long-term plan for the future development of all spheres of science. Psychology, being part of this plan, worked out the blueprints for its reconstruction.

Because of the sabotage and interference of the Gang of Four, there is a gap between our work and the contributions from overseas. We Chinese psychologists are now working ever harder, with renewed vigor and vitality, in the revival of psychology, to compensate for the time lost during the past ten gloomy years.

In August 1977 the Chinese Psychological Society resumed its activity, and a national assembly was held in Peking to discuss plans for development. In May of the following year, a larger meeting took place in Hangchow; representatives from nearly all the provinces of China reported on their current research and teaching projects as well as on plans for future development; 101 papers were delivered. This meeting particularly emphasized the importance of developmental and educational psychology for the reconstruction of the educational system of our country in the aftermath of the destruction caused by the Gang of Four. This meeting also called on psychologists to write commemorative papers on the centennial of the founding of the first psychological laboratory by Wundt in Leipzig in 1879. In December 1978 the Chinese Psychological Society held its annual meeting in Paoting, with 230 participants and 248 papers. In December of the following year, the annual meeting took place in Tientsin, attendance rose to 350, and over 400 papers were submitted. Problems relating to how psychology should cope with the modernization of China were discussed.

The Chinese Psychological Society, with a total of 800 members, now has 26 branch societies in various provinces of the country, and its Executive Office is located at the Institute of Psychology in Peking. It has seven branch committees: (a) Developmental and Educational Psychology, (b) Medical Psychology, (c) Physiological Psychology, (d) Psychology of Sports, (e) Experimental and General Psychology, (f) Industrial Psychology, and (g) Psychological Theory. Publication of *Acta Psychologica Sinica* was resumed in August 1979.

Late in 1978 an independent department of psychology was established at Peking University, and departments of psychology have recently been instituted at Shanghai Normal University and Hangchow University. Peking Normal University has plans for a psychology department in the near future. Current research in China is being undertaken along several lines, as discussed below.

### Developmental Psychology and Educational Psychology

Topics of study include development of the number concept in children of different age levels, development of language ability, and gifted and mentally retarded children. A variety of methods are used, including experimental methods, surveys, and descriptions of teaching experiences by advanced teachers. A nationwide collaborative study in developmental psychology has been organized.

It seems acceptable to divide the development of the number concept in children into three stages—the stage of knowing the quantity of physical objects by sensory and motor activities (children at about 3 years), the stage of association of numerals with the quantity of physical objects (3–5 years), and the stage of primary mathematical operations with numbers (above 5 years).

Psychologists have observed that when children begin to learn Chinese characters, they first try to associate the forms of characters with the actual shape of things they know. For instance, in the Chinese character for "basket," the upper part looks somewhat like a bamboo tree and the bottom part like an inclined basket, and children make use of these cues to learn this character. Later they are able to differentiate the small parts, or the components of the whole character, thus developing the ability to recognize Chinese characters. We are also trying to simplify Chinese characters (we call it the "reformation of Chinese characters") by reducing the number of strokes in a character and reducing the total number of characters in our language system.

In the area of mental retardation, a rating scale has been developed for diagnosing the intelligent behavior of mentally retarded children who pay visits to clinics and determining whether any progress has been made as a result of certain treatments. The rating scale assesses behavior in five categories: gross motor behavior, fine movement, ability in self-care, language development, and number concepts; each category is rated on a 6-point scale. This rating scale has proved to be quite effective. The mean incidence rate of mental retardation in a sampling from four districts of Peking is .34 percent of the population, a rate similar to that in other countries. Methods and suggestions on remedial work for mentally handicapped people have also been explored.

### General, Experimental, and Engineering Psychology

The main work in this area is in vision and is directed at meeting our nation's demands for industrialization. Many studies deal with the development of industrial standards related to visual work and speech communication. Topics under study include the luminous efficiency function of Chinese eyes and color standards for use in color television and color photography, covering tolerances of Chinese facial skin color, tolerances of commonly seen object colors, and memory of colors. Illumination standards based on studies of visual performance and standards of noise control in relation to loss of speech audibility are being developed. Much of this work serves practical ends, and some has been adopted for industrial uses. Activities within this area have recently shifted more in the direction of fundamental research, and the areas under current investigation include spatial vision, perceptual aftereffects, pattern recognition, and haptic perception.

## Medical Psychology and Physiological Psychology

The role of psychological factors such as suggestion, attention, and emotional states in acupuncture analgesia has been studied. Psychologists, in collaboration with medical doctors, study emotional changes before, during, and after surgical operations and their relation to physiological and biochemical changes. Because surgical operations are done under acupuncture analgesia, the patient is fully conscious and is able to describe his or her experience by answering questions posed by the experimenter. This kind of material is impossible to obtain with drug anesthesia. Explorative studies of the neural and biochemical bases of learning and memory have been conducted. The effects of electrical damage to different areas of the hippocampus and injection of pancreatic trypsin and ribonuclease show that during the early phase of learning and memory, the hippocampus plays an active role and is related to the synthesis of protein.

In pathological psychology, the effects of Chinese herbal psychedelic drugs, particularly the medicinal fungus *Boletus boletaceae,* are studied in animals. It was reported that hallucination took place 6–24 hours after the oral administration of this drug. Hypnosis has been tried in mental hospitals, and the application of psychology in the clinical field has recently been well received. Biofeedback and behavioral therapy are also being examined in China.

## Theoretical Studies in Psychology

At the 1978 annual meeting of the Chinese Psychological Society, 29 papers were devoted to theoretical problems. Topics encompassed the contributions of Wundt as well as the work of other prominent psychologists in the West. In addition, psychologists criticized the destruction of psychology by the Gang of Four.

A few words must be said about mental testing and social psychology. These two areas, formerly forbidden, are now open to research for the first time. Some psychologists have already begun a revision of the Wechsler Intelligence Scale for Children for use in China. Sociology

Selected Articles from China

has been readmitted into the family of science, and social studies in psychology are about to begin.

The experience we Chinese psychologists have gained from the thirty years of work since Liberation offers us the following lessons:

1. Dialectical materialism is the guiding principle for psychological science, but psychology cannot be replaced by philosophy. Marxism should serve as a guide to our research work, but rather than citing quotations from Marxist writers as evidence, we must adhere to the principle that the only standard for the verification of truth is practice.

2. Free and democratic discussion of scientific matters should always be encouraged and must persist, as we learned from the painful lesson of treating different scientific viewpoints as political problems.

3. Psychology is international and some theories or schools of psychology abroad may or may not fit into our own culture, but we must acquaint ourselves with them, borrowing anything that is good for and useful to us. The blindly antiforeign attitude can only result in loss for ourselves. We should promote scientific contact and exchange with colleagues overseas.

The above overview presents, I think, a general idea as to how Chinese psychologists, with the aim of building a scientific discipline, have proceeded along a course beset with storm and stress. Fortunately, the storm has cleared and we now have a stable and peaceful environment in which to develop our science and to make psychology of better service to our socialist construction. For this enterprise we need to work arduously and depend on our own effort, but it is equally crucial that we learn from the advanced experience of our colleagues overseas. With Chinese psychologists rejoining the international community, perhaps we can participate fully in the development and growth of our discipline.

# References

Chen Li & Wang An-sheng. A developmental study of color and form abstraction in children. *Acta Psychologica Sinica,* 1965, 2, 154–162. (a)

Chen Li & Wang An-sheng. A follow-up study of color and form abstraction in children of different ages. *Acta Psychologica Sinica,* 1965, 2, 163–164. (b)

Chen Li & Wang An-sheng. Color and form preferences. *Acta Psychologica Sinica,* 1965, 3, 265–269. (c)

Ge Ming-jen. Is this the scientific method and correct direction in psychological research? *Kwang Ming Daily,* October 28, 1965.

Höffding, H. *Outlines of psychology* (M. E. Loundes, Trans.). London: Macmillan, 1893.

Kornilov, K. N. (Ed.). *Advanced psychology*. Moscow: Pedagogical Publishers, 1948.

Lenin, V. I. *Materialism and empirio-criticism: Critical comments on a reactionary philosophy*. Moscow: Progress Publishers, 1973. (Originally published, 1947.)

Mao Tse-tung. On contradiction. In *Selected works of Mao Tse-tung* (Vol. 1). Peking: Foreign Languages Press, 1965. (a)

Mao Tse-tung. On practice. In *Selected works of Mao Tse-tung* (Vol. 1). Peking: Foreign Languages Press, 1965. (b)

Pavlov, I. P. *Lectures on conditioned reflexes* (Vol. 1; W. H. Gantt, Trans.). New York: International Publishers, 1928.

Smirnov, A. A. (Ed.). *Psychology*. Moscow: Pedagogical Publishers, 1962.

Teplov, B. M. *Psychology*. Moscow: Pedagogical Publishers, 1951.

Selected Articles from China

# Bibliography

"A Symposium on Psychology was Held in T'ai-yuan," *Translations from Kuang-ming Jih-pao.* U.S. Joint Publications Research Service No. 12524 (14 February 1962), pp. 106–107.

Adams, Frank. "Mental Care in Peking." *China Now,* Vol. 18 (January 1972), pp. 5–8.

Aisin-Gioro Pu Yi. *From Emperor to Citizen.* 2 vols. Beijing: Foreign Languages Press, 1964–65. 2 vols.

Allan, T., and S. Gordon. *The Scalpel, the Sword: The Story of Docotor Norman Bethune.* Toronto/Montreal: McClelland and Stewart, 1952.

Allodi, F., and J. Dukszta. "Psychiatric Services in China or, Mao versus Freud." *Canadian Psychiatric Association Journal,* Vol. 23, No. 6 (October 1978), pp. 361–370.

Barlow, John, "Mass Line Leadership and Thought Reform in China," *American Psychologist,* Vol. 36, No. 3, March 1981, pp. 300–309.

Bates, D. G. "Medical Education in China after the Gang of Four." *Canadian Medical Association Journal,* Vol. 120, No. 12 (1979), pp. 1578–1582.

Bazar, Joan. "Psychology . . . Making a Comeback." *APA Monitor,* Vol. 10, Nos. 9 and 10 (September/October 1979), pp. 17–19.

———. "Psychology—Such a Cultural Product." *APA Monitor,* Vol. 10, Nos. 9 and 10 (September/October 1979), p. 23.

Belden, Jack. *China Shakes the World.* New York and London: Monthly Review Press, 1970.

Bermann, Gregorio.. "Mental Health in China." *Psychiatry in the Communist World,* ed. A. Kiev. New York: Science House, 1968.

Braybrooke, George. "Recent Developments in the Chinese Social Science, 1977–79." *China Quarterly* (September 1979), pp. 593–607.

Breggin, Peter. "The Return of Lobotomy and Psychosurgery." *The Congressional Record,* Vol. 118, No. 26 (February 24, 1972).

Brown, L.B. *Psychology in Contemporary China.* Oxford and New York: Pergamon Press, 1981.

Butterfield, Fox. "Americans Make Rare Visit to Chinese Mental Hospital." *The New York Times,* June 30, 1979.

Cerny, Jan. "Chinese Psychiatry." *International Journal of Psychiatry,* Vol. 1, No. 2 (1965), pp. 229–247.

Chao Yi-ch'eng. "Neurology, Neurosurgery and Psychiatry in New China," *Chinese Medical Journal,* Vol. 84 (1965), pp. 714–742.

Ch'en Ta-jao. "How Does Psychology Serve Socialist Construction?" *Translations from Communist China's Political and Sociological Publications: The Movement in Psychology.* U.S. Joint Publications Research Service No. 1932-NY, pp. 31–40.

———. "How Psychology Can Be of Service to Socialist Construction." *Articles on Psychology in Communist China.* Translation of selected articles from *Hsin-li Hsueh-pao* (July–September 1959). U.S. Joint Publications Research Service No. 3424, pp. 3–10.

Chin, Robert, and Ai-li S. Chin. *Psychological Research in Communist China: 1949–1966.* Cambridge, Mass. and London: The M.I.T. Press, 1969.

Ching, C. C. "Psychology in the People's Republic of China." Special Colloquium, May 2, 1980, Department of Psychology and Institute of Human Development, University of Michigan.

————. "Psychology in the People's Republic of China," *American Psychologist,* Vol. 35, No. 12 (December, 1980), pp. 1084–1089.

Chu Chi-hsien. "Some Views on the Problem of the Object of Study of Psychology." *Translations from Communist China's Political and Sociological Publications: The Movement in Psychology.* U.S. Joint Publications Research Service No. 1932-NY, pp. 16–30.

Committee of Concerned Asian Scholars. *China! Inside the People's Republic.* New York, Toronto & London: Bantam Books, 1972.

Dittmer, Lowell. *Liu Shao-ch'i and the Chinese Cultural Revolution: The Politics of Mass Criticism.* Berkeley & Los Angeles: University of California Press, 1974.

Epstein, Israel. *From Opium War to Liberation.* third ed. Hong Kong: Joint Publishing Company, 1980.

Fuyu Medical Team, Provincial Hospital for Mental Diseases, Beian, Heilungkiang. "How We Operated a Small Hospital in the Countryside." *China's Medicine,* No. 6 (1968), pp. 347–350.

Galston, Arthur S., and J. S. Savage. *Daily Life in People's China.* New York: Thomas Y. Crowell Company, 1973.

Gardner, Howard. "China's Born-Again Psychology." *Psychology Today,* Vol. 14, No. 3 (August 1980), pp. 45–50.

Goldner, Virginia. "The Politics of Mental Health in China." *State and Mind* (Spring 1978), pp. 12–16.

Greenberg, Joel. "Mental Illness in China: A Contradiction Among the People." *Science News,* Vol. 115, No. 9 (March 3, 1979), pp. 140–141.

Grimes, Ken. "Mental Health Care in Shanghai." Unpublished, 1978.

Herrington, B. S. "Visitors from China Reflect on U.S., Chinese Mental Health Care." *Psychiatric News,* Vol. XIV, No. 14 (July 20, 1979), pp. 8, 22.

Hinton, William. *Fanshen.* New York: Random House/Vintage Books, 1966.

Ho, David Y. F. "Prevention and Treatment of Mental Illness in the People's Republic of China." *American Journal of Orthopsychiatry.* Vol. 44, No. 4 (July 1974), pp. 620–636.

————. "The Conception of Man in Mao Tse-tung Thought." *Psychiatry.* Vol. 41, No. 4 (November 1978), pp. 391–402.

Horn, Joshua S. *Away With All Pests.* New York & London: Monthly Review Press, 1969.

————. "Away with All Pests," talk at the Hotel Diplomat, New York, 1971. Denver, Col.: Blue Bus, producers (film).

Hsia Chen-yi (Xia Zhenyi). "Some Problems in Organic Psychosis." *Chinese Medical Journal,* Vol. 92, No. 1 (1979), pp. 45–50.

Hsia Chen-yi, Yan Heqin, and Wang Changhua. "Mental Health Work in Shanghai." *Chinese Medical Journal,* Vol. 93, No. 2 (1980), pp. 127–129.

Hsia Chen-yi, and Zhang Mingyuan, "History and Present Status of Modern Psychiatry in China," *Chinese Medical Journal,* Vol. 94, No. 5 (May 1981), pp. 277–282.

Hsu, L. T., C. C. Ching, and Ray Over. "Recent Developments in Psychology in the People's Republic of China," *International Journal of Psychology,* Vol. 15, No. 2 (1980), pp. 131–143.

Kagan, Leigh. "Report from a Visit to the Tientsin Psychiatric Hospital." *Far East Reporter* (April 1973), pp. 12–18.

Kao, John J. *Three Millenia of Chinese Psychiatry.* New York: The Institute for Advanced Research in Asian Science and Medicine Monograph Series, 1979.

Kety, Seymour S. "Psychiatric Concepts and Treatment in China." *China Quarterly,* Vol. 66 (June 1976), pp. 315–323.

Kleinman, A. M., et al. "Psychiatry in Mainland China: Additional Sources." Letter, *American Journal of Psychiatry,* Vol. 129, No. 4 (1972), p. 482.

Kleinman, and D. Mechanic. "Some Observations of Mental Illness and Its Treatment in the People's Republic of China." *Journal of Nervous and Mental Disease,* Vol. 167, No. 5 (1979), pp. 267–274. (See also Mechanic and Kleinmann.)

Koran, Lorrin M. "Psychiatry in Mainland China: History and Recent Status." *American Journal of Psychiatry,* Vol. 128 (1972), pp. 970–978.

Kraft, Alan, and Susan Swift. "Impressions of Chinese Psychiatry December 1978," *Psychiatric Quarterly,* Vol. 51, No. 2 (Summer 1979), pp. 83–91.

Krcek-Frank, Rosanne. "Psychosomatic Problems in the People's Republic of China." *Journal of Psychiatric Nursing and Mental Health Services* (December 1980), pp. 15–18.

Kuang Peizi, Luo Shengde, and Liu Shanxun. "Development of Physiological Psychology over Thirty Years Discussed." *China Report: Science and Technology,* No. 53. U.S. Joint Publications Research Service No. 76,320 (August 28, 1980), pp. 62–78.

Kuo Shu-su. "Using Materialist Dialectics to Cure Common Diseases." *Selected Essays on the Study of Philosophy by Workers, Peasants and Soldiers.* Beijing: Foreign Languages Press, 1971.

Kuo, You-yuh. "Psychology in Communist China." *Psychological Record,* Vol. 21 (1971), pp. 95–105.

Kupers, R., and T. Kupers. "Mental Health in China: An Evening with Al Wasserman." *Rough Times,* Vol. 3, No. 3 (December 1972), pp. 16–17.

Lazure, Denis. "Politics and Mental Health in New China." *American Journal of Orthopsychiatry,* Vol. XXXIV (1964), pp. 925–933.

Lee, Lee C. "Mental Health: A People's Project." *APA Monitor,* Vol. 10, Nos. 9 and 10 (September/October 1979), pp. 20–21.

Lee T'ao, Ch'eng Chih-fan, and Chang Ch'i-shan. "Some Early Records of Nervous and Mental Diseases in Traditional Chinese Medicine." *Chinese Medical Journal,* Vol. 81 (1962), pp. 55–59.

Lessof, Maurice and Jeremy Dale. "Meeting Enormous Health Needs: Medical Education," *China Now,* No. 87 (1979), pp. 15–18.

Leung, Sophia M. R. "Mental Health Home Care Program in the Communes of the People's Republic of China." *Journal of Psychiatric Treatment and Evaluation,* Vol. 3 (1981), pp. 53–58.

Leung, Sophia M.R., and Milton H. Miller. "Mental Health Care by the People: North America and the People's Republic of China," presented at the 57th

Annual Meeting of the American Orthopsychiatric Association, April 7–11, 1980, Toronto.

Leung, Sophia M.R., Milton Miller, and S. Wah Leung. "Chinese Approach to Mental Health Service." *Canadian Psychiatric Association Journal,* Vol. 23, No. 6 (October 1978), pp.. 354–359.

Li Ch'ung-p'ei, Hsu Yu-hsin, Keng Chen-mei, & Wang Ming-te, "Some Problems Concerning the Cuase of Psychasthenia and Attempts to Find Quick Treatments." *Collection of Theses on Achievements in the Medical Sciences in Commemoration of the 10th National Foundation Day of China,* Vol. II. Beijing, 1959. Translated by U.S. Joint Publications Research Service No. 14829, pp. 652–670.

Li Xintian, Xu Shulian, And Kuang Peizi. "Thirty Years of Medical Psychology." *China Report: Science and Technology,* No. 53. U.S. Joint Publications Research Service No. 76,320 (August 28, 1980), pp. 43–61.

Lin Chiao-chih. "The Party Keeps Me Young." New Women in New China. Beijing: Foreign Languages Press, 1972.

Lin Yang, "Medical and Health Service," *Beijing Review* , Vol. 23, No. 25, (1980), pp. 17–27.

Ling Ming-yu. "Psychiatry in China Today." *National Reconstruction Journal,* Vol. 6, No. 3 (1946), pp. 20–30.

Liu Ju-chin. "Our Neighborhood: Study Brings a Broader View." *China Reconstructs,* Vol. XXII, No. 8 (1973), p. 7.

Liu Xiehe. "Mental Health Work in Sichuan." *British Journal of Psychiatry,* Vol. 137 (1980), pp. 371–376.

———. "Psychiatry in Traditional Chinese Medicine," *British Journal of Psychiatry,* Vol. 138 (1981), pp. 429–433.

Liu Xiehe, Huang Mingsheng, Zhang Rongsong, Zhang Yuping, and Hu Guangcai. "Survey of Psychosis in Sichuan." *China Report: Science and Technology,* No. 53. U.S. Joint Publications Research Service No. 76,320 (August 28, 1980), pp. 24–32.

Livingston, Martha. "Mental Health Care."*Encyclopedia of China Today,* eds. F. Kaplan et al., New York: Harper & Row, 1979.

Livingston, Martha, and Nancy Henningsen. "How China Got Rid of Drugs." Scripted slide show and filmstrip, U.S.-China Peoples Friendship Association, 1975.

Lowinger, Paul, "How China Solved the Drug Problem, *The New York Times,* June 2, 1973.

———."Psychiatry in China: A Revolutionary Optimism." *Medical Dimensions* (December 1976), pp. 25–31.

———. "The Solution to Narcotic Addiction in the People's Republic of China." *American Journal of Drug Abuse,* Vol. 4, No. 2 (1977), pp. 165–178.

———. "Brainwashing: Truth Comes Home to Roost." *Los Angeles Times,* December 11, 1977, p. 2.

———. "Psychiatric Opinions in Peking." *Psychiatric Opinion,* Vol. 15, No. 5 (May 1978), pp. 36–39.

———. "Mental Health in China," *China Now,* No. 90 (1980), pp. 23–24.

———. "Mental Health in China Today," *MD,* Vol. 25, No. 5 (May 1981), pp. 179–181.

———. "Why Do We Have Drug Abuse?—Economic and Political Basis," Chapter 48 in *Substance Abuse,* Joyce Lowinson and Pedro Ruiz, eds., Baltimore: William and Wilkins, 1981.

———. "Mental Health in China Today," *Young Traditional Practitioner,* Vol. 1, No. 2 (November 1981), pp. 7–8.

Lu, Yi-chuang. "Social Values and Psychiatric Ideology in Revolutionary China." Paper presented at the annual meeting of the American Sociological Association, New York, August 30, 1973.

———. "The Collective Approach to Psychiatric Practice in the People's Republic of China." *Social Problems,* Vol. 26 (October 1978), pp. 2–14.

Ma Chung-lin. "Primary Education: A Lesson from Life." *China Reconstructs,* Vol. XXII, No. 6 (1973), p. 13.

Malraux, André. *Man's Fate.* New York: Random House/Vintage Books, 1961.

Mao Tse-tung. "The Bankruptcy of the Idealist Conception of History." (September 16, 1949). *Selected Works of Mao Tse-tung,* Vol. IV. Beijing: Foreign Languages Press, 1967, pp. 451–459.

———. "Be Concerned with the Well-Being of the Masses, Pay Attention to Methods of Work" (January 27, 1934). *Selected Readings from the Works of Mao Tse-tung.* Beijing: Foreign Languages Press, 1967, pp. 42–47.

———. "On Contradiction" (August, 1937). *Selected Readings from the Works of Mao Tse-tung.* Beijing: Foreign Languages Press, 1967, pp. 70–108.

———. "On the Correct Handling of Contradictions Among the People" (February 1957). *Selected Readings from the Works of Mao Tse-tung.* Beijing: Foreign Languages Press, 1967, pp. 350–387.

———. "On Correcting Mistaken Ideas in the Party" (December 1929). *Selected Works of Mao Tse-tung,* Vol. I. Beijing: Foreign Languages Press, 1967, pp. 105–116.

———. "On Practice" (July 1937). *Selected Readings from the Works of Mao Tse-tung.* Beijing: Foreign Languages Press, 1967, pp. 54–69.

———. "Preface to Rural Surveys" (March 17, 1941). *Selected Works of Mao Tse-tung,* Vol. III. Beijing: Foreign Languages Press, 1967, pp. 11–13.

———. "Some Questions Concerning Methods of Leadership" (June 1, 1943). *Selected Readings from the Works of Mao Tse-tung.* Beijing: Foreign Languages Press, 1967, pp. 234–239.

———. "Speech at the Assembly of Representatives of the Shensi-Kansu-Ningsia Border Region" (November 21, 1941). *Selected Works of Mao Tse-tung,* Vol. III. Beijing: Foreign Languages Press, 1967, pp. 31–34.

———. "Talks at the Yenan Forum on Literature and Art" (May 1942). *Selected Readings from the Works of Mao Tse-tung.* Beijing: Foreign Languages Press, 1967, pp. 204–233.

———. "The United Front in Cultural Work" (October 30, 1944). *Selected Works of Mao Tse-tung,* Vol. III. Beijing: Foreign Languages Press, 1967, pp. 185–188.

———. "Where Do Correct Ideas Come From?" (1957). *Selected Readings from the Works of Mao Tse-tung.* Beijing: Foreign Languages Press, 1967, pp. 405–406.

Marvin, Jeff. "Mental Health in China Today." *Canada-China Friendship Association Newsletter* (Vancouver), Vol. 4, No. 4 (September 1973), pp. 12–14.

Masengill, Ann. *Letters from Americans in China* (San Francisco: U.S.-China Peoples Friendship Association, 1980), pp. 1–2.

McCartney, L. "Neuropsychiatry in China: A Preliminary Observation." *Chinese Medical Journal,* Vol. 40 (1926), pp. 617–626.

Mechanic, David and Arthur Kleinman. "Ambulatory Medical Care in the People's Republic of China: An Exploratory Study," *American Journal of Public Health,* Vol. 70, No. 1 (1980), pp. 62–66.

"Medical Care for 700 Million: Some Questions Answered." *China Reconstructs,* Vol. XXI, No. 11 (1972), pp. 13–15.

"Mental Health in China." *U.S.-China Friendship Newsletter* (San Francisco), Vol. 2, No. 4 (1972), pp. 1–2.

"Mental Health in China." *Canada's Mental Health,* Vol. XXI, No. 6 (1973), p. 14.

"Mental Health in China." *Science Digest,* Vol. 80, No. 5 (November 1976), pp. 11–12.

Miller, Marvin F. "Psychiatry in People's Republic of China," *World Studies of Psychiatry,* Vol. 2, No. 2 (1978). Distributed by E. R. Squibb & Sons, Inc.

"The National Mental Illnesses Prevention Work Plan (1958–1962)." *Compendium of Laws and Regulations in the People's Republic of China,* translated by U.S. Joint Publications Research Service No. 14,335, pp. 562–575.

*Neurology-Psychiatry in the People's Republic of China.* Bethesda, Md.: DHEW (NIH) No. 74–56, 1973 (translated).

"New Treatment for the Insane." *China Pictorial,* Vol. 11 (1971), pp. 13–15.

Orleans, Leo A. "Birth Control: Reversal or Postponement?," *The China Quarterly,* Vol. 1, No. 3 (July–September, 1960), pp. 59–69.

Our Correspondents. "A Visit to the Tungting People's Commune (VI)." *Peking Review,* Vol. 16, No. 18 (May 4, 1973), pp. 12–14.

Pan Shuh. "China's Recent Work on Psychology." *Psychologia,* Vol. 2 (1959), pp. 193–201.

Parise, Goffredo. "No Neurotics in China." *Atlas,* Vol. 13 (1967), pp. 46–47.

"Peking's Former Prostitutes." *China Weekly Review,* July 29, 1950, pp. 148–150.

*Philosophy is No Mystery: Peasants Put their Study to Work.* Beijing: Foreign Languages Press, 1972.

Poo, Lucille S. "Street and Neighborhood Committees in China: Firsthand Report." *Far East Reporter* (April 1973), pp. 19–24.

Pope, Lillie. "Notes on Education." *APA Monitor,* Vol. 10, Nos. 9 and 10 (September/October 1979), p. 22.

Ratnavale, David M. "Psychiatry in Shanghai, China: Observations in 1973." *American Journal of Psychiatry,* Vol. 130 (1973), pp. 1082–1087.

Ratner, Carl. "Psychology in the People's Republic of China." *Eastern Horizon,* Vol. XVIII, No. 5 (May 1979), pp. 13–17.

Rickett, Allyn, and Adele Rickett. *Prisoners of Liberation.* Garden City, New York: Anchor Press/Doubleday, 1973.

Robinson, Nancy M. "Mild Mental Retardation: Does it Exist in the People's Republic of China?" *Mental Retardation,* Vol. 16, No. 4 (August 1978) pp. 295–299.

Rosner, Steven. "Treatment in China." *MH* (formerly *Mental Hygiene*), Vol. 60 (Summer 1976), pp. 5–9.

Sainsbury, Maurice J. "Psychiatry in the People's Republic of China." *The Medical Journal of Australia,* Vol. 1, No. 17 (1974), pp. 669–675.

Science for the People. *China: Science Walks on Two Legs.* New York: Avon, 1974.

Selden, Mark. "China: Revolution and Health." Health Policy Advisory Center *Health-PAC Bulletin No. 47* (December 1972), pp. 2–18.

Shapiro, Phillip. "Mental Illness: A Social Problem with a Social Cure." *Getting Together,* Vol. 5, No. 3 (February 1–5, 1974), p. 7.

Shen Yu-tsun. "Application of Artificial Hibernation in Practice." *Collection of Theses on Achievements in the Medical Sciences in Commemoration of the 10th National Foundation Day of China,* Vol. II. Beijing, 1959. Translated by U.S. Joint Publications Research Service No. 14829, pp. 618–651.

Shen Yu-tsun, Zhang Weixi, Shu Liang, Yang Xiaoling, Cui Yuhua, Zhou Dong-feng, Shi Hengyao, and Su Entao, "Investigation of Mental Disorders in Beijing Suburban District," *Chinese Medical Journal,* Vol. 94, No. 3 (1981), pp. 153–156.

Shen Yu-tsun, and Zhang Wenhe. "5-Hydroxytryptamine Metabolism in Schizophrenics." *Chinese Medical Journal.* Vol. 92, No. 12 (1979), pp. 817–821.

Sheringham, Eve. "Visit to a Mental Hospital in China." Unpublished, 1974.

Sidel, Ruth. "Social Services in China." *Social Work,* (November 1972), pp. 5–13.

————. *Women and Child Care in China.* New York: Hill & Wang, 1972.

————. "Mental Diseases and their Treatment." *Medicine and Public Health in the People's Republic of China,* ed. J. R. Quinn. Washington: NIH, Fogarty International Center, HEW Publication 72-67, U.S. Government Printing Office, 1973.

————. *Families of Fengsheng.* Baltimore: Penguin Books, 1974.

Sidel, Ruth, and Victor Sidel. "The Human Services in China." *Social Policy,* Vol. 2, No. 6 (1972), pp. 25–34.

————. *Serve the People: Observations on Medicine in the People's Republic of China.* New York: Josiah Macy, Jr. Foundation, 1973.

————. "The Delivery of Medical Care in China." *Scientific American,* Vol. 230, No. 4 (1974), pp. 19–27.

————. *The Health of China.* Boston: Beacon Press, 1982.

Snider, Arthur. "Psychiatrist Says Mental Illness Uncommon in China." *Chicago Sun-Times,* March 21, 1979, p. 40.

Snow, Edgar. *Red Star Over China,* rev. ed. New York: Grove Press, 1968.

————. *Red China Today.* New York: Random House/Vintage Books, 1971.

Staff Reporter. "Our Neighborhood: Street Factories." *China Reconstructs,* Vol. XXII, No. 8 (1973), pp. 9–11.

Taipale, Ilkka, and Vappu Taipale. "Chinese Psychiatry: A Visit to a Chinese Mental Hospital." *Archives of General Psychiatry,* Vol. 29 (1973), pp. 313–316.

T'ao Kuo-t'ai. "Healing and Preventive Work in the Field of Childhood Mental Diseases." *Collection of Theses on Achievements in the Medical Sciences in Commemoration of the 10th National Foundation Day of China,* Vol. II. Beijing, 1959. Translated by U.S. Joint Publications Research Service No. 14829, pp. 683–699.

Tavris, Carol. "A Plague of Meetings: In China, Everybody Is a Psychologist." *Psychology Today* (May 1974), p. 48.

"Theoretical Problems of Psychology in the Realization of Class Struggle." *Articles on Psychology in Communist China,* translation of selected articles from *Hsin-li Hsueh-pao* (July-September 1959). U.S. Joint Publications Research Service No. 3424, pp. 1–2.

"Three Senior Citizens Tell their Stories." *China Reconstructs,* Vol. XXVIII, No. 7 (July 1979), pp. 34–38.

Ting Tsan, "How to Develop Medical Psychology in China." *Articles on Psychology in Communist China,* translation of selected articles from *Hsin-li Hsueh-pao* (July-September 1959). U.S. Joint Publications Research Service No. 3424, pp. 11–17.

Ts'ao Jih-ch'ang, "What Does Psychology Study?" *Translations from Communist China's Political and Sociological Publications: The Movement in Psychology,* translated by U.S. Joint Publications Research Service No. 1932-NY, pp. 1–15.

———. "Why Should We Discuss the Nature of Psychology?" *Selections from Kuang-ming Jih-pao,* translated by U.S. Joint Publications Research Service No. 4937 (31 August 1961), pp. 29–33.

Ts'ao Jih-ch'ang, and Li Chia-chih. "Industrial Psychology in China." *Articles on Psychology in Communist China,* translation of selected articles from *Hsin-li Hsueh-pao* (July-September 1959). U.S. Joint Publications Research Service No. 3424, pp. 18–35.

Veith, Ilza. "Psychiatric Thought in Chinese Medicine." *Journal of the History of Medicine and Allied Sciences,* Vol. 10 (1955), pp. 261–268.

Visher, John S., and Emily B. Visher. "Impressions of Psychiatric Problems and their Management: China, 1977." *American Journal of Psychiatry,* Vol. 136, No. 1 (January 1979), pp. 28–32.

Vogel, Ezra F. "A Preliminary View of Family and Mental Health in Urban Communist China," in *Mental Health Research in Asia and the Pacific,* William A. Caudill and Tsung-yi Lin, eds., Honolulu: East-West Center Press, 1969.

Walls, Philip D., Lichun Han Walls, and Donald G. Langsley. "Psychiatric Training and Practice in the People's Republic of China." *American Journal of Psychiatry,* Vol. 132, No. 2 (February 1975), pp. 121–128.

Wan, F. E., and T. H. Chang. "Psychosurgery." *Chinese Medical Journal,* Vol. 68 (September-October 1950), pp. 273–280.

Wang Ching-hsiang. "Insulin Treatment." *Collection of Theses on Achievements in the Medical Sciences in Commemoration of the 10th National Foundation Day of China,* Vol. II. Beijing, 1959. Translated in U.S. Joint Publications Research Service No. 14,829, pp. 671–682.

Westbrook, C. H. "Psychiatry and Mental Hygiene in Shanghai." *American Journal of Psychiatry,* Vol. 110 (1953), pp. 301–305.

Whyte, Martin King. *Small Groups and Political Rituals in China.* Berkeley and Los Angeles: University of California Press, 1974.

Williams, John. "Child Health and Psychiatry in China Today." *The Medical Journal of Australia,* Vol. 44 (October 26, 1957), pp. 630–631.

Wong, K. C. "A Short History of Psychiatry and Mental Hygiene in China." *Chinese Medical Journal,* Vol. 68 (January-February 1950), pp. 44–48.

Wray, Joe D. "Child Care in the People's Republic of China: 1973," *Pediatrics* Vol. 55, No. 4 (April 1975), pp. 539–550.

———. "Child Care in the People's Republic of China—1973: Part II," *Pediatrics* Vol. 55, No. 5 (May 1975), pp. 723–734.

———. Interview with Paul Lowinger, 1979.

Wu Chen-i. "New China's Achievements in Psychiatry." *Collection of Theses on Achievements in the Medical Sciences in Commemoration of the 10th National Foundation Day of China,* Vol. II. Beijing, 1959. Translated by U.S. Joint Publications Research Service No. 14,829, pp. 594–617.

Wu Chen-i and Zhang Ji Zhi, "The Last Fifteen Years of Progress in Our Country's Treatment of Mental Diseases," *Chinese Neuropsychiatric Journal,* Vol. 12, No. 3 (1979).

Yang Desen, and Chen Yongde. "A Survey Report on Psychosis in Hunan Province." *China Report: Science and Technology,* No. 53. U.S. Joint Publications Research Service No. 76,320 (August 28, 1980), pp. 32–42.

Yee, A. H. "Psychology in China Bows to the Cultural Revolution." *APA Monitor,* Vol. 4, No. 3 (1973), p. 1.

Zweig, Michael. "Unemployment in the People's Republic of China," unpub- Service No. 76,320 (August 28, 1980), pp. 32–42.

Yee, A.H. lished paper presented at the annual meeting of the Eastern Economics Association in Philadelphia, April 1981.

———. "China's Economy: Present Policies Address Past Mistakes," *China and Us,* Vol. 10, No. 2 (Summer 1981), pp. 1–3.

———. "Urban Unemployment in the People's Republic of China," talk presented to the Department of Economics Seminar, State University of New York at Stony Brook, November 4, 1981.

# Index

religions and psychiatry